Repackaging Libraries for Survival

Research libraries face many challenges in today's declining economy. The essays in this book explore these challenges and were originally delivered at a conference entitled "Climbing Out of the Box: Repackaging Libraries for Survival," sponsored by the University of Oklahoma Libraries and held March 4-5, 2010, in Oklahoma City. The authors, recognized leaders in academic librarianship, broach sensitive, but necessary, discussions in how academic libraries provide services and resources today while planning for the future. As academic libraries continue to transform, each of the cases included provide specific examples of strategies used to place libraries in a position of competitive values for future research, teaching, and learning in higher education. Each situation is unique to the culture and economic conditions of particular institutions. However, the research cases provide all academic librarians with examples of how our libraries can repackage roles and content in order to survive in the twenty-first century.

This book was originally published as a special issue of *Journal of Library Administration.*

Sul H. Lee is Peggy V. Helmerich Chair and Dean of the University of Oklahoma Libraries, a position he has held since 1978. His academic background is in political science, international relations and library and information science and has authored more than two dozen books in the field of librarianship.

Repackaging Libraries for Survival

Climbing Out of the Box

Edited by
Sul H. Lee

Routledge
Taylor & Francis Group
LONDON AND NEW YORK

First published 2012
by Routledge
2 Park Square, Milton Park, Abingdon, Oxon, OX14 4RN

Simultaneously published in the USA and Canada
by Routledge
711 Third Avenue, New York, NY 10017

Routledge is an imprint of the Taylor & Francis Group, an informa business

First issued in paperback 2013

This book is a reproduction of the *Journal of Library Administration*, vol. 51, issue 1. The Publisher requests to those authors who may be citing this book to state, also, the bibliographical details of the special issue on which the book was based.

British Library Cataloguing in Publication Data
A catalogue record for this book is available from the British Library

ISBN13: 978-0-415-69743-9 (hbk)
ISBN13: 978-0-415-85033-9 (pbk)

Typeset in Times New Roman
by Taylor and Francis Books

Disclaimer
The publisher would like to make readers aware that the chapters in this book are referred to as articles as they had been in the special issue. The publisher accepts responsibility for any inconsistencies that may have arisen in the course of preparing this volume for print.

Contents

1. Introduction
Sul H. Lee 1

2. Climbing Out of the Box and Into the Cloud: Building Web-Scale for Libraries
Jay Jordan 3

3. Why Libraries Persist: Hermits, Clouds, Confucius, Bubbles, and Hortense Foglesong
Dennis Dillon 18

4. Year 2 of the "Great Recession": Surviving the Present by Building the Future
Charles B. Lowry 37

5. Finding the Right Metaphor: Restructuring, Realigning, and Repackaging Today's Research Libraries
Joan Giesecke 54

6. Advancing From Kumbaya to Radical Collaboration: Redefining the Future Research Library
James G. Neal 66

7. Repackaging the Library: What Do Faculty Think?
Kevin Guthrie and *Ross Housewright* 77

8. Times of Crisis Accelerate Inevitable Change
Allen Powell 105

9. From Surviving to Thriving
Carla J. Stoffle and *Cheryl Cuillier* 130

Index 156

Introduction

SUL H. LEE
University of Oklahoma, Norman, OK, USA

The articles included in this special issue of the *Journal of Library Administration* examine the many issues research libraries currently face as we transform our spaces and services. These articles were originally delivered at a conference entitled "Climbing Out of the Box: Repackaging Libraries for Survival," sponsored by the University of Oklahoma Libraries and held March 4–5, 2010, in Oklahoma City. In this issue, Jay Jordan, president and chief executive officer of OCLC, begins this examination by evaluating the current state of Web-scalability in libraries. Jordan argues that cloud computing, which has become standard practice in information technology sectors, will equally become pervasive in libraries in the future. This model will present different methods for providing and evaluating services in the future but contains the potential for a shift in resource allocations away from the parent library.

Dennis Dillon, associate director for research services, University of Texas–Austin Libraries, extends this debate on the effects of cloud computing—and the subsequent redesign of library workflows—for research libraries to transition to a competitive market environment. Confronted with many internally and externally driven environmental factors, Dillon contents that a reevaluation of librarians' thinking and practice is necessary to make another shift in the evolution of our organizations. Charles Lowry, Executive Director of the Association of Research Libraries (ARL), equally addresses these issues from the system-wide perspective of the research library collaborative. Basing his research on ARL surveys conducted on the 2009 financial recession, Lowry contends that many of the budget cuts institutions of higher education saw during the past few years will not be reinstated in library acquisitions and staffing budgets, and that the economic crisis escalated a growing trend in academic libraries. However, Lowry offers several propositions that can help offset these deficits, such as reorganization of services and staffing, changing the way we deliver information, and multi-institutional collaboration.

Joan Giesecke, dean of libraries, University of Nebraska–Lincoln, suggests that we can recreate our libraries by searching for different metaphors that drive our organizational thinking. Ranging from the library as body to the library as an ecological system, Giesecke presents a poignant interpretation of how we must change our thinking about research libraries from the metaphors of the industrial age to those that reflect the transformative changes of a technology-driven society. And James Neal, vice president for information services and university librarian, Columbia University Libraries, weaves the concept of metaphor throughout his article, suggesting that research libraries engage in "radical collaboration" that disrupts many of the locally held organizational mental models that are currently in place. From shared print and digital collections to educating the populace effectively, Neal argues that an emphasis on quality improvement through continual evaluation will be detrimental to our survival in the future.

Kevin Guthrie, president of Ithaka, shifts focus toward constituent views of academic libraries in one of his recent faculty user studies. Faculty members have become more advanced in their use of discovery tools to find information, thereby dramatically shifting their expectations of librarians' roles away from traditional practices. Allen Powell, president of EBSCO Information Systems, integrates these same types of concepts by focusing on the economic crisis of 2009 as a catalyst for significant change in libraries. Although information as a commodity continues to press the market for subscription increases, library budgets have not risen at a concurrent rate, and even vendors have been subsequently affected. Powell contends that libraries, vendors, and publishers each stand to benefit from mutually acceptable strategies that reflect the changing use of information in the future.

Carla Stoffle, dean of libraries, University of Arizona, and Cheryl Cuillier, University of Arizona Libraries, provide several examples of how continuous organizational change and professional thinking can help transition research libraries from merely surviving to actually thriving in the 21st century. From the use of team-based organizational structures and balanced scorecard models of assessment to information discovery tools and changing library services, Stoffle and Cuillier suggest that this transformation is continual and difficult but not without great reward for the future of research libraries.

The articles included in this issue of the *Journal of Library Administration* broach sensitive but necessary discussions in how academic libraries provide services and resources in the future. As academic libraries continue to transform, each of these cases provides specific examples of strategies used to place libraries in a position of competitive values for future research, teaching, and learning in higher education. Each situation is unique to the culture and economic conditions of particular institutions, however, the research cases in this issue provide all academic librarians with examples of how our libraries can repackage roles and content in order to survive in the 21st century.

Climbing Out of the Box and Into the Cloud: Building Web-Scale for Libraries

JAY JORDAN
Online Computer Library Center (OCLC), Dublin, OH, USA

ABSTRACT. *Libraries have made significant investments in computer resources and infrastructure. They now incur the costs of supporting an array of systems across workflows for print, licensed, and digital materials. Similarly, libraries have fragmented presences on the Web, where they must compete with search engines and other information resources in meeting the information needs of people. The Online Computer Library Center (OCLC) is building its next generation of services in the computing cloud, where applications and data are stored on the Internet rather than on a local computer, and libraries can use an application without having to worry about the supporting technology. Web-scale services will provide libraries with powerful new applications and services when and where needed.*

This conference challenges us to climb out of the box and repackage libraries for survival. This presentation reviews the current state of library automation and opportunities to move to a Web-scale, cloud computing environment.

Let me start by paying homage to someone who really thought outside the box: Charles Darwin. A quotation that is frequently attributed to him is this: "It is not the strongest of the species that survive ... but the ones most responsive to change" (van Wyhye, 2010).

EVOLUTION OF SEARCH ENGINES

In the past 10 years, the concept of "search engine" has changed dramatically. Today, search engine is synonymous with Google, or Yahoo, or Microsoft's Bing. But, there are new approaches to search engines that are evolving. For example, Wolfram/Alpha calls itself a computational knowledge engine. According to its Web site, it is the first step in an ambitious, long-term project to make all systematic knowledge immediately computable by anyone. When you enter a question or calculation, Wolfram|Alpha uses its built-in algorithms and a growing collection of data to compute the answer. Wolfram|Alpha now contains more than 10 trillion pieces of data, 50,000+ types of algorithms and models, and linguistic capabilities for more than 1,000 domains. You can ask it to: compare the gross domestic products of France and Italy; find the number of Internet users in Europe by country; or find what the weather was like on your birthday in the town where you were born.

Another new search engine is Aardvark, which was recently acquired by Google. You have to be on a social network like Facebook to use Aardvark. Then, when you send a question to Aardvark via instant message or e-mail, its software looks among your Facebook friends for volunteers to answer it. Aardvark uses information about registrants to select to whom it should forward questions. Humans, not software, supply the answers. This is similar to the Online Computer Library Center (OCLC) QuestionPoint virtual reference service, in which reference librarians pool their time and expertise to answer questions from library users.

A third example is Hakia, which is described as a general purpose "semantic" search engine that is dedicated to quality search experience. According to the Hakia Web site, its quality search results satisfy three criteria simultaneously. They: (a) come from credible Web sites recommended by librarians; (b) represent the most recent information available; and (c) remain absolutely relevant to the query. Hakia search results are organized in a tabbed format that clearly distinguishes results as Web results, Hakia Credible Sites, images, and news.

For shorter and popular queries, Hakia generates a page of categorized results, known as *galleries*. Hakia galleries provide a balanced presentation for any given query, by generating results for various aspects of the search term, rather than just 10 blue links. For example, a search for "Boston" will categorize results in areas such as history, hotels, restaurants, sports, parks, real estate, and so forth. This presentation of information is equivalent to conducting at least 10 searches on other Web sites, according to Hakia.

Libraries are also getting involved in alternatives to search engines. Since 2008, with grant funding from the John D. and Catherine T. MacArthur Foundation, researchers and developers from OCLC and the information schools of Syracuse University and the University of Washington have been working on what they call a "credibility engine." This innovative approach will deliver search results based on the citations and recommendations of reference librarians. The researchers have just received another round of funding—$350,000—to continue their work on the Reference Extract Project and the credibility engine.

Clearly, search engines continue to evolve. The same can be said for library systems and services.

EVOLUTION OF LIBRARY SYSTEMS

As we know, libraries now incur the costs of supporting an array of systems across workflow for print, licensed and digital materials.

In 2007, Marshall Breeding estimated those costs: "In aggregate, libraries spend at least half a billion dollars per year on automation products and services" (Breeding, 2007).

I think you will agree that half a billion dollars is a lot of money, funds that are not being spent on collections or on other projects. So, where is this half a billion dollars being spent? Here is a partial list of individual systems and services available in North America:

- 100 ILS systems,
- 14 discovery layer interfaces,
- 41 document delivery systems,
- More than 24 interlibrary loan services,
- 150 digital repositories,
- 6 virtual reference services,
- 3 cataloging services, and
- 11,000 databases.

In addition, libraries invest in link resolvers, metasearch capabilities, electronic resource management modules, and circulation and acquisition systems.

The OCLC WorldCat Registry lists:

- 16,139 U.S. libraries with book catalog (OPAC) links registered,
- 1,228 U.S. libraries with Virtual Reference link registered, and
- 3,664 total OpenURL resolvers for over 2,000 unique institutions around the world.

It is interesting to note that the WorldCat Registry provided resolver information 1.2 million times in May 2009 alone.

The systems picture is further complicated by the fact that the very nature of academic collections is changing, partly because of publishing practice in the journal world and partly because of changed user expectations. The Association of Research Libraries's(2008) statistics report in 2008 shows that year after year, libraries are increasing the rate of spending for electronic resources much more quickly than they are increasing the rate of expenditures on physical materials.

As libraries consider their place in the information landscape we might ask ourselves some difficult questions.

Have the systems libraries use to deliver services kept pace with the changing nature of users and collections? Do libraries have too many systems to support? Are libraries investing too much in maintaining the systems they use to deliver their services?

Moreover, is a fragmented presence on the Web keeping libraries from success with their users? Does this fragmentation make it difficult for information seekers to find libraries and their services? Does this fragmented presence prevent libraries from taking advantage of new technologies that would allow them to share data and infrastructure with a greater cloud of libraries so they can increase work flow efficiencies?

These are difficult questions. The remainder of this presentation will present some answers and possible solutions to the challenges raised by these questions.

As a nonprofit, membership organization, OCLC has a tradition of transparency when it comes to sharing our strategic directions with member libraries. This transparency assists libraries in their own long-range planning processes, and it also provides us with the opportunity to get feedback from the membership and adjust our course when necessary. OCLC's current strategic direction can be summed up as Web-scale for libraries.

In April 2009, OCLC announced its strategy to build Web-scale services for libraries, and this announcement created quite a stir in the community. (It is interesting to note that based on traffic in the *LJ Academic Newswire*, 2010, OCLC's strategic directions were the number one story in the past year.)

It is useful to define the terms *cloud computing* and *Web-scale*.

Gartner, Inc. (2009), a research and advisory firm, defines *cloud computing* as a style of computing in which scalable and elastic information technology–enabled capabilities are delivered as a service to external customers using Internet technologies. Put another way, it is Web-based applications with shared data and services.

Lorcan Dempsey, OCLC's vice president for research and chief strategist, defines *Web-scale* as:

> Increasingly, libraries, like other organizations, need to focus on creating value for their users and reducing the effort they spend on routine and common tasks. The emerging concept of Web-scale is strongly aligned with OCLC's historic mission of operating a computer network and infrastructure that creates economies of scale, enabling more and more libraries to reduce costs and share resources. (Dempsey, 2008)

Web-scale means concentrating computer resources, applications and data to deliver benefits to large numbers of users through the Web.

For the OCLC cooperative, Web-scale means the more libraries, records, and network effects there are, the greater the value for everyone.

Although there are many organizations that can rightly claim to be cloud-based, there are very few that can claim to be Web-scale. Genuine Web-scale providers include such organizations as eBay, Amazon.com, Facebook and Google. They have these things in common: a cloud infrastructure; an aggregated mass of data; an aggregated mass of users or community.

What is not often observed is that OCLC was conceived by Frederick G. Kilgour as a cloud computing organization way back in 1967, when there was no Web, no Internet, and no search engines or graphical user interfaces.

Kilgour's (1984) strategic plan was to develop a total online system for libraries that provided for six subsystems:

- online union catalog and shared cataloging,
- serials control,
- technical processing (acquisitions),
- interlibrary loan,
- retrieval by subject, and
- remote catalog access and circulation control.

By 1998, OCLC had implemented three subsystems: cataloging, interlibrary loan, and subject retrieval. Earlier subsystems for serials control and acquisitions had been started but then discontinued.

In 2009, OCLC implemented a new approach to serials control with eSerials Holdings and a new approach to acquisitions with OCLC Selection, and a new approach to circulation with WorldCat Local. In other words, it has taken OCLC a mere 40 years to realize Kilgour's original system design!

We at OCLC are not just moving functionality to the cloud, however. We are creating the same network effects in new operations as we have done in our existing services, bringing collaborative effects and benefits to thousands of libraries. The goal is to simultaneously lower the total cost of managing library collections while enhancing the library user's experience. Broadly, the benefits of this approach are:

- increased visibility and accessibility of collections for users,
- reduced duplication of effort from networked technical services and collection management,
- streamlined workflows, and
- cooperative intelligence and improved service levels.

It is useful to briefly review the past 30 years of library automation to see how we got to where we are today.

In the 1970s the very basic ILS came into existence. Books were cataloged and circulated and an OPAC was put up front for users, replacing the card catalog. Each of these relationships and activities came with its own sets of data and services.

In the 1980s some acquisition functions were added along with connections to consortia and national systems as well as cataloging utilities such as OCLC. Users got some ability to do some minor self-service, such as placing holds on books, viewing their fines, and renewing books. Libraries also started working with partners as well as vendors, utilities, consortia, and national and global systems.

In the 1990s things got even more complicated with the appearance of electronic resource management systems, A-to-Z lists of e-journals, resolver services to get from citation databases to e-journal subscriptions, and some interaction with e-vendors.

In the first decade of the 21st century, libraries faced increased challenges with digital materials. Libraries either managed or needed to interact with institutional repositories. They implemented metasearch products and tried to get the acquisition system to talk to the new electronic resources management system. The result is a complex infrastructure that is costly to maintain both in staff time and dollars spent.

Amazon.com has stated that on average, developers spend 70% of their time building and maintaining and worrying about infrastructure, and 30% focused on the ideas that propel their business forward. Amazon's proposition is that Web scale can invert the 70/30 ratio, enabling businesses to spend 70% of their energy doing things that will make them more successful (Code Project, 2006).

How does this relate to libraries?

Although libraries have taken some advantage of new technologies that move to Web scale, much of their management process is still based on pre-Web technology. As a result it is likely they are only spending 30 percent of their time creating and implementing innovation.

So, following Amazon's thinking, if libraries were to externalize the routine management functions, in other words move into a cloud computing infrastructure, they should be able to increase their focus on innovation and service. At the same time, they can take advantage of shared data and services to streamline their workflows to match today's changing collections.

What if we could take the current picture of many systems requiring local support and move these systems up to a Web scale solution, or cloud computing?

Things are starting to get more streamlined. First we gain efficient storage and use of data in the cloud. There will continue to be data commonly shared for all to see and consume such as bibliographic records, library holdings and user contributed data including lists, reviews and tags. The value of the cloud is the ability of all libraries to share this data pool in the most efficient workflow possible. A new element is the ability to view and consume shared data pools which groups of libraries have agreed to share access to. This can simplify workflows and create easier collaboration between libraries. It will also save costs on creation and maintenance of certain classes of data for each library.

Of course, there will always be data that is private to a specific library and must be kept secure though it is in the cloud.

Cloud computing provides an opportunity for increased interoperation with all types of systems through shared Applications Programming Interface (APIs) and massively aggregated data. As a result, libraries will be able to reach more users, improve their supply chain and generally work better with all kinds of partners. Libraries can also improve their workflows through integration in the cloud. Each step of managing and delivering library collections is woven together, from selection and acquisitions to cataloging to discovery to delivery and to preservation.

OCLC member libraries have been building Web-scale services for 40 years.

As noted in Kilgour's original system design, the vision for the OCLC cooperative was to create much more than a cataloging and resource sharing network. It was to build truly shared solutions for managing library collections.

The members started by sharing cataloging efforts. This allowed improved options for resource sharing. And as the Web appeared, online databases became available through the cooperative. As the Web matured, the members built virtual reference services, shared in collection analysis and began implementing next generation discovery with WorldCat.org and WorldCat Local. Cloud computing now affords members the opportunity to connect to Web-scale management services, thereby placing their routine core management needs into a shared infrastructure that can simultaneously reduce costs and increase efficiency.

The benefits of cloud computing and Web-scale that were discussed earlier can now be recapitulated with more specificity. Web-scale lets libraries share all types of data, moving beyond bibliographic data to include library policy data, vendor data, ordering data and patron data. Web-scale simplifies the building of interoperability between services and partners and suppliers, thus creating more efficient and cost-effective workflows. Web-scale can free up staff to work on new initiatives instead of maintaining systems.

In 2010, OCLC launched pilot tests of its new Web-scale management services at these sites:

- CPC (Craven, Pamlico, Carteret) Regional Libraries in North Carolina,
- Idaho Commission for Libraries, including Boundary County Public Library, Payette County Public Libraries, and the Cooperative Information Network (CIN),

- Orbis Cascade Alliance and Linfield College Libraries, and
- Pepperdine University Libraries.

The Library Advisory Council is assisting us in creating a Web-scale service strategy that will meet the needs of libraries across various sectors and geographies. We greatly appreciate the willingness of the pilot participants and the advisory council to get involved in the development of our Web-scale services. This is in the great tradition of the OCLC cooperative.

An acquisitions module will provide unified acquisitions for physical and electronic collections, including license management and cataloging. It will allow for cooperative intelligence with other libraries based on shared, aggregated data. It also includes next generation discovery with WorldCat Local. It continues to support the circulation of physical collections. It is all built on a workflow engine to give libraries the flexibility to organize services to match their needs. The pilot libraries are already testing circulation and patron management modules. They will continue iterative testing and product feedback as new functionality becomes available.

OCLC's strategy for building Web-scale services has several other important aspects. We are focusing on four broad objectives.

- create a compelling user environment
- make OCLC Web Services a valued part of library operations
- increase OCLC's global relevance and position of trust
- create system-wide efficiencies in library management

These objectives complement each other. Together, they are taking us to the next-generation of OCLC services.

CREATE A COMPELLING USER ENVIRONMENT

OCLC's first major initiative in creating a compelling user environment began in 2006 with WorldCat.org. This search box made collections in OCLC member libraries visible on the Web to people everywhere. The goal is to have a person who is searching for information on the Internet using a search engine to end up in a library. WorldCat.org is experiencing steady growth. About 1 million referrals to libraries are coming in from the Web each month. These millions of searches started out on the Web and ended up in a library service. We are clearly increasing the visibility of libraries on the Web.

We are also running a pilot program based on WorldCat.org to make collections from libraries visible through mobile devices. We started in Canada and the United States and have now extended the program to France, Germany, the Netherlands, and the United Kingdom. In 2010, thanks to an iPhone application called RedLaser, it became possible for a user to scan a barcode on a book and then find that book in a nearby library using data from WorldCat. The RedLaser application costs $1.99 and presently works only in the United States. For book barcodes, the application uses the WorldCat Search API and WorldCat Registry API to deliver localized library results based on the user's location, providing library holdings, library location, contact, and mapping information. A similar free application, Pic2Shop, also uses the WorldCat Search API and works for libraries in Europe and around the world.

With WorldCat Local, OCLC is creating a compelling user environment that provides a single interface to the collections of a library. It enables a library or group of libraries to customize WorldCat.org as a solution for local discovery and delivery services. It interoperates with locally maintained services such as circulation, resource sharing and resolution to full text to create an integrated experience for library users. About 670 libraries are now using WorldCat Local.

We have added a quick-start program to WorldCat Local in which a library can easily activate its own configuration of the service in the computing cloud. About 500 libraries are exploring this option. This is another step toward Web-scale cooperative library management services. WorldCat Local is a cloud service provided to the library across the Internet that eliminates or reduces costs to the library for hosting, operating and maintaining software.

We are also creating a compelling user environment in reference. We developed the QuestionPoint virtual reference service with the Library of Congress and launched it in 2002.

More than 2,300 libraries in 30 countries now use the service, and some 1,500 libraries participate in the 24–7 reference cooperative in which reference librarians answer questions for each other. The global knowledge base contains more than 21,000 records in nine languages. Since 2002, the system has handled more than 5 million questions. QuestionPoint is also available on Facebook and MySpace, and it can be used from a mobile phone to chat with a reference librarian. OCLC is also developing a text-messaging capability. This is yet another way that OCLC is developing services that provide information to users when, where, and how they want it.

We are also creating a compelling user experience with Web services that enable us to present the data that we already have in new and ever more useful ways.

For example, WorldCat Identities creates a summary page for the more than 25 million personal and corporate authors mentioned in WorldCat. The summary page for Will Rogers lists 675 works in 1,077 publications in 5 languages with over 57,000 library holdings.

The RedLaser app and WorldCat Identities are not only creating a compelling user environment. They are also related to our second area of focus—Web services.

MAKE OCLC WEB SERVICES A VALUED PART OF LIBRARY OPERATIONS

Web services enable applications to interconnect over the Web through machine-to-machine interfaces. They cover a wide range of activities that let people tap into the computing power on the Web. In addition to WorldCat.org, WorldCat Local and the WorldCat Identities mentioned above, OCLC has also introduced these Web services in the past five years.

The International Standard Book Numbers (ISBN) service, developed by OCLC Research, supplies ISBNs associated with an individual intellectual work, based on information in the WorldCat database. It finds all related editions of a book, including paperback, hardback, audiobook, foreign, and out-of-print. Easily incorporated into library catalogs, the service is available free to OCLC cataloging members and available for a fee to others.

In 2008, OCLC established the WorldCat Developers Network by inviting a small group of developers from OCLC cataloging institutions in North America and Europe to use the WorldCat API to build applications that would guide people from the Web to library services. These developers could then link WorldCat information to Internet applications as well as presentations, blogs, and e-mails. This shared development will enhance the creativity and usage of WorldCat. The Developers Network sponsored events such as the WorldCat Hackathon held at the New York Public Library in 2008, a Mashathon in Amsterdam in 2009, and events in Seattle, Washington, and Melbourne, Australia, in 2010. These events bring developers together in a creative, collaborative environment. This open-source, code-sharing infrastructure improves the value of OCLC data for all users by encouraging new Web services uses.

The QuestionPoint Qwidget is another Web service that gives libraries the ability to embed a snippet of HTML code throughout their Web pages and in a variety of environments such as Facebook or MySpace. Other Web services that have been developed include:

ISBN, ISSN, OCLCNUM, the OpenURL Gateway, Terminologies and Metadata Crosswalk.

We have just released a new API called WorldCat Basic. It enables users to develop their own library-related applications. As a very simple interface to WorldCat, the WorldCat Basic API results include information about authors, titles, ISBNs, and OCLC numbers. Records are returned in the five standard bibliographic citation formats.

OCLC's WorldCat Registry is a free Web tool that provides a single location from which any library can manage and distribute data that describes its institutional identity and services. The registry record includes library system links, like OpenURLs, virtual reference, and online catalog links. WorldCat Registry record metadata can be provided to multiple services such as WorldCat Local, WorldCat.org, and openURL Gateway. The registry connects to these functions:

- WorldCat.org "Search for a Library" feature,
- WorldCat.org "Library info" pages (library profiles),
- WorldCat.org "Deep links" to take an end-user from the WorldCat detailed record to the specific library catalog item, and
- WorldCat Mobile pilot "Find a Library" feature and location for other mobile apps like RedLaser

In WorldCat Local the OpenURL Gateway within the registry can automatically direct an authenticated end-user to the available electronic resource for an item. Clearly, there are benefits to using shared data in a Web-scale environment. For WorldCat Local "quick start" libraries, a self-configuration login will also work for the WorldCat Registry. OpenURL resolvers in a library's registry profile can be shared with its WorldCat Local configuration.

For developers, adding APIs into registry data let them build apps and mash-ups that showcase electronic resources available (through the OpenURL Gateway) and also look up institutions by IP address.

INCREASE OCLC'S GLOBAL RELEVANCE AND POSITION OF TRUST

OCLC's third area of focus is increasing OCLC's global relevance and position of trust. One of the main ways we do this is through research that we share with the global library community. Frederick G. Kilgour founded the OCLC Office of Research in 1978, and it has been conducting research and sharing it with the library community ever since. OCLC research staff, under the able leadership of Lorcan Dempsey, vice president of research and chief strategist, have developed a work agenda that includes:

- supporting new modes of research, teaching and learning,
- managing the collective collection,
- renovating descriptive and organizing practices,
- modeling new service infrastructures,
- architecture and standards, and
- measurement and behaviors.

OCLC Research provides the OCLC cooperative with an infrastructure and interactive process for helping libraries, museums and archives deal with the rapidly changing digital, global community. Here are two research projects that are under way.

Constance Malpas, OCLC Research Program Officer, is leading a research project at OCLC in which the WorldCat database is being used to determine the overlap of holdings of New York University Libraries, the Hathi Trust and the Research Collections and Preservation Consortium (ReCAP). The goal is to determine the feasibility of combining large-scale virtual and print repositories as surrogates for onsite, physical, research library collections. We believe that cooperative agreements with large print and digital preservation repositories could enable North American research libraries to reduce their local collection inventory and associated management costs by 20%.

ReCAP is jointly owned and operated by Columbia University, New York Public Library and Princeton University. It holds more than 7.5 million volumes from member libraries and delivers requested items within 24 hours.

Another view of extending our global relevance and position of trust can be seen in a major international cooperative effort—the Virtual International Authority File (VIAF). In the past year, the project has grown to 13 institutions:

- Bibliotheca Alexandrina (Egypt),
- Bibliothèque nationale de France,
- German National Library,
- ICCU (Italy),
- Library of Congress,
- Narodni Knihovna (Czech Republic),
- National Library of Australia,
- National Library of Israel,
- National Library of Portugal,
- National Library of Spain,
- National Library of Sweden,
- Vatican Library, and
- OCLC Research

The VIAF participants are extending and enhancing the Virtual International Authority File, which virtually combines multiple name authority files into a single name authority service. The long-term goal of the project is to include authoritative names from many libraries into a global service that will be freely available via the Web to users worldwide.

OCLC has also formed some important strategic alliances with digital repositories and others.

The Hathi Trust and OCLC are working together to adapt OCLC's WorldCat Local service as a public discovery interface for its digital repository that contains more than 7.5 million digitized volumes from the nation's research libraries. We are working with Hathi partner libraries on specifications, with a goal of deploying the interface this year. In the meantime, Hathi is

deploying a temporary public beta using VuFind. We at OCLC are pleased and honored to be working with the Hathi Trust on this important project.

The University of Michigan and OCLC have successfully moved the OAIster database to OCLC. OAIster is a union catalog of digital resources hosted at the University of Michigan since 2002. Launched with grant support from the Andrew W. Mellon Foundation, OAIster was developed to test the feasibility of building a portal to open archive collections using the Open Archives Initiative Protocol for Metadata Harvesting (OAI-PMH). OAIster has grown to become one of the world's largest aggregations of records pointing to open archive collections with more than 23 million records contributed by over 1,100 organizations worldwide. OAIster records are now fully accessible through WorldCat.org, and will be included in WorldCat.org search results along with records from thousands of libraries worldwide that add their holdings to WorldCat. In 2010, OCLC has released a freely accessible, discrete view of the OAIster database, which will be updated regularly. This will allow WorldCat.org searchers to view only items harvested through OAIster. OAIster records will also continue to be available on the OCLC FirstSearch service to Base Package subscribers, providing another valuable access point for this rich database and a complement to other FirstSearch databases.

CREATE SYSTEM-WIDE EFFICIENCIES IN LIBRARY MANAGEMENT

Our fourth area of focus in building Web-scale is to create system-wide efficiencies in library management. We are not doing it all by ourselves; we are also enlisting new partners.

For example, OCLC and Google are exchanging data to facilitate the discovery of library collections through Google search services. OCLC member libraries participating in the Google Book Search program may share their WorldCat-derived MARC (machine-readable cataloging) records with Google to better facilitate discovery of library collections through Google, with links from Google Book Search to WorldCat.org that will drive traffic to library OPACs and other library services. Google shares data and links to digitized books with OCLC, which makes it possible for OCLC to represent the digitized collections of OCLC member libraries in WorldCat.

Thanks to an API released by Google last year, WorldCat.org users now have an easy, seamless way to view digitized books available in the Google Book Search collection, right on the WorldCat.org Web site. A Google Preview Button will appear in the record display when the text of a work—either excerpts for in-copyright works or full text for public domain materials—is available online. Visitors can click on the button to access the content within WorldCat.org via an embedded Google viewport. This is a significant enhancement to the discovery process on WorldCat.org. The Google Book Search APIs represent an important advance in accessing

the content scanned on behalf of libraries participating in the Google Book Search Library Project. Working together enables us to increase the presence of these libraries and their collections on the Web.

The WorldCat database has been creating system-wide efficiencies in library workflow management since 1971. The OCLC cooperative continues to contribute to WorldCat and use its records second-by-second throughout the day and around the world. Today, WorldCat contains more than 175 million records and more 1.5 billion location listings. WorldCat is now growing faster than ever. For the fiscal year that ended on June 30, 2009, libraries added an impressive 31 million records to WorldCat. WorldCat was at 139 million then. As of March 1, 2010, libraries had added 36 million records in the current fiscal year.

It's interesting to note that it took the OCLC cooperative 31 years, from 1971 to 2002, to add the first 50 million records; six years (2002–2008) to add the next 50 million; and just 1.5 years to add the most recent 50 million. Clearly, WorldCat and shared cataloging continue to provide value for the cooperative.

Going forward, we are extending WorldCat to represent the collective collection of the OCLC cooperative, including physical holdings such as books and journals, licensed digital content, and the growing array of local content that is being digitized.

We began adding article metadata to WorldCat a few years ago.

We have been systematically indexing entire databases in WorldCat Local, beginning with FirstSearch databases and moving on to content that we do not host, such as EBSCO.

We are also reaching out to others to synchronize their data with WorldCat—eBook providers, OAIster, CONTENTdm, Google Books, and HathiTrust, to name a few.

Approximately 4.5 million article-level records for content in the JSTOR archive are now indexed in WorldCat.org and delivered in WorldCat.org search results.

Scholars and researchers will now be able to identify JSTOR resources through WorldCat.org and connect with the full-text content using the authorization provided by their library. This is an exciting development.

CONCLUSION

We have seen that libraries have made significant investments in computer resources and infrastructure and now incur the costs of supporting an array of systems across workflows for print, licensed, and digital materials. Similarly, libraries have a fragmented presence on the Web, where they must compete with search engines and other information resources in meeting the information needs of people. In response, OCLC is building its next

generation of services in the computing cloud, where applications and data are stored on the Internet rather than on a local computer. Libraries can use an application without having to worry about supporting technology.

In 1971, with the launch of the OCLC WorldCat database and shared cataloging via a central system running on a mainframe computer, OCLC made it possible for libraries to take advantage of hardware and software that most of them could not afford on their own. As the OCLC network of libraries grew, so did the computer system. By 1981, the OCLC cooperative owned 17 mainframe computers, and by 1994, they were all decommissioned, replaced by newer server technology. For OCLC and its member libraries, 2010 is starting to look a lot like 1971 all over again, only this time, instead of big iron, the computing power has moved to the cloud, where libraries will once again have access to resources that none of them could singly afford. Web-scale services will provide libraries with powerful new applications and services when and where needed. To echo Charles Darwin on being responsive to change, we are indeed climbing out of the box and into the cloud.

REFERENCES

Association of Research Libraries. (2008). Electronic resources vs. total materials expenditures, 1993–2008/Yearly increases in average expenditures. *ARL Statistics 2007–2008*, 19.

Breeding, M. (2007, February). Working toward transparency in library automation. *Computers in Libraries, 27*(2), 23–25.

Code Project. (2006, November 6).*What is Amazon Web Services?* Retrieved from http://www.codeproject.com/KB/showcase/AmazonWebServices.aspx

Dempsey, L. (2008). Building Web scale for libraries. *OCLC Annual Report 2007OCLC Annual Report 2007*, 20–21.

Gartner, Inc. (2009, January 27). Experts define cloud computing: Can we get a little definition in our definitions [Web log post]. Retrieved from http://blogs.gartner.com/daryl_plummer/2009/01/27/experts-define-cloud-computing-can-we-get-a-little-definition-in-our-definitions/

Kilgour, F. G. (1984). Initial system design for the Ohio College Library Center: A case history. In *Collected papers of Frederick G. Kilgour, OCLC years* (p. 108). Dublin, OH: Online Computer Library Center.

LJ Academic Newswire. (2010, January 7). *The top 10 stories in LJ Academic Newswire in 2009.* Retrieved from http://www.libraryjournal.com/article/CA6713750.html

van Wyhye, J. (2008, February). *It ain't necessarily so.* Retrieved from http://www.guardian.co.uk/science/2008/feb/09/Darwin.myths/print

Why Libraries Persist: Hermits, Clouds, Confucius, Bubbles, and Hortense Foglesong

DENNIS DILLON

University of Texas at Austin, Austin, TX, USA

ABSTRACT. *This article is a look at hermits, cowgirls, pioneer librarians, information habits, and how networks are changing the information supply chain. The Internet operating as a ruthlessly effective supply chain direct from the cloud to the individual poses a fundamental risk to libraries. Libraries have to adapt, as they have successfully done in the past, or follow the well-documented pathway to institutional failure. Adaptation is difficult and requires a reexamination of core values and the processes by which those values are implemented, including questioning the concept of what constitutes research, information, and customer service.*

Just west of Big Bend National Park in the protective embrace of the Chihuahuan Desert, lies prime hermit country (Texas style). Four-wheel drive pick-up trucks with off-road tires and brush guards are the basic means of transportation. Advertised to the uninitiated as one of the 20 cell-phone-free vacation spots in the U.S., cell phone reception is guaranteed to be unreliable at best. Boots are a not a fashion choice but protection against an environment in which every plant species sports thorns and rattlesnakes lie waiting beneath the rocks on every side of you.

Here between the hamlets of Study Butte and La Jitas, lies the even smaller collection of widely spaced buildings known as Terlingua. There is no Wi-Fi at the Terlingua store, but if you sit on the porch and look up 6,000 feet up into the clouds and then 100 miles eastward, you can pinpoint the nearest place you can get it. That would be in the basin of the Chisos

Mountains near the restrooms and check-in desk at the National Park Lodge. The only practical nearby threat to a violation of the general terms of the official hermit's oath is a small quality book store, more of a room actually, just behind the store's cash register and across from the beer cooler and an impressive display of knives.

CLOUDS

One of the foundations of current technological thinking is that the network is now a key component of human progress. This cloud of interlinked devices provides for instant access to data, ideas, commentary, vacation photos, and other useful content. It brings improved medical services to rural areas and expands education opportunities in the third world. A repeated corollary to our growing reliance and belief in the powers of the network is that this electronic collaborative is more powerful than the individual nodes of which it is composed. Because the network consists of many cooperating nodes, it is in the collective power of the whole, where transformational efficiencies can be achieved. What any one computer knows, all computers can know. It is this network that will eventually transform life as we know it for everyone who uses a keyboard, pulls a touch screen out of their pocket, or gets up in the morning braced to face the ever expanding mysteries of the human experiment.

Libraries are nodes on this network, as is a west Texas hermit who calls his Web site "a field laboratory for sustainable living." Web sites and hermitry may seem like mutually exclusive concepts, but the cloud has a power to establish social bonds between even the most unlikely and antisocial among us. It also appears to be profoundly shifting our personal information processing models. We read fewer printed newspapers, subscribe to fewer magazines, buy less from neighborhood bookstores—all changes in personal behavior that will continue to have implications for libraries in the foreseeable future. It would be amiss for librarians to fail to consider what these behavioral changes mean for the future of libraries, just as it would be in the best interest of libraries to step back and ask the broader question of why it is that some institutions fail, while others are able to adjust and even thrive, as the world changes around them.

In the early days of U.S. librarianship, Hortense Foglesong (1907) of Dayton, Ohio, noted that: "The library system of today has brought order out of chaos, has brought books to light that were buried, has made knowledge accessible, not only in organized libraries, but in endless branches and byways where its principles may be applied—an incomparable service, and an evolution with remarkably few crooks." The observation about crooks aside, this statement could have easily been made today. The sense that librarians were part of a grand effort to bring order out of chaos was a common one in 1907, and one that imbued early librarians with a strong sense of mission as they constructed the foundation on which U.S. librarianship has been built.

OX CARTS AND THE SUPPLY CHAIN

One of the first lessons that U.S. librarians learned is that librarians do not have to bring order out of chaos alone. In the early 1800s, 500 books were individually wrapped in blue paper and dragged through mud and forests, across rivers, and up hills, from Connecticut to Ohio, by oxcart (Ohio History Central, n.d.). The books were then stored in various families' homes and circulated to nearby residents of the area. Fifteen of the books can still be found in their original blue paper covers at the North Olmsted, Ohio, branch library. Nowadays, printed books for the North Olmstead library are supplied by approval plans and shipped over interstate highways, while the library's mp3 audio books are downloadable over the network, and their Web-based eBooks are accessible via the Internet. The network of hosts for the original library (the log homes of the residents who kept the books) has been replaced by library content served via computers on the global networked cloud. The library supply chain, which used to consist of transporting books via four legged animal power, now consists of moving digital impulses over optical cables and wireless transmissions to whatever digital receiving devices each local resident prefers. The supply chain from author to reader has changed, but the library mission, to enable the communication between author and reader, over time and geographic barriers has continued.

Reengineering library workflows from the handling of oxcarts to mp3 files takes a bit of effort. But because libraries are middlemen in a supply chain between content providers and content consumers, libraries long ago became adept at becoming responsive self-correcting organizations (e.g., adjusting with minimal disruption to e-journals, eBooks, and institutional repositories). However, the current recessionary economy has brought a disturbing number of layoffs among longtime friends in publishing, a noticeable number of mergers of once powerful library vendors into combines of ever-dwindling numbers, and widespread reductions in library funding, all of which have helped to reemphasize the fact that libraries are not immune to global economic hurricanes.

Libraries are not only part of the worldwide technological cloud and supply chain; libraries are also part of the global financial system with all of its ups and downs, bubbles and excesses, and its shifts in consumer enthusiasms. The current economic situation cannot help but to underline the fact that one of the experiences that accompanies every economic disruption is an upwelling of new approaches to solve old problems. This familiar tale unfolds once the easy money which propped up the old way of doing things begins to recede. This then sends once satisfied individuals out to look for new efficiencies, and makes human beings more willing to embrace alternatives. We are already seeing some of these innovations as bestselling authors skip new print editions and sell their work to customers as eBooks, thereby reducing the prices paid by the reading public, and increasing their own author royalties ("Top Author," 2009). This is an example of a win–win innovation, except that if it catches on, libraries may find themselves on the outside looking in, unable to license books and other electronic content because it is now limited to direct sales to retail customers. This is the type of unintended disruption that is part of the "creative destruction" phase of healthy capitalism. If libraries end up getting locked out of this particular aspect of the supply chain, then libraries will adjust or risk becoming a relic of the past, a victim of the ever-shifting dynamism of capitalism.

WHY INSTITUTIONS FAIL

When the economy turns bad, companies fail. Companies, however, fail even when the economy is good. A recent book, *How the Mighty Fall* by Jim Collins (2009), is a study of why institutions stumble and become vulnerable to decline. Collins found that there are several commonalities in institutional decline, and that failing organizations typically pass through five stages:

1. Hubris born of past success (which results in a sense of entitlement, arrogance, and a neglect of the fundamental purpose and priorities).
2. Undisciplined pursuit of more (which results in the growth of activities that divert attention and resources from the core business thereby straining the organization and eroding cost discipline).
3. Denial of risk and peril (by this stage the warning signs are mounting, but negative data is discounted, external praise is highlighted, and big bets or goals are undertaken without empirical evidence or need).
4. Grasping for salvation (by this stage the institutional decline is becoming obvious; there is a search for silver bullets, for a leader who can turn things around; people are no longer able to articulate the core values of the institution).
5. Capitulation to irrelevance or death (at this point the company is sold or the institution hangs on but is simply irrelevant).

Collins' advice on how to avoid this fate is to hang onto the institution's core values, continue to ask why a certain activity or service or approach is being undertaken, and to put the organization in the hands of internally grown leadership—on the shoulders of those who know the core business the best, and not to rely on outsiders or big new schemes or fundamental business shifts to save the organization.

Of course, every analysis of complex situations (such as the demise of long standing institutions) is simplistic in one way or another. The two principal criticisms of Collins' analysis have been that:

1. Sometimes the initial cause of the problem is the result of an unavoidable decline in the core business, followed by overreaching for solutions that do not work. For example, the steady demise of travel companies, newspapers, popular magazines, and other businesses that were based on specialized information and whose declines have been brought about by easy access to information on the Internet.
2. Sometimes the initial cause is a result of companies listening too much to their established customers and employees, and failing to respond to emerging needs and changed circumstances. This is the classic cause of institutional failure that is acerbated by surveys and focus groups and was first brought to worldwide attention by Clayton Christensen (1997) in his seminal work, *The Innovator's Dilemma*. Christensen found that customers are inevitably invested in the current methods of doing things, and are seldom able to imagine anything other than incremental improvements to current operations. Taking advice from these customers reinforces beliefs among an institution's leader that it is alright not to seek significant change, which in turn makes the institution ripe to be supplanted by more aggressive organizations that are less invested in the past. In libraries, one example of this problem surfaced when many libraries were slow to embrace the Web, e-journals, eBooks, or even online databases, thereby providing an opening for the popularity of information searching to develop outside the library during the 1990s.

From the early days of the Internet, commentators have noted that traditional institutions whose businesses are based on information, have additional cause for concern. Usually these warnings are couched in the language of ongoing fundamental shifts in the way people create, consume, and share information—and in the implications this has for business. A popular example of this type of work is Thomas Friedman's (2005) *The World is Flat*, in which he talks of the ease with which goods, people, information, and business practices are now able to move around the world. A recent report in a similar vein entitled "Measuring the Forces of Long-Term Change" from the Deloitte Center for the Edge, noted that those most at risk were "Twentieth Century institutions [that] built and protected their knowledge stocks—proprietary resources that no one else could access. The more the business environment changes . . . the faster the value of what you know at any point in time diminishes" (Hagel, Brown, & Davison, 2009, p. 137).

The overall context of this report is that worldwide business has become more competitive, that information now moves faster than ever before, and that the value of proprietary knowledge bases continues to decline as the importance of quick flowing informal, Web 2.0, and personalized information sources increases. Using the sometimes irritating babble favored by consultants and technologists, the report goes on to say, "In this world success hinges on the ability to participate in a growing array of knowledge flows in order to rapidly refresh your knowledge stocks." In other words, the Deloitte study makes the hardly earthshaking observation, that every type of organization now needs to be part of near instantaneous information flows or they face the danger of being pushed aside by other organizations that are better able to take advantage of the new information ecosystem (a world that is suddenly smaller, flatter, and more connected than ever before). These observations leave research libraries in a quandary however, because there is no evidence that these Web 2.0 trends are having any effect on the formal pathways of scholarly communication that control promotion and tenure (articles in journals, etc.) ("Assessing the Future," 2010). This lack of traction in changing scholarly communication flows, despite years of campaigning by a determined group of advocates seeking to alter the publishing landscape through the use of the Web, leaves libraries in the position of having little choice but to support both the traditional forms of communication, which are the core function of academic libraries, and to embrace the new forms of communication, which continue to grow in the margins of academia and are an increasing part of popular culture.

BUBBLES

But for academic libraries there are additional concerns. The current unwinding of the decades-long economy of easy money, excess, and bubbles that existed from the early 1990s until the crash of 2007 is a forewarning that the levels of higher education funding that once existed in libraries are going to be difficult, if not impossible, to sustain. This will alter the nature of libraries for the next generation of users, much as the technological revolution changed the nature of libraries for the previous generation. For the last two decades the abundance of cash sloshing about the post–Cold War world led to the rapid expansion of new degree programs throughout higher education, the development of campus-wide computer networking, a building boom (including new recreational facilities that increased colleges' abilities to compete for students), and the development of a suddenly smaller networked world awash in excess publishing production, all while consumers and libraries were both flush enough with pocket change to continue to support highly speculative up front purchasing of both books and journals.

The opportunities to buy were everywhere. Libraries could buy in print, they could buy online, they could buy from multiple consortia, and they could have access to content now and pay later. Every sub-sub-subdiscipline of a couple dozen academic researchers felt a longing to create their own journal—and institutions were funded just well enough to be able to indulge these wants. The end result was that journals that at one time had actual human subscribers, now became purely institutional products, priced well beyond the ability of any individual to subscribe. Because the journals were no longer relevant enough to engage the interest of an entire discipline, they were priced to recover the production costs associated with their low-revenue-generating smaller audiences (the decreased revenue being a reflection of the journals' narrower and ever more minuscule concerns). Like the tulip mania in 17th-century Holland, every misbegotten journal was able to find a few institutions willing to pay any price to gain possession of that journal's singular micrograms of academic appeal. However, as this institutional money recedes, swept away by lower endowment payouts and reduced government revenues, it is beginning to unveil the true magnitude of the "journal bubble" that libraries are inheriting from previous decades of nonstop shopping for content in the belief that someone, somewhere, would always be around to pay the bills.

The "journal bubble" was originally marketed by clever salesmen as a solution to tight budgets, libraries were enticed to sign long-term contracts at reduced but ever-inflating rates, for bundles of journals that libraries were not allowed to cancel. By agreeing to this model, libraries in turn were able to slow down the impact of rising prices on their current budgets and to satisfy some of the unmet needs of their users. This slowly inflating bubble then spread across the academic world, with the vector being the newly created library consortia. What the bubble left behind were academic libraries with journal contracts in which costs continually escalated, rising in a manner eerily similar to the situation in which American homeowners found themselves during 2007–2008 with the continually escalating costs of subprime mortgages (which had originally been marketed as simple solutions for individuals with tight budgets). Every year the costs of the library journal bundles rose and every year the publishers tweaked the model to add even more journals (and costs) to the bundles in an ever-spiraling tornado of prices. And all of this effort was expended for journals that in the saner pre-Web environment of title-by-title subscriptions, libraries would never have considered purchasing. But the higher education climate of the times left libraries little choice. Every year, higher education had more students, more faculty, more research labs, more computers, and researchers everywhere demanded more journals.

As the funding behind this once-in-a-century journal market now begins to dry up, we can expect increasing vendor consolidation, tooth and claw fights for market share, and companies with depleting capital operating as only slightly more than empty shells. Some publishers will hang on as a librarian's nightmare version of the walking dead, while others will increasingly abandon those parts of the market that are no longer fat with potential profit. The deflating of this bubble to a more manageable size will be one of the principle librarian tasks of the next decade. But it will not be an easy task. There is no going back to simpler times, not in libraries, not among publishing conglomerates, not in academia, and not among the members of the intertwined global information cloud. One would hope that new forms of publishing and new methods of scholarly communication would arise out of the subprime-like journal bubble. If it does, there may be an additional role for libraries. But so far, practical nonideological solutions are not in evidence, and as Jim Collins notes, the long-term record of institutional failure by organizations looking for silver-bullet solutions is not a comforting one. The simple answer may be that most universities will have to learn to live within their now shrunken means, no matter how grand their prior vision.

The basic problems outlined above: the speeding up of new types of informal information flows "outside of the library supply chain," the stubborn persistence of traditional forms of scholarly communication, the economic bubble in journal publishing that has saddled libraries with difficult cost burdens, and the declines in university revenues—are challenges for libraries, but they are far from insurmountable.

HERMIT PUBLISHING

There are few among us clueless enough to doubt that we are in the midst of the biggest change in communication and information sharing since the invention of the printing press, and there is no doubt that libraries will emerge from these shifts with radically altered agendas and approaches. Even our West Texas Big Bend hermit is now engaged in a modern form of publishing. A generation ago the publishing world was simpler, the library world was simpler, and the path forward for both enterprises was more certain. Following the same business plans as the previous year was almost always guaranteed to be sufficient. Authors wrote, publishers published, readers bought books from bookstores or borrowed them from libraries. Hermits did not have Web pages and Web cameras, and cowgirls did not have Facebook pages. Nowadays, part of this once-timeless and traditional publishing model has moved into the digital realm and part has not. We are simultaneously inhabitants of the 15th century and the 21st century. There are layers on layers of communication formats with which each of us must contend. The choices can be daunting. What do we plug into, turn on, bookmark, read, buy, friend or unfriend, twitter, or listen to? What information pathways do we enable, and which ones will help each of us establish the connections that will make it easier to do our jobs and lead our lives?

THE LIBRARY OF CONGRESS BOOK TRAIN

Libraries have a long history of embracing innovations to improve the flow of information. One forgotten example of this type of innovation was the 1897 Library of Congress book railroad. Congressmen at the nearby Capitol would write an order for a book and drop it into a pneumatic tube in their office. The order would be received at the library desk and routed through another pneumatic tube to the appropriate level of the book stacks where a page would retrieve the book. The book would then be placed on the book railroad, which moved automatically and ceaselessly in an endless loop through all nine stories of the library's stacks. When the books reached the basement they were removed and rerouted to the underground book trolley, which then sent the books speeding at 600 feet per minute to the Capitol. The total time from request to delivery was said to be 4 minutes, only slightly more time than it takes to access an eBook from your local library today ("The Book-Delivery," 1897).

The book train never gained widespread acceptance, but the Internet has, and with it, we have seen a continued breakdown of the traditional methods of distributing, organizing, and sorting information. As the new tributaries of information multiply, information in digital form not only moves faster, it threatens to persist long past the time it should have expired. How long does each of us want our exuberant sophomore protestations of undying love to show up in a Google search? Even in the more serious and reliable realms of news, history, and scholarly communication: mistakes, rumors, myths, and multiplying inaccuracies threaten to overwhelm us as the written record is replaced by unkillable vampire-like manifestations akin to digital graffiti that proliferates in the endless gullible recycling of the unfiltered and unedited Internet, an Internet that provides page after page of incontrovertible proof that the world is flat and that aliens live among us.

As institutional repositories have proliferated, libraries are now a tentative part of this process of adding non–peer reviewed content to the Internet. Content that a generation ago would have been discarded is now able to find its way into the institutional repository. While most of this repository content has some value and lumping it in with the "digital graffiti" is unkind, there are nevertheless reasons for being cautious about diverting increasingly scarce library funds into experimental repositories. Studies such as the United Kingdom's "Peer Behavioural Research: Authors and Users vis-à-vis Journals and Repositories" (Department of Information Science, Loughborough University, 2009), or the United States' "Assessing the Future Landscape of Scholarly Communication" (Center for Studies in Higher Education, 2010)—which together interviewed and surveyed well over 3,000 researchers—have found that although many faculty are aware of repositories, they are not particularly inclined to use them or to view their contents as having passed through scholarly validation. At the moment, it is hard to know if institutional repositories are a classic case of hubris and overreaching by libraries uncertain of their future organizational mission (as Collins warns us), or whether they are an example of libraries charging out in front of a need that is yet to be realized, which, as Christensen notes, is a necessary step for forward-looking organizations. Whichever scenario turns out to be true, there are few reasons to envision repositories being a game-changer for academic publishing anytime soon. Despite a decade of experiments by more than 1,000 institutions, repositories remain a solution in search of a problem, with minimal faculty uptake and the certitude of increased budgetary scrutiny on the horizon. It is not surprising that a group as egocentric and independent as most faculty, have difficulty imagining a change in their own research and publication behavior, or that they are likewise reluctant to imagine a change in the process by which their discipline communicates. This is entirely in keeping with librarian experiences with slow-to-change faculty as e-journals were introduced, and with Christensen's research into the inability of those who are most closely involved with an existing product to envision that it could be replaced by something entirely new (Christensen, 1997).

RESEARCH

One of the classic definitions of research comes from the U.S. playwright and owner of Hollywood's Brown Derby restaurant, Wilson Mizner, who said, "If you copy from one author, it's plagiarism. If you copy from two, it's research" (Macmillan, 1989). As previously noted, one of the unstoppable wonders of the Internet is that myths, hoaxes, and fraudulent information take on a life of their own. For every fact there is now an antifact. You can find citations, publications, and "research" to support every point of view. Many years ago, before the concept of Internet-based research became a staple of all our lives, we more readily recognized that "research" was a slippery animal.

In 1939, David Gilchrest, the Association of Research Libraries's first executive secretary, said, "I don't know what a research library is; I don't even know how to define the word 'research.' "The title has been a source of embarrassment ever since it was chosen." This echoes his opinion of 2 years earlier in which he said, "My private opinion is that there's no such thing as a research library" (George & Blixrud, 2008). But founding fathers must sometimes be forgiven for the clarity of their vision. Luckily, years of repetition by less reflective minds have worn away our original misgivings about the concept of research libraries. Today the term *research library* has managed to become institutionalized and has assumed a useful place as an effective public relations tool for the profession, despite the shaky and unstable ground on which it was originally built. Carving out an understanding of research libraries that clearly differentiates future library content from digital graffiti, in a world in which information moves faster and more informally than ever before, is one of the challenges in front of thoughtful librarians who are hoping to guide the profession into a sustainable future.

MARY TITCOMB

Among the ground-breaking work done by early U.S. librarians were the spirited efforts of Mary Titcomb, of Hagerstown, Maryland, who in 1905 began traveling the nearby mountains in a black book wagon, bringing books to families who lived down long dirt roads that were virtually impassable for much of the year. In autumn, each family was allowed to borrow 20–30 books that would be their companions until the following spring. Originally Mary Titcomb's black wagon spread fear among the citizenry, who were afraid that it was the undertaker pausing in front of their homes for some unknown but deeply terrible reason; she later on painted the wagon red to make her appearances more acceptable. In 1910, her horse-drawn wagon was destroyed when it was hit by a freight train, but in 1912 it was replaced by a specially constructed International Harvester truck in which she carried on in the best traditions of U.S. librarianship (*Annals*, 1924; "On the Trail," 1909; Titcomb, 1909). Mary Titcomb had an independent mind; she was not comfortable doing things as they had always been done, and instead innovated to reach those on the periphery who were not going to simply walk into her library. She recognized that part of library's role was to provide easy access to information, even if that meant the user never set foot in the library. If she is not the mother of the eBook, she is at the very least the mother of the mobile book.

THE TERLINGUA BOOKSTORE

Back at the Terlingua store, just a few hundred yards away from Mexico over dirt, ocotillo, cactus, and more dirt—the telecommunications grid is an intermittent visitor and there are no eBooks, but the bookstore nevertheless remains an information node in the old-fashioned sense of the word. It is a reliable source of outside information for a community of a couple hundred Texas souls. The bookstore is solid with fiction, history, social commentary, books on building your own home with adobe and rock, books on the local mountains and desert, and books on the tangled and complex relationships with neighboring Mexico. Through some accident of demography and ornery migration patterns, the local population here reads, and reads well. The landscape attracts individualists, and they often stop by for a "cold one" and then find themselves lingering for further discussion in the shade of the porch. If anybody in the area has heard of the collapse of print, they are not letting it affect their consumption of books or their curiosity about the world around them. One of the criticisms of Web 2.0 and the social media has always been that it devalues intellectual achievement and substitutes in its place a form of enlightened virtual gossip and ego-centeredness (i.e., fewer newspapers, more Facebook and twitter), this kind of debate is not an issue in places where tarantulas significantly outnumber cell phones, where bookstores still thrive, and where people do much of their talking face-to-face, however.

A TEXAS COWGIRL

Among the local citizens is a woman we will call Amanda. She is in her early 30s and left her career in the big city to come back and help run cattle on the family ranch. This is not an unusual story. She bought some goats, learned how to make goat cheese, and began selling it to restaurants and grocery outlets in the surrounding neighborhood of 100 miles or so. She is a West Texas cowgirl. A generation ago, cowgirls did not think about digital clouds or cell phone reception or worry about keeping their biographies and connections up-to-the minute on a Facebook page or whether or not the batteries of their eBook readers or mobile devices were properly charged. Texas songwriter Guy Clark sings of this state of affairs affecting a similarly out-of-place and independent Texan, asking, "She's a real deal old fashioned analog girl in a digital world. What's an analog girl to do?" (Clark & Thompson, 2006).

Analog-based humans can still choose not to be swallowed up by the tyranny of the digital cloud—but the number of holdouts is decreasing. Nowadays every cowgirl's Facebook page is a node and every hermit's "field laboratory" is part of the cloud, and everything either one does leaves behind a digital trail. Amanda's life and her relationship with information have become more complex. But because the grid is an unreliable visitor in Chihuahuan Desert country, Amanda's goat cheese success has up until recently, been by word of mouth, although now news of it occasionally surfaces on the Web. She has been profiled in the local newspaper (which is partially online) and even here, on the outer edges of the cloud, she is leaving behind digital life crumbs, whether intended or not, that will not go away. Our hermit, who was originally living entirely off-the-grid, has had a landline put in and now has a Web camera that documents his sort-of-off-the-grid life without electricity, water, job, and most of the other aspects of connectedness, but he does choose to make sure his laptop batteries stay charged and his Internet connection active so that he can remain a contributing part of the virtual information community.

It is hard to argue against the value of sharing information digitally, but nevertheless, the number of bookstores is continuing to decline, as are the number of people employed in print-based publishing industries. Librarians who have concerns about the control licensing and digital rights management systems provide over the distribution of electronic information cannot help but note that it has always been difficult to control who bought a printed book, or to control what happened to the printed book after it was sold.

The printed book remains one of the best truly open formats in libraries today. Electronic information, however, can be licensed, which means that the producers then have control over who has access to the information and even who has access to which chapters or versions of the information. Producers can easily decide that they want to maximize their income by not selling to libraries (because libraries share content and thus can harm sales), or they can easily decide that they will only sell electronic versions that self-destruct in 5 years (so they can sell more copies later). Of course, none of this would be in the public's best interests, but the network cloud provides the financial incentives that, for the first time, make this future a distinct possibility.

INFORMATION

Human relationships of a generation or two ago, although never simple, had fewer communication pathways and fewer opportunities for communication missteps. The denizens of the age before everyone had a personal communication device in their pocket were also less inclined toward casual use of the word "information." Wendell Berry has noted that "information" (i.e., informing) has traditionally inferred that facts, observations, and experiences play a role in the formation of the mind and character of the individual human being (Berry, 2005). This is a much more substantial and weighty concept of "in-formation" than the common use of the word today. Berry elaborates that "in-formation" involves the forms, patterns, structures, concepts, themes—indeed the very order and context that is created in an individual mind as ideas are formed—and then latter solidified and molded by experience. Nowadays, this deeper and fuller conception of "in-formation," as a process with a meaning that is more knowledge oriented, has become drowned in the lesser and more simplistic view of information as a collection of random observations: some factual, some disputed, some simply not true. If our time on earth is going to end up being defined as the information age, one potential role for libraries is to provide a shelter of context, depth, and substance for "in-formation," as opposed to the lesser and impoverished concept of "information" as it is used and understood in the wider world.

Libraries have always been repositories of information, but what is the value of the information libraries save? In the United States, with our longstanding national philosophical bent towards pragmatism and utilitarianism, the value of information lies in the aid it provides in manipulating the natural world (for improving the economy, society, relations among people, etc.). Our hermit and cowgirl, however, might say that information provides them with the ability to lead a rich, complex, and fulfilling life in an environment where others see only scorpions, broken bits of rock, and an unforgiving sun known for searing the veneer off everything it touches. In other words, the value of information might be said to lie in its potential to improve society and enrich individual lives. But how do libraries connect the useful information bits in the amorphous worldwide cloud, to the individual who may be able to make meaningful use of them?

COLLABORATION

Traditionally libraries have connected users with the information they need through metadata. They have collaborated in the development of that metadata, and as organizations, have stayed connected to their users by keeping organizational priorities straight. Early library collaboration took many forms, but among the most notable were efforts at cooperative cataloging, which were first proposed by Charles Coffin Jewitt of the Smithsonian in 1850. This concept then traveled a circuitous path before achieving significant success via the 1901 program of the Library of Congress to distribute printed catalog cards to subscribing libraries. Catalogers of the day, who were used to penning catalog records in the "library hand," viewed the very concept of printed cards from the Library of Congress and other sources as a threat to their jobs. But once underway, the new cards proved so cost effective that there was no stopping their spread (Baker, 1993). Libraries continued to enlarge their cooperative cataloging efforts in what could be called a Web 2.0 manner, long before the invention of the Web, and long before the rest of the world discovered the merits of this type of widespread collaboration. This spirit of cooperation, be it with publishers through cataloging-in-publication data and electronic data interchange, or with Google through the digitization of millions of books, has helped libraries remain in the mainstream of the process of cultural exchange and information flow, and has helped librarians to perpetually test and debate the library's appropriate priorities.

LIBQUAL PRIORITIES

Academic libraries know where their funding comes from, they know what classes are being taught, and they know what research is being done on their campus. They know how many users they have for each of their services, and if they have been conducting LibQUAL surveys, their faculty and students have been unambiguously ranking the priorities they want the library to focus on year after year (LibQUAL, n.d.). In general, these priorities vary little from year to year, or from one library to the next. Yet, despite the clarity of information at hand, it is not unusual for libraries to continue to offer services for which users say they find little value and allocate funds in ways that only imperfectly match up with research and educational efforts of the university. Part of this disconnect is historical, part is political, and part is because libraries are also trying to collaborate across nodes and reform their institutions to meet common challenges. These collaborative efforts can sometimes get libraries momentarily crossways with the priorities of local customers and also with the priorities of their funding institutions. Usually these types of debates about priorities are just part of the normal push and pull of healthy organizations, but when budgets take a turn for the worse, the question of priorities takes on a more critical importance.

If we are to take Collins's advice, the best way to secure the future is to look at the number one reason for an organization's existence, and to concentrate on doing that one thing well. A mature and well-run organization is not distracted by mission creep away from the core, or given to flighty frantic shifts in organizational mission.

If we are to learn from Christensen, one component of effective organizations is that they do not just listen to the surface of customer requests and employee suggestions—but instead look deeper at the more fundamental needs that are being commented on, and then think ahead and determine how the organization can perform its primary business and its primary function more effectively. This may mean making some changes before customers are aware that change is exactly what they have been wanting. For example, broadcasters provided color television broadcasts even when most of their customers only had black and white televisions; just as libraries provided Internet access to library services even before many library customers had any idea what a modem was, and just as libraries invested in e-journals and eBooks while 90% of their users were still print-based. However, in each case, the organization did not allow itself to stray too far from the basic mission, which in the case of academic libraries has historically been to provide value added information services to a specific group of users.

If we are to learn from those who believe the Internet represents a fundamental shift in the handling of information, a shift in which an increasing amount of information will move online, and in which information available for sale to the public will not always be available to libraries—then libraries will have to be quick to adapt to changes in the supply chain or they will become increasingly irrelevant. It is not clear that libraries will be able to do this, nor that they will have the fortitude to break from the comforts of traditional group-thought even if institutional credibility hangs in the balance.

If history is any guide, neither will any of us will learn anything from the latest financial meltdown. Financial and economic advice of any kind is often worthless because people either tend to believe that "this time is different," or they just do not possess viable skills of fundamental economic and financial analysis and are easily and unknowingly manipulated and misled by colleagues and salesmen. Nevertheless, it is a good bet that this budget crisis will eventually pass, to be followed by yet another budget crisis, and so forth and so on, for generation after generation.

LIBRARY VALUES

All of the aspects of librarianship already discussed: the innovative focus on the individual needs of the user by Mary Titcomb, the embrace of the new technological opportunities provided by speaking tubes and book railroads at the Library of Congress, the use of cooperation and outsourcing to achieve efficiencies by early 20th-century catalogers, the symbiotic relationship libraries have with the information supply chain, and even librarians' knowing acceptance of the consequences of the journal bubble (done to benefit users, embrace innovation, and participate in the changing supply chain), all of these aspects of librarianship, including the need to wrest order out of the chaos of the Internet, are examples of what Hortense Foglesong (1907) called "making knowledge accessible in the branches and byways where the principles [of librarianship] may be applied." These principles have long been part of the fundamentals of the profession. Focusing on individual users, embracing technology, changing with the times, and cooperating and employing outsourcing as needed, all these precepts have, so far, served libraries well as a response to the challenges each generation of librarians has found in the world around them. Libraries have persisted.

This persistence is more than just happenstance. Libraries predate all of the world's major religions and eastern philosophical traditions. Libraries are older than every nation on earth, they have survived both the mini-skirt and plunging hemlines, they are older than baseball and cricket, and they were around when writing itself was considered an innovation. Technological devices come and go, empires rise and fall, but libraries persist.

DUALITY

What is it about the library impulse that has insured its survival? Part of that impulse is simply the desire to pass on knowledge to the next generation. But there are other ways to achieve this end without libraries. Why do libraries take the particular form that they do?

The Greeks can be said to have spawned two complementary philosophical traditions: that of Aristotle (celebrating the practical and commercial) and that of Socrates (focusing on the individual and the eternal). These same complementary impulses later surfaced in Rome, which besides running the world's largest functional empire (focusing on practical and commercial concerns) had to deal with their primary opponents, the Cynics, who favored simplicity and poverty. Meanwhile, in China this duality emerged as Confucianism (practicality and commercialism) versus Daoism (the simple, humble, and eternal). In Roman times, the Cynics and similar movements became associated in the popular imagination with the desert hermit who lives in a cave. Later in China, the Dao was written by Laozi as he retreated from civilization to take up life as a hermit in the mountains. In the United States, these two dual impulses, the intrinsic worth of the individual and the values of the simple life on the one hand (best embodied by Henry David Thoreau), and of the practical engagement in the community and commercial side of life on the other (pragmatism), have figured in much of our community, state, and national debates.

The genius of libraries is that they serve both sides of this fundamental human duality. Libraries are able to simultaneously meet the needs of the individual and the community. Libraries serve both practical and eternal impulses. Everyone's needs are met and everyone is included. It is easy for any community to understand the practical value that comes from sharing the cost of a library when that library strives to make both the citizens and the community: kinder, smarter, and richer, and does so in a straightforward and pragmatic way.

THE VALUE OF INEFFICIENCY

Unfortunately, focusing on the individual is never efficient. Google is efficient, libraries are less so. A world full of hermits would be inefficient. Efficiencies come from mainstreaming and simplifying operations, not from handcrafted customization for every individual customer. Libraries have tried to be both efficient and to focus on quirky individual needs, but this inevitably creates tension and difficulties. From an efficiency standpoint the best course of action would be for libraries to cooperate and buy one copy of every book and share it among every library in the country. Libraries do not do this because: (a) it would be stupid, and (b) it is not efficient for the user. Libraries do not exist solely to be efficient for librarians; they exist to be efficient for users. It would have been more efficient for Mary Titcomb to wait for users to come down off the mountains and hunt up the books in her library, but instead she harnessed up the horses and brought the library to the users. It would have been more efficient for the Library of Congress to make turn-of-the-century congressmen bide their time waiting for a library book, but instead they devised an automated system to deliver the book to the congressman's desk within minutes. Of course, libraries that make the mistake of not continually reengineering themselves to become more efficient, end up moribund, fat, and sloppy, with too much staff doing too many things that no longer need to be done. Inefficient libraries eventually find that their profligacy has left them with insufficient money to devote to their core purposes, and then they self-correct (or get corrected by their parent funding agencies), redirecting the necessary funds back into their core function, just as the Library of Congress eventually retired the book train, and Washington County, Maryland, eventually retired the book wagon, all in the interest of budgetary constraints.

But it is nevertheless the spirit of this inefficient focus on the individual that separates libraries from Google. Libraries have always been about more than the efficiencies that can be achieved from channeling massive amounts of digital bytes down preengineered pathways. The Google search algorithm has been endlessly tweaked to insure that the results of any search will be the set of pages that most people find useful. It thereby becomes a tool of assured mediocrity where the results are those that others (not as smart, creative, or independent-minded as you) have found to be acceptable, results that conform to the preconceived mundane expectations of what the most mediocre answer possible should be.

In a library, herd behavior does not determine the library's contents. This is one of the reasons libraries persist, because they provide individuals with a combination of content and services they cannot get anywhere else, and because they do so in a practical but somewhat idiosyncratic way as determined by practical but idiosyncratic and individualistic librarians, who are stubbornly focused on serving the customers standing in front of them. It is the inefficiencies, indulgences, and sheer joyous stupidities that separate humans from the computer chip, and it is these human inefficiencies and values that lie at the core of why we have libraries.

There can be little doubt that the Internet, operating as a somewhat randomly effective supply chain direct from the cloud to the individual, poses a fundamental risk to the future of libraries. Likewise there is little question that economic challenges lie ahead for the foreseeable future—but these are challenges libraries have seen before, surmounted before, and ones that they can incorporate into normal planning for libraries of the future. No matter what transpires over the next few years, libraries will continue to focus on the needs of the individual while constructively balancing those needs with the provision of practical services to the community at large. Libraries have a lot to be proud of. Libraries (done correctly) have always outlasted everyone who doubted them, and they have always adjusted and self-corrected while keeping their priorities in focus.

> *The library system of today has brought order out of chaos, has brought books to light that were buried, has made knowledge accessible, not only in organized libraries, but in endless branches and byways where its principles may be applied—an incomparable service, and an evolution with remarkably few crooks.* —Hortense Foglesong, 1907

REFERENCES

Annals of the American Academy of Political and Social Science. (1924). 116–118, 66.

Center for Studies in Higher Education (2010). *Assessing the future landscape of scholarly communication: An exploration of faculty values and needs in seven disciplines*. Retrieved from http://escholarship.org/uc/item/Okr8s78v

Baker, B. (1993). *Cooperative cataloging: Past, present, and future*. Binghamton, NY: Haworth.

Berry, W. (2005). *The way of ignorance*. Emeryville, CA: Shoemaker & Hoard.

Christensen, C. (1997). *The innovators dilemma: When new technologies cause great firms to fail*. Cambridge, MA: Harvard Business School Press.

Clark, G., & Thompson, V. (2006). Analog girl. EMI April Music and Whipsaw Music/Victor Tango Music. Performed by Guy Clark on *Workbench Songs*, Dualtone Music.

Collins, J. (2009). *How the mighty fall: And why some companies never give in*. New York: Collins Business.

Foglesong, H. (1907). Library work viewed from the byway. *Public Libraries, 12*(7), 293–297.

Friedman, T. (2005). *The world is flat: A brief history of the twenty-first century*. New York: Farrar, Straus and Giroux.

George, L. A., & Blixrud, J. (2008). *Celebrating seventy years of the Association of Research Libraries, 1932–2002*, p. 28. Washington, D.C.: Association of Research Libraries.

Hagel, J., III, Brown, J. S., & Davison, L. (2009). *Measuring the forces of long-term change: The 2009 shift index*. Retrieved from www.edgeperspectives.com/shiftindex.pdf

LibQUAL (n.d.). *LibQual+: Changing library service quality*. Retrieved from http://www.libqual.org/home

Macmillan dictionary of quotations. (1989). New York: Macmillan.

On the trail of the book wagon. (1909). *Bulletin of the American Library Association, 3*, 354–355.

Ohio History Central (n.d.). *Ox Cart Library*. Retrieved from http://www.ohiohistorycentral.org/entry.php?rec=2718

Department of Information Science, Loughborough University (2009, September). *Peer behavioural research: Authors and users vis-à-vis journals and repositories*. Retrieved from http://www.peerproject.eu/reports

Stone, B., & Rich, M. (2009, December 14). Top author shifts e-book rights to amazon.com. *New York Times*.

The book-delivery system at the Congressional library. (1897, August 14). *Harper's Weekly*, 815.

Titcomb, M. (1909). A country library. In *Papers and proceedings of the general meeting of the American Library Association* (pp. 150–152). Chicago: American Library Association.

Year 2 of the "Great Recession": Surviving the Present by Building the Future

CHARLES B. LOWRY
Association of Research Libraries, Washington, DC, USA

ABSTRACT. *During Fiscal Year 2008–2009 the Association of Research Libraries (ARL) surveyed its 123 members on the impact of the worldwide contraction and reported the results (see http://www.arl.org/sparc/meetings/ala09/index.shtml). The findings indicate the emergence of drastic steps needed to "right size" budgets that were reduced to meet institutional loss of income from a variety of sources, particularly tax support and endowment earnings. The impact of the 1st year of the downturn was taken primarily from operations and staff with large efforts to protect acquisitions. Every indicator pointed to this trend not being sustainable for the next fiscal period. A 2nd survey, conducted in the fall of 2009, indicated that the crisis has grown worse for Fiscal Year 2009–2010. It is anticipated that the steep decline in institutional revenues will continue throughout the year with repeated reductions and cyclical need to constrain expenditures. The necessary budget cutbacks are having an impact on all segments of ARL member library budgets—operations, staff, and acquisitions. It is clear that the elements of recovery being seen worldwide will have no positive impact for higher education in North America for the current fiscal year and likely beyond. Primary income sources have not recovered—state tax revenues are down, endowment expenditures are being eliminated in hopes of growing capital, and tuition is increases are being restrained. The depth of the recession has accelerated a process in the research library community that has been underway for some years. This process is aimed at fundamentally reshaping the mission of the research library to meet transformational changes eventuating from the higher education and scholarly communication environments.*

We are all facing the most difficult fiscal challenge of our careers—libraries and information providers alike. Indeed, the recent economic events are unprecedented for anyone born in the last 75 years. The primary fiscal concerns for library managers in my 35 years in the profession—concerns about annual price increases in acquisitions in excess of inflation and other similar experiences—seem like small bumps in the road. I will address a distinct slice of the library world, that of North American research libraries, but it goes without saying that what happens in the Association of Research Libraries (ARL) alone will have a major impact on the world of scholarly publishing, if for no other reason than collectively our 113 university members have annual expenditures totaling $3.1 billion, and $1.3 billion (42%) of that is spent purchasing information. That excludes the 10 nonacademic members, such as New York Public Library, Boston Public Library, and the national libraries of both the United States and Canada. If one adds to that the thousands of other academic libraries in North America and elsewhere, the impact may well be profound. Any large reduction in their collective expenditures, indeed even flat funding, will have a significant impact on the market. A hopeful phenomenon that we see emerging in the ARL member libraries is that they are using their limited funds wisely—not merely to hang on and muddle through but to seed the future. My topic is not only the near-term impact on fiscal behavior because of the recession but also the longer term transformation that we will see in libraries. This future will be explored after a discussion of the unpleasant here and now.

It is rather in the nature of dealing with such crises that there is an impetus to identify the causes in order to avoid them in the future, as was the case in the aftermath of the Great Depression. There is also a desire to punish the guilty, as demanded by the recent populist outcry not to mention massive amounts of "bloviation" in the media in the United States and elsewhere. However, it is also valuable to understand the causes to estimate the duration of the current crisis. Any reasonable list of causes would include those most recently enumerated by Jacob Weisberg of *Newsweek*. The bursting of the U.S. housing bubble in 2007 precipitated a series of events, but the root causes lie in what Weisberg calls "plausible necessary and enabling conditions":

- The policies of Federal Reserve Chairman Alan Greenspan.
    - Low interest rates 2003–2005, spurring the bubble; and
    - Long-term aversion to regulation, turning innovative financial products into lethal weapons.
- Global savings imbalances;

- Misjudgment by bond raters;
- Lack of transparency about banking risks;
- Excessive reliance on mathematical models; and
- Flawed compensation models that encouraged excessive risk taking by traders and financial firms (Weisberg, 2010)

I would add my own personal favorites to the list—the repeal of the Glass–Seagal Act, which had separated investment and commercial banking, and the attendant rise of unregulated derivatives, along with the lending policy of quasigovernmental mortgage agencies Fannie Mae and Freddie Mac.

As we look at the rebounding markets in 2009–2010, we should definitely not take heart. The defunding of North American research libraries, I believe, is the "new normal." To understand why, we need to look at the sources of income for higher education as a whole. They are similar in both the United States and Canada. There are three main sources of income among our academic ARL members:

- Institutional allocations:
  - Tuition/student fees (i.e., private and public);
  - Tax-based funding (i.e., public);
- Gifts and endowments; and
- Auxiliary funds, grants, and contracts (i.e., overhead)

A recent private survey of ARL by Carla Stoffle (University of Arizona) gave us granular detail on the mix of revenues on which our individual member institutions depend (Stoffle, 2009).[1] On average, funding for libraries in public institutions is based on about 90% institutional allocations, with the balance from endowments and grant income. By contrast, research libraries in private institutions, on average, receive slightly over 83% of revenue from institutional funding, nearly 14% from endowment, and just under 6% from auxiliary, grant, and contract funds. There are, of course, a few significant exceptions in ARL, such as a public institution that is more than 90% dependent on student fees and a private institution that is in excess of 54% dependent on endowment. Today, the only ARL member universities that are not at apparent risk are the few that are private and principally tuition- and research-revenue based. The revenue mix for most of our members is based on highly vulnerable income sources—tax revenues, endowments, or both.

There is plenty of external data to verify what ARL has learned from surveying its membership, and it is worth looking at this briefly to understand the condition of the universities of which our member libraries are a part. A recent survey of members of the Association of Public and Land-grant Universities (APLU), "Coping Strategies of Public Universities During The Economic

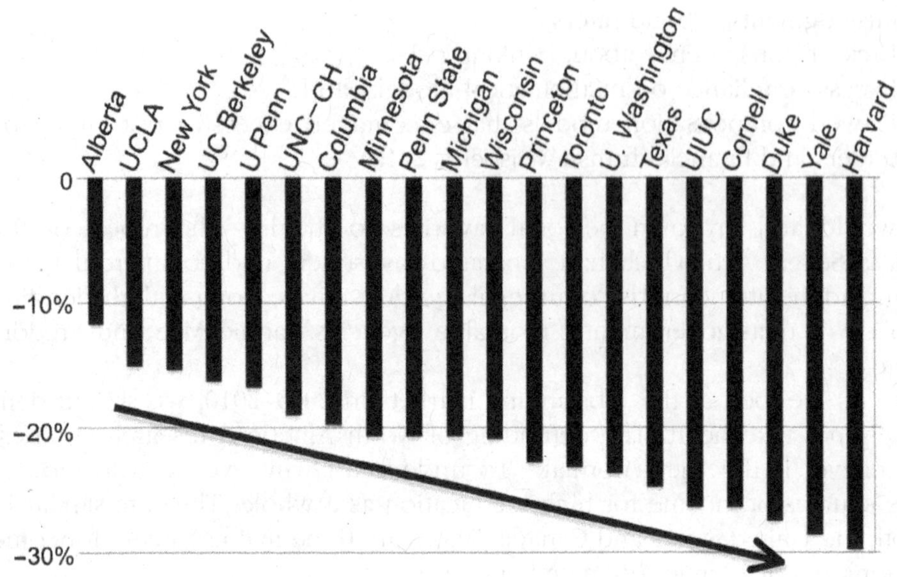

FIGURE 1 Top 20 Association of Research Libraries Institutions' Endowment Decline by Percentage.

Recession of 2009," provides the data to give some important insights into the long-term nature of the problem for tax supported institutions.

> Governors and state legislatures, working with unprecedented declines in state revenues as the result of the global economic recession, faced significant budget gaps for fiscal years 2009 and 2010. Most states closed the 2009 budget gap with a combination of service reductions, revenue increases [such as fee and tuition hikes], and appropriation recisions [*sic*]. Despite the presence of $53.6 billion in stabilization funds from the *American Recovery and Reinvestment Act* for the 2010 budget cycle, states again were forced to cut programs and services. Appropriations for public universities and student financial aid were not spared in most states.
>
> Decreasing state appropriations are not a new experience for public universities. State contributions to public research universities have steadily declined in real terms by more than 15% in the last 20 years. However, the current financial situation is especially precarious due to the magnitude of the recent cuts and the cumulative effects of decades of declining financial support. (Keller, 2009, p. 3; see also Hebel, 2010)

ARL institutions are also retrenching because of relative dependence on endowments (see Figure 1) ("College and University Endowments," 2010). Recent media reporting on the annual National Association of College and University Business Officers (NACUBO) survey of endowments in U.S.

colleges and universities paints a grim picture. Among the hardest hit are the topped-ranked universities with the largest endowments—all reporting losses greater than 10%. Among the top 20 ranked ARL institutions, 5 had declines in their budgets of more than 25–30%; 8 had more than 20–25%; 6 had more than 15–20%; and only 1 had a decline of less than 15%. For all of these institutions, the size of their endowments has been a vital factor in sustaining their ranking, not to mention quality. They are not unique in experiencing these declines when compared to the whole membership of ARL. Among private institutions, this has had a large impact on one of the main sources of revenues. Of course, public institutions in ARL also suffered sharp endowment declines, albeit they were not as dependent on this income as the private institutions.

We do not expect the major sources of revenues for our institutions to recover soon, since state tax funds are declining and endowments will remain submerged for up to two years. Thus, recovery—that is, getting back to where we were in 2007—will be a long slog. "The long-term implications of the funding cuts and the impact on public [and private] universities in North America are of consequence beyond the higher education community. . . . It is clear public [and private] universities provide significant contributions to the national economy and the well-being of [US and Canadian] citizens" (Keller, 2009, p. 4). They are also a significant market for all manner of commercial interests—no less so their libraries.

The data results of surveys of ARL member libraries taken over the last two years are significant. In the summer of 2008, ARL began getting many questions about how its members were faring in the emerging budget crisis. As time passed, it became apparent that we had much anecdotal and no empirical perspective on exactly what was happening. This led us to develop the "ARL Survey on Base Budgets, 2008–2009" that was administered March–April, 2009. Out of 123 members, 100 responded; and they were emphatic about repeating the survey for fiscal year 2009–2010. We opened this second survey in September 2009. In this round the responses were slower in coming because budget conditions had grown more unstable, and the impact of the recession was broader. We had a total of 93 responses from our 123 members. This was a smaller return than the 100 received last year and indicative that some were unable to give stable numbers well into the fiscal year. In fact, 26% of the respondents did not even have final budgets at the beginning of the fiscal year, which for most was July 1, 2009.

It is useful to compare data for the two fiscal year cycles (see Table 1). A total of 84 member libraries responded in both years, and we asked for a look back at the experience for last year in the current survey (2009–2010). This allowed us to compile a comparison of the experience of 90 member libraries for these two budget cycles from the two separate surveys. Those that had cuts of less than 5% (row one) in year one did not fare as well in the second year. Similarly, if first-year cuts were higher than 5% (Rows

TABLE 1 Comparison of Budget Impact, Fiscal Years (FYs) 2008–2009 and 2009–2010

	2009–2010 FY budget					
2008–2009 budget	< 5% decrease	5%–10% decrease	> 10% decrease	Flat	Increase	One-year response*
< 5% decrease $N = 48$	18	7	4	5	5	9
5–10% decrease $N = 17$	1	9	1	—	1	5
>10% decrease $N = 2$	—	2	—	—	—	—
No cuts $N = 42$	14	3	2	5	13	5
Total $N = 109$	33	21	7	10	19	19

*19 institutions responded to only one of two surveys.
Total responses = 109.

2 and 3), the second-year experience was—with one exception—as bad or worse, with cuts clustering between 5–10% or higher than 10%. For those that had no cuts in the first year (Row 4), the picture generally turned ugly in the second year. Clearly, for this group, the delayed budget challenges have now emerged strongly in the second year of the recession. However, it is worth noting that, for a small group of 13 libraries that had no cuts last year, things have not grown worse, and they received increases this year. These are the lucky few with the revenue mix previously discussed. Their revenue is based on tuition and research overhead with little or no dependence on endowment and none on tax funding.

The hard data we have for our fiscal year (FY) 2009–10 is based on the 93 responding ARL member libraries. The broad-brush picture indicates that over 79% had flat or reduced budgets from year one. Among the 57 libraries that gave us details about the real dollar budget reductions, the maximum budget cut was a striking –22%, the mean was –5.00% and the median was –4.49% (see Table 2).

As previously indicated, the serious impact on endowment income was caused by portfolio declines. For libraries that provided detailed figures (see Table 3), we can see the stark reality; but, again, it is important to

TABLE 2 Percentage of Net Budget Change for ARL Members, 2009–2010

2009–2010 budget change	%	Range minimum	Range maximum	M	Median
Decrease	77	−0.01%	−22.00%	−5.00%	−4.49%
Increase	23	+0.45%	+6.90%	+3.00%	+2.59%

Total responses = 74.

TABLE 3 Percentage of Change in Endowment for Association of Research Libraries Members, 2009–2010

2009–2010 endowment change	%	Range minimum	Range maximum	*M*	Median
Decrease	80	−0.20%	−100.00%	−16.00%	−16.00%
Increase	20	+2.54%	+145.06%	+20.15%	+5.009%

Total responses = 59.

remember that these data refer to income not the endowment corpus. The most draconian decline for income was 100%, and the average was lower but still a dispiriting decline of 16%. As you can imagine, such reductions cause drastic action and rethinking of the way research libraries do business. If one includes income that was flat, the overall picture for endowments is more instructive. Of the reporting institutions, 85% experienced flat or reduced endowment income. There is an attendant problem. When endowments go underwater—that is, when the book value declines to an inflation-adjusted amount that is less than the original benefaction—as a matter of common practice, endowment payout ceases. Even with the rebounding markets, some institutions have made strategic decisions not to take a draw on endowments so that they may recover lost ground fully, but this is at the expense of serious retrenchment; and the impact falls hardest on a significant number of ARL private institutions. Of the 19 private institutions reporting, 12 (63%) indicated that a significant part of their budgets came from sources other than institutional allocation. The amount ranged from 15–54%, and this translates into significant cuts when the endowment spigot is turned off.

It is informative to observe where members adjusted their budgets using the rough categories of staff, acquisitions, and other operations (see Table 4). Here we see illustrated how the three budget components were used to meet cuts. Staff budget adjustments ranged from –14% to 4.3%, but the mean was –2.74%, and the median was –2.50%—indicating that staff numbers are declining for a second year in a row. Likewise, the mean for operations was –5%, and the median was –3%. However, unlike year one, fewer members were able to completely ameliorate the impact on acquisitions expenditures, and cuts reached a maximum of –25% of some acquisition budgets.

TABLE 4 Percentage Net Change for Base Budget Hard Funding of Association of Research Libraries Members

2009–2010	Range minimum	Range maximum	*M*	Median	*SD*
Staffing change N = 65	−14.00%	+4.30%	−2.74%	−2.50%	−.04
Operations change N = 62	−41.00%	+17.90%	−5.00%	−3.00%	.08

Total responses = 73

TABLE 5 Reduction Impact on Budget Categories

	2008–2009 $N = 49$		2009–2010 $N = 59$		Future $N = 72$	
Categories	*n*	%	*n*	%	*n*	%
Staffing and/or operations	31	63%	35	59%	32	44%
Staffing, operations and/or acquisitions	18	37%	24	41%	40	56%

But it is more illuminating, perhaps, to look at the shifting strategies across these categories for both years (see Table 5). In 2008–2009, there was a decided effort to take reductions principally from staff and operations, sparing acquisitions; and over 63% of libraries made all cuts here, although 37% were forced to make some cuts in acquisitions nonetheless. Exempting acquisitions is difficult to do repeatedly; and, in 2009–2010, 59% of the cuts involved staff and operations alone, while 41% included acquisitions. This shifting ratio is reflected in what members tell us about the expectations for the remainder of the fiscal year. Only 44% of the libraries will be able to spare acquisitions the remainder of the current year if there are additional cuts. Let me underscore that this means there is approximately a 20% shift in libraries that have been forced to turn to their acquisitions budgets for reductions in the last two years. Cutting acquisitions late in the year is almost unprecedented. Keep in mind, though, that lack of budget reductions for acquisitions does not mean that there will be no reductions in purchases because even libraries with flat acquisitions budgets have to adjust book, serial, and database purchases to meet publishers' price increases. Research libraries have never adjusted to price rises with uniform cuts across all material categories and publisher lists. I do not think they will do so now; therefore, different parts of the scholarly publishing industry will suffer differentially.

However, there are a number of standard strategies for reducing acquisition expenditures (see Table 6). The first thing to note among the 56

TABLE 6 Acquisition Reductions Strategies, 2009–2010

Action taken	*n*	%
Reduced monograph purchases	23	41%
Cancelled serial/journal titles	30	54%
Cancelled databases	17	30%
Shifted journals—print to e-only	12	21%
Miscellaneous stragegies	14	25%
Insufficient description of strategies	9	16%
No reductions needed	5	9%

Total responses = 56.

TABLE 7 Staff and Librarian Pay Increases, 2009–2010

2009–2010	Librarians $N = 92$	Other Staff $N = 90$
Merit/ATB increase	41 (45%)	42 (47%)
No increase	51 (55%)	48 (53%)

libraries that reported details is that fewer than 10% avoided reductions in acquisitions. It should be noted, too, that the categories of "action taken" are not mutually exclusive, and most libraries adopted more than one of these strategies. Among the strategies employed, journal cancellation was most common and used by 54%, followed closely by 41% reducing monograph purchases, and 30% eliminating databases. Since around the year 2000, libraries have moved from purchasing print and e-versions to e-only; and 21% used the strategy this year when it could reduce serial subscription cost.

Let me turn to some details of what we know about staff reductions. It is not surprising to see staff budgets become a target for reductions in 2 consecutive years, given the proportion they take of a typical research library budget. The average is 45% of the total budget among ARL institutions. However, a significant number of institutions were able to give raises this year (see Table 7). It may seem inconsistent that, in 47% of our libraries, staff received modest pay increases, and librarians did in 45% of the cases. But this is more apparent than real, since the increases averaged less than 3% in over three-quarters of those libraries giving them. Moreover, union contracts required some increases. In addition, those lucky few libraries that received budget increases all rewarded their staff and, therefore, skew this statistic.

At the same time, reductions in force usually accompanied pay increases and were the de facto source of the funding for salary improvement (see Table 8). In most cases, there was an attempt to protect currently employed

TABLE 8 Required Staffing Changes for Fiscal Year 2009–2010 Among Association of Research Libraries Members

Variable	n	%
Staffing changes were/ will not be needed	20	23%
Eliminate vacant positions	59	66%
Hiring freezes	38	43%
Staff layoffs	25	28%
Early retirement program	22	25%
Staff furlough(s)	9	10%
Salary reductions	4	5%
Salary givebacks as charitable contributions	2	2%
Other	20	23%

Total responses = 70.

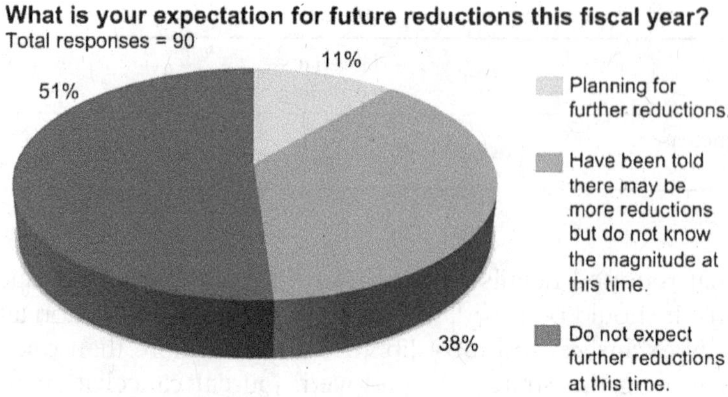

FIGURE 2 Expectation for Future Reductions in Fiscal Year 2009–2010. Total responses = 90.

staff by eliminating vacant positions in 66% cases and hiring freezes in 43%. However, to achieve reductions in staff force, 28% of ARL libraries turned to layoffs, 25% to early retirement programs, and 10% to furloughs; and straight salary reductions were used by 5%. These are not normal times.

What did members say about expectations for the remainder of this fiscal period (see Figure 2)? Of our 93 total respondents, 90 were able to make some observations about how things looked, based on the current state of campus planning. Around 51% expect to see no further cuts this year, but 49% are either actively planning for cuts or have been warned to expect them. As we have seen, these further reductions will likely be taken from all sources; and it is clear that, unlike last year, acquisitions will not be well protected.

All of this bad news supports ARL's early reporting last year. We are not crying wolf as has been asserted by some. Indeed, there is plenty of other evidence that libraries of all types are in crisis. The recently published CIBER (Centre for Information Behavior and the Evaluation of Research) University College London (2009) report, "The Economic Downturn and Libraries: Survey Findings," which was presented at the 2009 Charleston conference, assessed budgets for libraries of all types and sizes. Its conclusions are little different from those reported here for ARL. If there is any message that one should take away from our ARL data, it is that there is close to zero tolerance and, more important, little capacity for price rises next year and beyond.

What does this mean in the larger ecosystem of research libraries and scholarly communications? We have constant reporting from our members that they are now addressing fundamental change in the way they do business—indeed, transformational change that reflects how unstable the research library model has become. I believe, too, that this instability and need to change were in the making already but have been greatly accelerated by the current fiscal crisis. One of the key reasons for this instability is the change in scholarly communication, which is itself caused by market instability, technology, and shifts in funding. Accordingly, among ARL members there is a very high level of interest in how libraries may influence positive change in the current model of scholarly communication.

The magnitude of the challenge that academic and research libraries face is dramatized by what we have seen in the budget numbers. Under the circumstances, it is not surprising that the main theme of the May ARL Membership Meeting last spring in Houston was "Transformational Times," and it was intended to depart from our norm. This spring in Seattle, the theme will be "Globalization of Higher Education and Research Libraries." I believe that these are the beginning of a conversation focused on collaboration that will lead to sustained action and the development of new models useful to academic libraries in general. ARL is a member-driven organization, and so our objective is to move from conversation, to plan, to transformative action. Some of these conversations and actions take place among members in regional consortia, some are bilateral, and some occur within ARL's committee structure—a structure that is designed to be adaptive and to respond to leading edge issues.

Let me emphasize—I believe that the current economic crisis is accelerating trends that would have emerged more slowly. It is compelling a rapid rethinking of how we do business in research libraries and, more fundamentally, what a research library is going to be. The evidence is found in the subtle shift in the way members are talking about how they are managing budgets—a shift from the terminology of "cuts" to that of reshaping their organizations to fit not only new economic realities but also fundamental change in the landscape of technology, scholarly communications, teaching, and research. The examples of this shift may not sound too revolutionary or very new. What I hope to make clear is that taken together they are *sui generis*. That is, taken together, their collective force goes beyond incremental, and their increasing momentum will take us rapidly to a place of rethinking the way we respond to the core mission of research libraries.

I classify the adaptive transformations into three general categories. The first is a real movement toward the elimination or at least drastic restructuring and reduction of investment in low-impact activities to better use human and fiscal resources. In one sense, this is merely a continuation of the long-term efforts to eliminate routines that once were of central importance but that have been overtaken by technology, changes in the processes of scholarly communication, and the emergence of new teaching and research strategies. At the same time, I believe we have reached a fiscally driven tipping point. Libraries that are unable to accelerate the rate of adaptation to emerging best practice will risk failure in their mission.

The challenge here often arises from organizational inertia, resulting from historic budget commitments to staffing and collections for which there may still be considerable support. Library staff and faculty especially, but also students, may see any change in the structure of service offerings as a departure from a commitment to what they consider important parts of the library mission, even if they have not used or benefited directly from them. Classic examples are the closing of the catalog, the installation of compact shelving, and the implementation of off-site storage, which often engendered outrage—and about which I can provide a half dozen personal and (in retrospect) amusing war stories. But, let me turn to some obvious current targets that reflect direct experience:

- *Technical service routines like copy cataloging that can be outsourced and automated with significant opportunities to reallocate highly valuable staff to vital new work.* It makes little sense to invest so much in providing access to commonly held monographs and spend so little to provide effective access to the electronic resources where use is dramatically greater. The commitment of technical services staff will shift from externally acquired collections to locally created content and special collections. There is new work to be done in technical services—how do we mobilize to do it?
- *"Obsessive collection development" (tao use a pejorative).* This is that propensity we see toward collecting that is carried forward by its own inertia. Today, the idea that a journal run ought not be broken may appear laughable, but it once was not. More current is the inertia in changing the way we do business in U.S. government information—for instance, the pressure to be sure that every document in a regional Federal Depository Library Program depository is represented in all its instantiations. Similarly, how do we ever call a halt to collecting current imprints or special collections in a subject area in which our institutions no longer teach and there are no researchers? After all, building content collections is not an end but a means to supporting education and research.
- *The commitment of staff resources where demand has declined.* The decrease in ARL circulation and reference statistics tells us that we have provided users alternative paths to the information they need. This is a sign of success. But there are staffing patterns that support the old work and that resist change. How do we reallocate significant effort to the new work?

The second category that I posit is a significant redefinition of the way we deliver information that redefines large-scale organizational strategies. The core structures of the research library emerged in the first third of the twentieth century, were ascendant in the second, and began to erode in the third. That erosion is reflected in numerous trends, but I will name a few:

- *The elimination and consolidation of branch libraries is an irreversible trend.* There was once a furious debate in the library literature about the central versus branch service model that seems strikingly absent today. This leads to new questions. For instance, how do we best use new strategies like the embedded (or feral) librarian? (Shkolnick, 1991; Neal, 2006)

- *Moving low-use collections out of primary library facilities has become the commonplace in ARL libraries, but this is now causing us to posit new questions.* Is there a national strategy for these collections that would establish a threshold for minimum holdings of a copy of a title? If so, how do we avoid the "free rider" problem? What is the agency through which assured national cooperation could be accomplished?
- *New models of service delivery, which are weakly supported, need strengthening.* I think we are still having the conversation about services like online reference, the information commons, and digital repositories that reflect uncertainty about their future. In the last 35 years, when new core services like library automation or preservation emerged, there was the struggle to determine, first, how they fit into the organization and, second, how to incorporate them into the standard budget processes. This was often daunting, even in good times. How do we now adjust budgets in face of current challenges to incorporate new service models, and where do we place them organizationally in bad times?
- *There is the compelling issue of digitization of legacy collections.* To understand how important digitization can be, I only have to reflect that I can now use Google Books™ search to find what has been written about the region of Lower Cape Fear in the 18th century. Whether or not the Google Book settlement is accepted will not, I think, alter this reality. Monographs are being drawn into the same vortex of change that has already transformed the information presentation of those things we used to call journal articles. E-books are about to become a major resource, and I believe we will stop hearing that students and faculty do not use them for linear reading but only to find specific information. There is something resonant in the recent prediction by Jason Epstein in a *New York Review of Books* piece:

> Amid the literary chaos of the digital future, readers will be guided by the imprints of reputable publishers, distinguishable within a worldwide, multilingual directory, a function that Google seems poised to dominate—one hopes with the cooperation of great national and university libraries and their skilled bibliographers, under revised world copyright standards in keeping with the reach of the World Wide Web. Titles will also be posted on authors' and publishers' own Web sites and on reliable Web sites of special interest where biographies of Napoleon or manuals of dog training will be evaluated by competent critics and downloaded directly from author or publisher to end user while software distributes the purchase price appropriately, bypassing traditional formulas. With inventory expense, shipping, and returns eliminated, readers will pay less, authors will earn more, and book publishers, rid of their otiose infrastructure, will survive and may prosper." (Epstein, 2010)

The next frontier, one I have no doubt will be successfully challenged, is the vast holdings of unique materials in special collections. There is the tightly related area of digital collection development, characterized by "collecting the Web." We are still asking, how can we create this change? Rest assured though, digitization is changing the game fundamentally.

My third category is multi-institutional collaboration. This may sound old fashioned, but I think it is more. No doubt, collaboration has been a library hallmark; but, in general, I would say it has been a way to share local resources and staff effort, and it is important but not fundamental. Consider for a moment the kind of cooperation that might actually be game changing. In the last 35 years, the singular example that comes to my mind is Online Computer Library Center (OCLC)—so fundamental that we cannot imagine what our world would look like without it. I take a risk in identifying developments that fit this threshold, but indulge me:

- Google Book Search does not exist without the participation of libraries that have built and made accessible the collections being digitized; and, to that extent, it is a collaboration among the contributors. Even in its limited form, it is profound, but imagine what things will look like after the court case. Whether or not the settlement is disallowed, the U.S. Department of Justice has already signaled that it thinks the digitization, searching, and snippets display are a "fair use." If Judge Chin rules against the settlement, what is likely to happen? Google will work to define "opt-in" strategies for all publishers as it already is doing for those who fall outside the proposed settlement. Book publishers, eager to find new markets and to create competition for Amazon, which has owned them, will not ignore the temptation.
- The Committee on Institutional Cooperation (CIC) members of ARL have formed the Hathi trust. Among the key goals of the trust are:
  - To build a reliable and increasingly comprehensive digital archive of library materials converted from print that is co-owned and managed by a number of academic institutions;
  - To dramatically improve access to these materials in ways that, first and foremost, meet the needs of the co-owning institutions;
  - To stimulate redoubled efforts to coordinate shared storage strategies among libraries, thus reducing long-term capital and operating costs of libraries associated with the storage and care of print collections; and
  - To create and sustain this "public good" in a way that mitigates the problem of free-riders. ("Hathi Trust," n.d.)

  This effort has attracted significant non-CIC participation and is a promising answer to the challenge of long-term preservation of collections we have digitized locally. The total participation is now 26 libraries.
- The 2CUL project of Columbia and Cornell libraries

With the support of the Mellon Foundation,

> Cornell and Columbia [are planning] . . . significant partnerships in collaborative collection development, acquisitions and processing. The two universities will form a separate service entity to facilitate the collaboration. Ithaka, a not-for-profit organization . . ., will provide project management and assist in the planning. Initial work will focus on several global collecting areas, as well as collaborative funding and support of technical infrastructure in various areas. (Cornell University Library, n.d.)

2CUL serves as a model that, if successful, begins to erode the historic tradition of "not done here" that has framed—if not undermined—our efforts at inter-institutional cooperation.

- New models for automation have emerged. Open-source cooperation is a trend that may well have profound impact on higher education and has been heavily supported by the Mellon Foundation and characterized by the Kuali Foundation and community (Kuali Foundation, n.d.). Among research libraries, open source has grown and flourished. Duraspace was an inevitable outcome if Fedora and DSpace were to grow and thrive over the long haul. Likewise, "The goal of the Open Library Environment Project is to define a next-generation technology environment based on a thoroughly reexamined model of library operations and connected to other enterprise technology systems" (Ole, n.d.). It has now moved from planning to the development phase. At the same time, we also see the emergence of new network level capabilities. OCLC's WorldCAT Local is but one prime example.
- The concept of the North Atlantic Storage Trust was first championed by Paul Gherman. The purpose of the trust was to coordinate the effective management of collections held in over 50 library shelving facilities, principally among ARL institutions. The ultimate goal was to limit growth in those stored collections and achieve economies by eliminating redundancy while preserving access (Gherman, 2007). Since the first work by southeastern libraries, OCLC has taken a lead; and the program has morphed into the "Cooperative Collection Management Trust (CCMT) [that] is a group of institutions connected by the need to reduce the costs and footprint associated with physical storage and management of print materials while maintaining access to the content. OCLC is leading a pilot program that seeks to address these needs across a variety of institutions in North America" (OCLC, n.d.). While we have yet to see a practical implementation, I believe the time is right for this project to gain traction.
- ARL as a member-driven organization has been asked to serve as a convener of efforts. During our 2009 strategic plan review, a new focus for our strategic directions emerged (ARL, n.d.). Without going into all the details, the directions were conditioned by membership's desire that we

focus on helping create the vision for the future research library. We are, for instance, beginning a "Future Scenarios Development" project that will shape just such a vision. Similarly, we have begun an active conversation with the Association of American University Presses on how to reshape collecting in the emerging e-book environment. We will soon publish a study on how independent small campus journals and libraries can cooperate to preserve these vital publications in an environment in which scale has dwarfed quality. I expect such efforts to proliferate rapidly over the three-year life of our current strategic plan.

In discussing what I view as the various categories of current change that are converging to reshape fundamentally the library institution, I have asked a series of related questions. Perhaps there is a simple question to guide us—"What should we do now that will in the future best serve the mission of the research library in the service of teaching and research?" We should test the answer to that question with another—"Is this answer generated out of the inertia of historic routine, the psychology of our own self-esteem, the incoherence of university community understanding, or fundamentally because the vision of the future lacks persuasive clarity?" If the answer is not motivated by these considerations, then we have a brightening path ahead.

NOTE

1. The author shared a spreadsheet of the data that included responses from 70 member libraries. Only two were non-academic members.

REFERENCES

ARL. See Association of Research Libraries. Association of Research Libraries. (n.d.). *About ARL: Governance and leadership*. Retrieved May 20, 2010, from http://www.arl.org/arl/governance/strat-plan/index.shtml

CIBER University College London. (2009, December). The economic downturn and libraries: Survey findings. *Charleston Survey Report*. Retrieved May 20, 2010, from www.ucl.ac.uk/infostudies/research/ciber/charleston-survey.pdf

"College and University Endowments, 2008–2009." (2010). *The Chronicle of Higher Education*. Retrieved from http://chronicle.com/premium/stats/endowments/results.php?year=2010

Cornell University Library. (n.d.). *Columbia and Cornell libraries announce new partnership*. Retrieved from http://www.library.cornell.edu/news/091012/2cul

Epstein, J. (2010, March 11). Publishing: The revolutionary future. *New York Review of Books*. Retrieved from http://www.nybooks.com/articles/archives/2010/mar/11/publishing-the-revolutionary-future/?page=1

Gherman, P. (2007). The North Atlantic Storage Trust: Maximizing space, preserving collections. *portal: Libraries and the Academy*, 7(3), 27–5.

Hathi Trust (n.d.). *Hathi Trust: A shared digital repository.* Retrieved from http://www.hathitrust.org/mission_goals

Hebel, S. (2010, March 14). State cuts are pushing public colleges to peril. *Chronicle of Higher Education.* Retrieved from http://chronicle.com/article/In-Many-States-Public-Higher/64620/

Keller, C. M. (2009, November). *Coping strategies of public universities during the economic recession of 2009: Coping strategies of public universities during the economic recession of 2009:.* Washington, DC: Association of Public and Land-Grant Universities.

Kuali Foundation. (n.d.). *Search.* Retrieved May 20, 2010, from http://www.kuali.org/search

Neal, J. G. (2006, February 15). Raised by wolves. *Library Journal, 131*(3), 42–4.

OCLC. (n.d.). *Cooperative Collection Management Trust (CCMT pilot).* Retrieved from http://www.oclc.org/productworks/ccmt.htm

Ole Project. (n.d.). *Overview.* Retrieved from http://oleproject.org/overview/

Shkolnick, L. (1991, July). The continuing debate over academic branch libraries. *College and Research Libraries, 52*, 343–51.

Stoffle, C. (2009). *ARL Libraries expenditures by source.* E-mail survey.

Weisberg, J. (2010, January 18). What caused the great recession? It's finally ending. Let the blaming begin. *Newsweek.*

Finding the Right Metaphor: Restructuring, Realigning, and Repackaging Today's Research Libraries

JOAN GIESECKE
University of Nebraska–Lincoln, Lincoln, NE, USA

ABSTRACT. *To change from collection-centric to user-centered research libraries and to survive in tough economic times, libraries face 2 major challenges: 1st, libraries need to change how they are viewed by their constituencies so they are seen as indispensable; and 2nd, libraries need to help the librarians and staff change their own mental models of their roles to remain relevant in these changing times. Metaphors are one way to help people connect terms in new ways so they develop new images of those terms. For more than 100 years, libraries have used metaphors to seek connections that will help people see libraries as something other than warehouses for books. This article will explore various metaphors being used in the library field and how these metaphors can help libraries introduce change to improve their chances of receiving the support needed to survive.*

Transitions. Change. Repackaging. Survival. These themes dominate our field as libraries seek to reinvent themselves in a 2.0 world to stay relevant in the competitive information environment. Libraries face two major challenges in implementing change in today's world. First, libraries need to change how they are viewed by their constituencies so they are seen as indispensable. Second, and equally challenging, libraries need to help librarians and staff change their own metal models of their roles to remain relevant in these turbulent times. Metaphors are one way to help people connect terms in new ways so they develop new images of those ideas.

What are metaphors or why is hail always the size of something else? Metaphors, as we all know, are phrases that connect unlike items that actually have something in common or phrases where one thing is used to designate another (Dictionary.com, 2010). Metaphors such as Shakespeare's "All the world's a stage, and all the men and women merely players," presents us with a different image of reality (Shakespeare, n.d.). As another example, Keith Fiels, executive director of the American Library Association (ALA), at the division leaders/BARC Midwinter meeting at the ALA meeting, January 2009, was describing the purpose of an initiative fund used for projects that relate to the ALA Strategic Plan. He noted that the fund helped ALA be more nimble, and then noted that this made ALA a nimble dinosaur. These metaphors are very useful examples of how metaphors help create images for people to see things differently. Metaphors can help us accept new ideas and to expand our views.

What does this have to do with the size of hail? Hail helps explain why metaphors work. There is an established chart for how to describe the size of hail. From the government National Oceanic and Atmospheric Administration (NOAA) Web site (2010) you learn that pea-size hail is one-quarter of an inch whereas golf ball–size hail is one and three-quarters of an inch. Scientists learned that people were more accurate in reporting the size of hail when they compared the hail to a known object than when they tried to guess the size in inches. The comparison approach provides an understandable standard way for people to describe an event.

Estimating Hail Size

- Pea = 1/4 inch diameter
- Marble/mothball = 1/2 inch diameter
- Dime/Penny = 3/4 inch diameter—hail penny size or larger is considered severe
- Nickel = 7/8 inch
- Quarter = 1 inch
- Ping-Pong Ball = 1 1/2 inch
- Golf Ball = 1 3/4 inches
- Tennis Ball = 2 1/2 inches
- Baseball = 2 3/4 inches
- Tea cup = 3 inches
- Grapefruit = 4 inches
- Softball = 4 1/2 inches

Metaphors have the same power. They help people think differently about an event or activity. They help us change or confirm our mental models. Because metaphors reflect conceptual or mental models, metaphors can be used to identify how someone perceives a particular institution, situation, idea, or how they look at things. Metaphors can provoke powerful images that can persuade others of a particular solution or point of view. They can frame a problem in a way that sets the direction for what solutions might be considered, but they do not result in canned solutions. For example, if the information highway metaphor for networked information conveys the idea that all information is available for free on the highway, then the need to support libraries as a source for information becomes questionable.

Librarians have been using metaphors to describe libraries and librarians since the modern library movement began in the late 19th century. These early leaders, such as Melville Dewey, used various images to "locate desirable meanings in other walks of life and associate them with their renewed but misunderstood institutions" (Nardini, 2001).[1] Library leaders in the late 1800s sought to redefine libraries in terms of education and schools. Others looked to religious metaphors to describe the importance of libraries to the local community. They sought to overcome the negative terms often used to describe libraries and librarians. Even in the 19th century, libraries were described as "just warehouses for books" or as "antiquarian museums" (Larner, 1998). Libraries were viewed as dusty collections of print material that were guarded by librarians and not meant to be used. This dismal image is a true contrast to the libraries of ancient Greece and Rome where the scholars who oversaw the private libraries were seen as important members of the community. In Rome, a librarian was a "stepping stone for the ambitious government servant" (Krasner-Khait, 2001).

Our library leaders of the 19th century tried a number of more positive metaphors to describe the profession. They argued that a community library was the people's university. In the academic world, the library was viewed as the laboratory for the humanities. Some leaders described branch libraries as the parish churches of literature and education. Each of these metaphors centers the library with a positive educational or community value.

The beginning of the 20th century saw libraries align themselves with business metaphors, emphasizing efficiency and incorporating business principles into the organization. Libraries also equated themselves with public utilities as institutions deserving public support. Libraries turned to department stores to describe the type of customer service that was needed to help library employees understand the service ethic that was becoming more important.

Not much had changed by the last decade of the 20th century. Danuta Nitecki, in a study of the use of metaphors by faculty, administrators, and libraries to describe academic libraries as reported in the *Chronicle of Higher Education* opinion pages, found that the following metaphors were used:

- library as storehouse,
- electronic access,
- activist,

- partners,
- location,
- measure of academic quality,
- object of ownership and
- economic setting. (Nitecki, 1993, p. 262)

Administrators were likely to describe libraries as partners with the campus, while faculty members were more likely to view libraries as repositories for physical information. Librarians attributed an activist role to libraries, yet also saw the library as a storehouse for information. These different perspectives help remind us that the impact of a particular metaphor is influenced by the background and positions of the senders and receivers of the messages as well as by the message itself. Nitecki also noted that additional metaphors found in the literature include library as salon, as a smorgasbord where specialists may diversify their diets, and a window on local events, as a watch tower, and as a multimedia kiosk (Nitecki, 1993, p. 260).

All of these concepts are very familiar to us. We are still seeking the right way to describe the library as more than a warehouse or museum for books. We bring in customer service training and turn to places such as the Disney Corporation to try to help librarians understand how to connect to their constituencies. We talk about our place on the information highway, the well-known metaphor for the Internet. We seek ways to be seen as flexible and agile.

LIBRARIANS

Metaphors have also been used to help recruit new librarians to the field. In Dewey's time, library leaders equated librarians with teachers and educators to bring more prestige to the profession. In the beginning of the 20th century, librarians referred to themselves as businesspeople promoting efficient operations and developing sound operating principles. These leaders hoped that equating libraries with educational institutions and business enterprises would help attract teachers and businessmen or department store employees to the library field.

By the end of the 20th century, the library field had incorporated numerous terms from the computer industry to describe librarians. Librarians were now information engineers, information professionals, and information specialists or information navigators on the information highway. We even referred to ourselves as the new search engines or as middleware. How odd that we equate ourselves to computer programs to raise our status among our constituencies. Research libraries could be described as part of the knowledge management system, participating in the dissemination and use of knowledge. Each of these images is an effort to improve the visibility of librarians and to change the way people think about and describe librarians. The images are also efforts to encourage librarians to change and adapt to the complex, information environment.

School librarians have used a number of terms to describe school positions from librarians to media specialists to learning specialists. Today, in the Lincoln Public Schools in Nebraska, the media specialists are also termed teacher–librarians and many are managing both the library and the computer laboratories. Again, librarians are seeking terms and metaphors that indicate librarians are professionals who do more than read and shelve books.

In the 21st century, academic library leaders have sought new metaphors to describe the changes needed in the workforce so libraries can take on new roles. Jim Neal (2006) referred to the "feral professionals" who hold professional positions in our libraries but do not necessarily have a master's degree in library science. These professionals include positions in human resources, development, special collections, and digital initiatives, to name just a few areas. The Council on Library and Information Resources (CLIR) used the term "hybrid librarians" to describe the post-doctoral fellowship program that brings PhD trained professionals into library positions to bridge the gap between the libraries and the teaching departments (Walter, 2008). CLIR fellows have been involved in a variety of projects often centering on new teaching models, digital scholarship, and special collections efforts.

Steven Bell and Jim Shank used the term blended librarians to describe the need for librarians to become more integrated in the teaching process by developing skills in instructional technology and instructional design ("Blended librarian," 2005). Blended librarians become partners with faculty and other academic professionals in designing courses and incorporating information literacy and research skills into academic programs to achieve student learning outcomes. Blended librarians therefore become part of the instructional development team (Bell & Shank, 2007). Blended librarians may be seen as a new metaphor for the librarian–educator metaphor that Dewey used.

John Budd (2009), University of Missouri School of Library Science, writes about the need for academic liaison librarians to be embedded librarians, closely tied to the academic departments they serve. Embedded librarians may have office hours in the academic department or even a joint appointment in an academic unit. This image expands the approach that branch librarians located in branches within academic buildings have taken to liaison librarians in a main or centralized library. Having the librarians physically closer to the faculty can increase informal communication and hallway conversations to keep the librarian well informed about and sharing information with the academic department.

In a recent article in *American Libraries*, Steven Bell (2009) suggested that we needed to move from the metaphor of gatekeeper to the metaphor of gate openers to describe our future. He argues that we need to shift from "a focus on creating access to resources to creating meaningful relationship with community members." We need to invite people into our libraries and to engage with them in their research. By creating great library user experiences we will create strong relationships with our users that can help generate support for our institutions. By creating meaning for users and developing relationships, librarians become an essential part of the community.

LIBRARY METAPHORS

Library as a Body Part

We are all familiar with the concept of the library as the heart of the university, a phrase attributed to Charles Eliot, President of Harvard in the 1860s.[1] At Yale University, that phrase was carved above the entrance of the Sterling Memorial Library, which opened in 1930. But certainly we are also aware of the conversations that the library may be losing its place as the heart and soul of the university. Perhaps those who argue that the World Wide Web had replaced librarians would suggest that the library as the heart of the university is a heart with clogged arteries and in need of bypass surgery. Can we describe libraries as healthy hearts? Will some other body part be a better metaphor for today's research library?

Lorcan Dempsey (2008) of OCLC in his Weblog posed a similar question on May 13, 2008. Is the library the brain, the blood, or the lungs (Dempsey, 2008)? One posting suggests the library is the foot on which the institution rests. The comments on Dempsey's blog entry did not yield a consensus. Edward Shepard, head of collection development at State University of New York, Binghamton, mused about the same question in a report on the October, 2008 Readex Digital Institute (Shepard, 2009). He wondered if the library is more of a muscle pumping information throughout the institution. Perhaps the library is the circulation system uniting the parts of the university. He concluded that the library should be seen as an active muscle to remain effective. While being the heart of the university may be comforting to some, it does not seem to be a metaphor that helps others see the library as an active part of the campus.

Library as Conversation

Another set of metaphors describes the library as the connector between content and the user of the content. Along these lines, J. Z. Nitecki (1993, p. 260) describes librarianship as a communication process involving information content and concepts, the ways that information is relayed, and the recipients of the content. R. David Lankes, Joanne Silverstein, and Scott Nicholson (2007) describe libraries as part of the conversation business, arguing that knowledge is created through conversation. They describe conversation theory, which is a means of explaining cognition and how people learn. People connect ideas and learn through conversations with others and as internal conversations between themselves and the written text. Librarians facilitate conversations or learning through information literacy activities, teaching critical thinking skills, and by preserving the social record so people can connect with history. Further, in today's technology environment, libraries become part of the participatory network or social networks that bring people and content together in ways that allow users to create their own connections. We have finally created the shared minds that Michael Schrage (1995), research associate at Massachusetts Institute of Technology's Sloan School of Management, described in *Shared Minds: The New Technologies for Collaboration.* He wrote about how libraries can bring people together through technology. Now, libraries join Facebook and Twitter, to engage our constituencies in our world.

Library as Place

As the need for libraries as physical spaces has come under discussion, the library field has created numerous metaphors to help people imagine the library as something other than a quiet place with dusty books and an unwelcoming environment. Some have equated libraries with bookstores and coffee houses. These are places where people can gather, access electronic information, interact with colleagues without being told to be quiet, and still enjoy a cup of coffee and a snack. Library as Starbucks or library as Barnes & Noble comes to mind. A recent posting on the *School Library Journal* blog contrasted the idea of library as grocery store and library as kitchen (Valenza, 2008). Library as grocery store is an image of libraries as places where one gets stuff whereas library as kitchen invokes the image of a place where people do things together. Kitchens are seen as social spaces, gathering spaces, and comfortable spaces where family and friends interact. This is the image many of us are trying to create for our libraries.

Other places are also used to describe libraries. As previously noted, the humanities disciplines describe the library as their laboratory. This metaphor is often tied to the need for some type of start up funds for new humanities faculty just as universities put together start up packages for lab scientists. For students we describe the library as their academic living room or place where they can gather and study. Recently our library at University of Nebraska–Lincoln (UNL) was rated by students as one of the best places on campus to grab a quick nap between classes. At least they see the place as safe and welcoming. We are beginning to describe our comfortable seating areas as the mini–bed and breakfast for the campus as students relax in a comfortable chair, get out their laptops, put down their cup of coffee or soda and fall asleep. Again, the challenge is to help students view today's academic libraries as a welcoming place for them and not as a large warehouse for books. As already noted, the metaphor of library as a warehouse or a museum for books has been with us for more than 120 years and is still one that we have not been able to eliminate from the conversations about libraries.

Digital, "e," and 2.0

There are an amazing number of metaphors describing libraries in terms of digital work, electronic resources, and 2.0 anything. We have library 2.0, librarian 2.0 as well as the coming 3.0 versions of these terms. We have digital libraries, digital collections, and digital librarians. We put the letter "e" in front of any format. We even have digital microfilm which again may be an effort to connect an understanding of one format with another format. In each case, these metaphors are being used to help librarians understand the need to change and to incorporate the social networking and technology of our users into our libraries. The terms are also an effort to help users see the library as technologically relevant in a world of Google and Amazon.com. Some research libraries, such as UNL, are now digital publishing services, creating institutional repositories and hosting open access journals. We still need a metaphor for the changing role of the library as publisher as well as the library as a collector of information.

Ecology

One set of metaphors that seems particularly helpful to today's research libraries is to think of the library as an ecosystem that promotes biodiversity. Scott Walter (2008), in an article in *Library Journal*, noted that libraries encompass "multiple species" including our users, traditionally trained librarians, and a variety of professionals from other fields, and the interactions and relationships among these different groups. In this ecosystem, mutualism and coevolution are key to the survival of the library rather than competition and survival of the fittest. In the ecosystem species will survive who provide mutual benefit to each other. Mutualism does not try to change each specie but rather emphasizes the strengths and benefits that each specie brings to the system. In the same way, in research libraries, each profession brings strengths to the system to help the system thrive and survive.

The metaphor also emphasizes the importance of building relationships and sees the library system as a set of relationships. It changes the library from a collection-centric institution to one that is user-centered. It can help library leaders think in terms of building partnerships on campus, continuing to build relationships among research libraries, and bringing together the variety of skills (or species) that are needed today to provide the services and collections that are essential to our survival. For example, at the 2003 Conference of the International Association of Aquatic and Marine Science Libraries and Information Centers, Peter Fritzler from the University of North Carolina at Wilmington used the metaphor of coral reefs to describe libraries.

Coral reefs, according to Fritzler (2003), are the rainforests of the sea, a very diverse, productive, and ever-changing environment. Fritzler used this image to capture the attention of the faculty and students at the university's Center for Marine Sciences (CMS). The image helps to describe the set of education and reference services that the libraries could provide to their remote CMS by establishing a symbiotic relationship between the CMS and the library.

Further, the ecosystem and biodiversity metaphors include the concept that each library needs to relate to its local environment. The library cannot just adapt ideas from other fields and implement them in an automatic way. Rather library leaders need to assess options and bring those ideas to their environment that will be mutually beneficial to their own ecosystem. The ecosystem metaphor of positive relationship building and interaction can be integrated with positive organizational psychology, learning organization theory, and strengths-based leadership to help libraries thrive in these difficult financial times.

Finally, the ecosystem metaphor can help libraries incorporate new roles and services that are mutually beneficial to the system. Increasing the visibility of and access to special collections materials is a strength libraries can pursue that will increase the diversity of resources available to researchers. Libraries creating robust institutional repositories and digital publishing units contribute to the overall ecosystem. Having students create digital content and products for use by others in the system builds a new cohort of researchers who can begin to see the library as more than a collection of books. With so many options available to librarians for how to change, the ecosystem metaphor can help leaders prioritize choices by thinking about the unique strengths of the library and how to best integrate those strengths in an environment of mutual benefit and increased biodiversity.

METAPHORS AT UNL LIBRARIES

At UNL, we have tried any number of metaphors to help our own librarians and staff to imagine new roles, cope with change, climb outside the box, and repackage our services. We have also tried different ways to help the university administration, faculty and students view the library as a vital, relevant part of the scholarly enterprise. Librarians at UNL have faculty status and tenure and have had to review and revise their view of promotion and tenure criteria as the campus has made changes in overall criteria and processes. These various reviews have allowed us to introduce different metaphors for describing the work of the librarians. A number of years ago the librarians adopted the model or metaphor of the scholar–practitioner to describe their role as faculty. The term was borrowed from the College of Education and Human Sciences and nicely describes the need for librarians to be active researchers staying current in the field, while providing good practice. The term also emphasizes that research informs practice so that the libraries can respond to the changing environment. The model has also made it possible for the library faculty to define themselves in broad enough terms that the library faculty includes members with PhD degrees but no MLS degree. It has allowed the faculty to add those involved in digital humanities research, digital initiatives, and electronic publishing to the library faculty on equal terms.

For the library, we have tried a number of different metaphors to describe our changing services. For students we have used the term academic living room, a metaphor that has been picked up by our admissions office and is used in student recruiting efforts to describe a space for students to study and to gather with colleagues. We have tried a number of terms to describe the addition of digital media services to the libraries. We tried digital learning librarians to describe those involved in digital media services who were hired to help faculty incorporate digital resources into their course assignments. We renamed the microforms area the media services area and moved the digital media computers from the computer area to the microforms room. We are still seeking a better way to describe the unit that helps students edit video and audio files, circulates cameras and video recording equipment, and now "houses" digital microfilm. As previously noted, we seem to run a bed and breakfast for some students, a social gathering place for others, and a snack and study zone for others. In each case we are seeking a way to relate our work to our constituencies in terms that will resonant with them.

We have emphasized library as partner to describe ways that we assist departments in electronic publishing efforts. For a number of years we have worked with other units on campus to create image databases using the ContentDM software. We learned early on that our art history faculty were not inclined to use published image databases but preferred their own slides. We partnered with the department on an internal teaching grant to develop a pilot set of digitized slides from the art history slide collection and to modify the equipment in their large teaching classroom to allow true full-sized dual-image projection of slides from a single computer station. The demonstration project was successful in part because of the partnership approach. The libraries were able to build on this demonstration project and partnered with museums on campus to add digital images of their collections to our database at no cost to the museums. Some groups that work with us do have resources to contribute to the project. For these groups we provide whatever level of support they need. For example, Nebraska Educational Television is using our software as the search engine for their database of streaming video. For this group, we showed them how to use the software and they took the project from there. They particularly like the fact that their videos can be searched through our catalog as well as through their own Web site or through Google. By customizing our approach to each group's needs, we have been able to create a variety of digital publishing projects. The partnership metaphor works well for us because it fits with the campus culture and signified that we were not looking for resources from others but came to the project with resources. The deans at UNL also use metaphors to describe the UNL culture. The deans will say that if you like to swim with the sharks, UNL is not the place to be a dean. The shark metaphor helps others understand our collaborative culture that encourages partnerships.

We are also trying to find a term that will better describe the search and discovery tool, Encore from Innovative Interfaces, that runs our catalog and integrates a variety of content databases into one search. We have partnered with our campus museums to add records for their specialized book collections to our catalog and to add images from their collections to our ContentDM databases. We have our institutional repository to preserve faculty and student scholarship, provide open-access journals, and publish original scholarly monographs. We have the digital humanities scholarship produced through our Center for Digital Research in the Humanities. And we have our digitized special collections. These various content types, with MARC, Dublin Core, EAD, or TEI records can all be searched through our catalog. We need a term that describes the complexity of a system that searches all these resources, includes faceted searching, and community tagging. We tried describing the catalog as central intelligence for the campus, bringing together a variety of resources, formats and publications together through one search engine, but that did not resonate with anyone. The best we have so far is to describe the catalog as "Google meets Amazon.com."

Finally then for UNL, where we are coping with financial constraints by partnering with other units on campus to remain visible and essential to the academic enterprise, we could be described as a group of scholar practitioners who manage the academic living room, are a publishing partner, and who bring a Google and Amazon.com experience to the search and discovery of scholarly resources to our students and faculty.

CONCLUSION

Library leaders have struggled for many years to find the right metaphor to describe the importance of libraries and librarians. No one has found the perfect metaphor that adequately describes the complexity of the research library in terms that resonant with the world outside our walls. However, the ecology metaphors can be helpful in describing for librarians, professional and technical staff the need to change and why we need new skills in our workforce to stay relevant in a changing environment. While we look for ways to stay relevant, integrate new businesses into our libraries, and a new business model for our library we will continue to seek the right metaphors to describe who we are, what we do, and why we need support.

NOTE

1. From the quote cum adage, "The Library is the Heart of the University," attributed to Charles William Eliot, President of Harvard University.

REFERENCES

Bell, S. (2009). From gatekeepers to gate-openers. *American Libraries, 40*(8/9), 50–53.

Bell, S., & Shank, J. (2007). *Academic librarianship by design: A blended librarian's guide to the tools and techniques.* Chicago, IL: American Library Association.

Blended librarian. (n.d.) Retrieved from http://blendedlibrarian.org/overview.html

Budd, J. (2009). Academic library data from the United States: An examination of trends. *Library and Information Science Research Electronic Journal, 19*(2), 1–21. Retrieved from https://libres.curtin.edu.au/

Dictionary.com (n.d.) *Metaphor.* Retrieved from http://dictionary.reference.com/browse/metaphor

Fritzler, P. (2003, October 5–9). Building REEAFS: Repackaging and personalizing library services to remote marine science facilities. *Conference Proceedings for the International Association of Aquatic and Marine Science Libraries and Information Centers, 29th Conference, October 5–9, 2003* (pp. 41–46). Mystic, CT: IAMSLIC.

Krasner-Khait, B. (2001). Survivor: The history of the library. *History Magazine, 4,* 1–7.

Lankes, R. D., Silverstein, J., & Nicholson, S. (2007, December). Participatory networks: The library as conversation. *Information Technologies and Libraries, 26*(4), 17–33.

Larner, F. (1998). *The story of libraries: From the invention of writing to the computer age* (pp. 24–26). New York, NY: Continuum Publishing.

Dempsey, L. (2008, May 13). [Weblog comment]. Retrieved from http://orweblog.oclc.org/archives/001636.html/

Nardini, R. (2001). A search for meaning: American library metaphors, 1876–1926. *Library Quarterly, 71,* 111–140.

Neal, J. (2006). Raised by wolves: Integrating the new generation of library professionals into the academic library. *Library Journal, 131*(3), 42–44.

Nitecki, D. (1993). Conceptual models of libraries held by faculty, administrators, and librarians: An exploration of communications in the *Chronicle of Higher Education. Journal of Documentation, 49*(2), 260, 255–277.

NOAA (n.d.). *Hail ... damage to property and crops ...* Retrieved from http://www.erh.noaa.gov/cae/svrwx/hail.htm

Schrage, M. (1995). *Shared minds: The new technologies for collaboration.* New York, NY: Doubleday.

Shakespeare, W. *As you like it,* Act 2, Scene 7. London, England: Iaggard and Blout.

Shepard, E. (2009, September). Heart or muscle? The library in the digital age. *Readex Newsletter,* Retrieved from http://www.readex.com/readex/newsletter.cfm?newsletter=242

Valenza, J. (2008, August 25). *Library as domestic metaphor.* Retrieved from http://www.schoollibraryjournal.com/blog/1340000334/post/90032209.html

Advancing From Kumbaya to Radical Collaboration: Redefining the Future Research Library

JAMES G. NEAL
Columbia University, New York, NY, USA

ABSTACT. *The research library community has developed an effective program of multi-institutional coöperation during the last 50 years. Conditions in technology, economics, and expanding service requirements demand a more radical approach to collaboration. The 2CUL initiative illustrates key opportunities to set aside the traditional models of research library operations and respond to new roles and responsibilities.*

Cooperation is part of the professional DNA of research libraries. From the conditions of knowledge scarcity over the centuries to the oppression of information and data overabundance in today's and tomorrow's library context, cooperation has been and will be a constant for service, success, and survival. The transformation of research library collections, services, and spaces continues to progress under the impact of rampant shifts in user behaviors and expectations, digital and network technologies, and deep fiscal challenges. But the definition and view of the research library as an independent and self-sustaining organization, collaborating and sharing resources on the margin, has persisted. The future health of the research library will be increasingly defined by new and energetic relationships and combinations, and the radicalization of working relationships among research libraries, between libraries and the communities they serve, and in new entrepreneurial partnerships.

The context for collaboration and innovation is rich and powerful. It combines rapidly evolving user requirements, a recognition of the need to rethink redundant inefficient library operations, an increasing emphasis on unique resources, a focus on the need to achieve scale and network effects through aggregation, a mandate for systemic change, and the unprecedented economic pressures.

The potential and reality of collaboration cuts across the core responsibilities of academic libraries. Whether it is information selection (choosing), information acquisition (getting), information synthesis (organizing), information navigation (discovering), information dissemination (delivering), information interpretation (assisting), information understanding (educating), information use (applying), or information archiving (preserving), libraries must find new ways to work together in support of teaching and learning, and of research and scholarship.

But academic libraries are assuming new roles as traditional boundaries shift. Libraries are learning how to be better consumers, often negotiating and licensing content and software collectively. Libraries are aggressive intermediaries and aggregators of information, and, as publishers, are creating new innovative modes of scholarly communication. Libraries are partnering with faculty to expand their educational involvement beyond traditional bibliographic instruction, and to advance operational investigations as research-and-development organizations. Libraries are more entrepreneurial organizations, more concerned with innovation, business planning, competition and risk, leveraging assets through new partnerships to produce new financial resources. Libraries are also increasingly successful information policy advocates seeking through political relationships to influence national and global laws and legislation.

Radical collaboration encourages academic libraries to move in four new directions. The first is mass production, including back-room operations like acquisitions, cataloging, electronic resource management, and preservation, for example, that might be based in regional distribution centers rather than in every individual library. The second is centers of excellence, deep and shared polycentric strategies for specialized expertise or services. The third is new infrastructure, building the technologies and functionalities for areas like digital ingestion, processing, and archiving. The fourth is new initiatives, new programs and projects based on shared investment in experimentation. In all four cases, the measures of success must be quality, productivity, and innovation. Are we producing something new, saving resources, and achieving something better together than working alone? Radical collaboration requires bi- and trilateral collaborations, as multilateral approaches are often too shallow or are not successful. It involves a business and sustainability plan, a legal framework and governance structure, risk capital to get it started, and a shared competitive spirit.

There are remarkable and expanding venues for research libraries to collaborate: in library systems, in local and regional consortiums, as part of state and multistate initiatives, in national programs, in international partnerships, with the cultural community, with researchers, with publishers, with campus technology organizations, with information technology vendors, and with corporations and other private-sector partners.

Collection storage facilities are often examples of deep library collaboration. The Research Collections and Preservation Consortium (ReCAP) located on the Forrestral campus of Princeton University in New Jersey is a high-density, environmentally controlled shelving facility jointly owned and operated by Princeton, Columbia, and the New York Public Library (NYPL). An inventory and retrieval system enables easy, dependable and effective access to the 10 million items housed at ReCAP for library users. A shared governance structure provides policy and budget control, and the management has been outsourced to Princeton.

Similar cooperative models are being implemented for shared repositories of digitized content from academic libraries. Launched in 2008, and housed at the University of Michigan, the Hathi Trust includes the member libraries of the Committee on Institutional Cooperation/Big 10, the University of California system, the University of Virginia, and Columbia. Hathi serves as a trusted repository, guaranteeing the long-term preservation of digital books created through mass digitization projects, and providing expert curation and consistent access.

Academic libraries have developed new strategies to build shared print collections. As the availability of online scholarly resources grows, libraries face increasing pressure to optimize management of print collections. Consolidation and rationalization of holdings within and across institutions enables economies of scale that benefit individual institutions and the wider academic library community by reducing costs and eliminating redundancies in holdings. Two noteworthy cooperative Research Library Group (RLG) projects have proceeded. One focuses on discarding print back runs of JSTOR titles as compared with the usual practice of moving these volumes into storage. A second seeks to identify the policy and business requirements for managing library print collections as a pooled resource, including optimal overlap to ensure long-term preservation, interinstitutional agreements to raise trust and confidence, and the technical infrastructure. RLG concludes that a new business model is needed that will enable academic libraries to establish partnerships capable of sustaining the long-term future of print collections, distributing the costs and benefits of acquiring and preserving content in tangible formats, and allowing aggregate holdings to be right-sized in alignment with aggregate demand.

Our academic library collection development programs cry out for new and innovative collaborative strategies. But in the short term, the following assumptions, in my view, will persist and dominate our investment in content. Academic research libraries will continue to develop comprehensive collections in all formats as research libraries acquire what the world produces. Collections will seek to align with university academic priorities and funding realities. This means that we will need to take on new areas and let go some collections of historical importance. Coordination of collection development across the research library community will remain marginalized. Cooperative collection development is a remarkable disappointment. Academic research libraries will increasingly focus on distinctive and unique collections in service to regional and national scholarly audiences. Academic research libraries will build innovative bilateral and trilateral partnerships to expand content access and delivery. Will there be true and rigorous coinvestment in collection development, access, and preservation? Preservation and archiving of the cultural and scientific record will remain balkanized and episodic with no leadership coordination. National and global information policies will not facilitate the deep collection collaboration needed. Copyright in particular is a major barrier to rigorous cooperation and to the reality of collective collection sharing. Work of collection building will require a new approach to professional staffing and organization. Where will we recruit the combination of subject, service, technical, and professional skills we need? Collections will need to align more intimately with teaching and learning processes, integration of content into the classroom, and the online learning environment. User communities will create their own tools for discovering, disseminating, and managing content. Academic research libraries will assume expanded roles as new scholarly communication business models are implemented. New publishing roles, content enrichment, data curation and archiving, and discovery will be critical. More focus will be placed on data capture and analysis to support collection development decisions.

Building the digital library where quality equals content plus functionality creates new innovative partnerships for academic libraries. The digital library includes: published and licensed content, primary content drawn from special and unique resources, open Web content (including sites and documents of quality and relevance that we need to collect and preserve), and institutional content (including the records of our universities and the grey literature produced across the institution)—all increasingly multimedia and integrated with services and requiring software tools. Digital libraries are all about collaboration.

Preserving and archiving the analog and digital content creates new and essential opportunities for collaboration. How will content be held, accessed, secured, and cared for if academic libraries do not develop new capacities as repository, curator and steward? Preserving content that is converted to digital or born digital requires a new shared commitment to architecture, policies, tools, workflows, and standards. Content that is often ephemeral, dynamic, and vulnerable, for which integrity is important, is where an academy-wide commitment is essential.

We painfully lack national policy and strategic leadership for preservation. I challenge anyone to identify an organization in North America that is championing and planning our preservation program. This means that we lack progress on the policy front, to build for example more expansive exceptions for preservation into our national copyright laws. This means that we lack significant national investment in preservation activities—state and federal funding of sufficient magnitude and sustenance to make a difference. The impact of these gaps is extraordinary and plays out in very damaging ways. I am concerned about a remarkable absence of research in so many areas of preservation. We need to move to best practices and standards which are based on science. I am heartened by the work being done at Johns Hopkins University, supported by the Mellon Foundation to apply rigorous scientific inquiry into our conservation work. I am concerned about an erosion of coverage of preservation in our library and information science education programs, and specialist degree initiatives at risk. And finally, the lack of a well-developed and well-supported national preservation program means that we miss opportunities to build strong relations and collaborations with other countries and regions that are investing in both analog and digital preservation studies and actions.

The repository movement has influenced dramatically where researchers deposit their work, and the ensuing chaos which has infiltrated the scholarly communication systems demands new collaborative strategies with academic libraries playing a key leadership role. Repository fatigue is setting in: publisher repositories, disciplinary repositories, academic unit repositories, institutional repositories, individual repositories, government repositories, national repositories, preservation repositories, and so on. What is the authoritative, official and citable version? What version will survive? What versions will be modified? Will a system of master versions develop? Can new identity registries help out? How do we work together to integrate and rationalize repositories and the open-access agenda into the system of scholarly communication and collection development in our libraries?

Preparing for accountability and assessment creates important opportunities for new partnerships. This is a product of heightened institutional expectations and government mandates. By working together, we can generate effective and broadly embraced measures of user satisfaction, market penetration, success, impact, and cost effectiveness. System design for user-centered, participatory, experimental, interactive, and user supportive outcomes means a new collaboration with library customers. Do academic libraries influence successful graduates, efficient administrators, and productive faculty?

Advocating the information policy agenda creates important partnerships for academic libraries in the work of advocacy, education and action. All policy arenas bring libraries together and into powerful new relationships to advance the political agenda: intellectual freedom, privacy, civil liberties, education programs, research programs, Internet development, telecommunications, government information, appropriations, workforce policy, and copyright.

Library space provides new opportunities for collaboration. We need to ask new questions about the conception and application of academic library space. Why do individuals enter a space (motivation or objective)? How do individuals navigate a space (transportation or circulation)? How do individuals use a space (experience or productivity)? What is the balance among function, usability, and aesthetics? How do individuals relate to each other (private, Collaborative, or public)? What is the symbolic role of space (emotional/spiritual)? How does a space reflect or advance the larger organization (mission, success, or feel)? How does space enable flexibility and adaptability?

Collaboration through library space means adopting new guidelines for planning and design. Focus less on statistical and operational formulas. Focus more on diversity of need and personal adaptability/customization. Design for the agile rather than the static. Start with the user and not the collection. Start with the technology and not with the staff. Bring the classroom into the library. Bring the academy into the library. Conceive the library five years ahead. Think more about playground and less about sanctuary. Prepare for anxiety, disruption and chaos.

The core responsibilities of research libraries align well with the needs of big science. Therefore, partnerships at the project, campus, discipline, national and global levels will advance scientific discovery and progress, and support the interests of individual scientists and teams of researchers, universities and research centers, and funding agencies. There is a productive marriage of capabilities and needs between library and science researchers.

When scientists map the universe, investigate the gene, monitor the environment, they create massive data sets that require management and structure. They want new tools for curation/findability and for extraction and application. As part of multidisciplinary teams, they increasingly care about distribution and collaboration and they seek sophisticated capabilities like visualization and simulation. Perhaps most importantly they are focused on permanent storage and availability. Can the research library add value to these processes?

We must raise the level of awareness and understanding. We must advance new approaches and standards for long-term digital data curation. We must identify new roles for libraries in e-science infrastructure and services to the scholarly community. We must outline new information profession skills and new roles for librarians as part of research teams. We must develop new relationships with government agencies and scholarly societies. But academic libraries are not routinely participating in the scholarly forums and the scientific funding arenas for research cyberinfrastructure.

Effective faculty relationships are essential to the success of the academic library. Faculty as researchers are among the primary consumers of library collections and services. They also produce, as authors and editors, the scholarly literature that is acquired by the library. Their teaching activities and course requirements determine the nature and intensity of library use by students. Faculty members occupy positions of administrative and policy leadership, which influence the financial and political status of the library in the institution.

Faculty members bring diverse but important priorities, interests, and expectations to their work at the university. They seek personal advancement and recognition in their disciplines and, in some cases, academic administrative opportunities. They want to contribute to the literature and prestige of their fields and, therefore, often actively pursue external funding in the form of grants and endowments to support their work and that of their students. They strive to produce high quality instructional content and experiences, and to advance students into successful careers or prestigious graduate and professional programs. They are interested in working on innovative projects and collaborating with interesting and accomplished colleagues. They expect financial recognition of their efforts in the form of compensation and, as appropriate, profit from their publications, inventions, software, or expert consultation. And increasingly, they demand access to the best laboratory, technology, and library capabilities, as well as opportunities to experiment with computers and networks in their teaching and research. It is important that the library understand these motivations as relationships with faculty are reshaped.

There is a taxonomy of faculty and library relationships that is historically based and explains the two cultures which often coexist in the academy. Academic libraries in the United States in the past were largely administered by senior professors, and this continues to be the case in countries around the world. In this century, with the advancing professionalization of librarianship, the situation has changed rapidly in some settings, though the tension between the faculty and the librarian administrator often persists. Another important consideration is the diversity of the faculty in terms of discipline, tenure status, years at the institution and comfort with technology, for example.

A classification scheme of faculty and library relationships can be outlined. The servant relationship places the library in a position of responding to faculty demands without an opportunity to influence expectations and without mutual respect. The stranger relationship is characterized by faculty and library communities which do not work together but coexist independently in the academic setting. The parallel relationship describes a situation where faculty and library activities do not intersect, where library collections and services are underused and where faculty information needs are satisfied from other sources. The friend relationship positions the faculty and library as cooperative and mutually supportive more out of tradition than an intense dependence. The partner relationship is built on a mutual reliance and a shared commitment to improving the quality of both the library and the university. The customer relationship places the library and the faculty in a market relationship with a recognition of the consumer and broker nature of the interaction. The team or knowledge management relationship realizes a fuller integration of interests and activities and high level of personal investment in the collaboration. These descriptions of faculty and library relationships are not complete or mutually exclusive, but they do illustrate the evolution of the quality and impact of the interaction and can assist future development of this critical association.

The points of intersection between library and faculty include some traditional elements. Faculty use libraries, assist with the building of collections, involve librarians in educating their students, seek assistance with course readings, consult with librarians on their research, expect effective access to local and distant collections, advise and advocate for library development, participate in the policy and priority setting, and contribute personal collections and financial resources. Technology and networking are expanding the functional relationships as faculty increasingly turn to the library for assistance in other areas: Internet access, guidance to quality Web sites, assistance in the integration of technology into teaching, digital collections, sophisticated searching tools and information finding aids, new literature alerts based on research profiles, high-level equipment, and partners in research, for example. The challenge faced by the library is that these new faculty needs do not replace the traditional expectations, but create an incremental, sometimes exhausting and always schizophrenic demand for resources.

The 2CUL Project between Columbia University and Cornell University libraries is a transformative and enduring partnership between two major academic research libraries based on a broad integration of resources, collections, services, and expertise. Research libraries have successfully collaborated in the licensing of electronic resources, cooperative cataloging, interlibrary loan and document delivery, information policy advocacy, offsite shelving facilities, and digital archiving.

The goals of 2CUL are to: (a) achieve major integration of operations, services, collections and resources; (b) reduce cost of overall library activities to direct resources to new priority areas; (c) increase revenues through joint proposals for funding, new products and services, and business opportunities marketed to academic and research customers; (d) establish an independent service entity and governance structure that supports 2CUL; and (e) expand 2CUL beyond initial partners, and model collaboration for other groups of research libraries and for other divisions at the university.

The Columbia University and Cornell University libraries have come together as major research libraries in New York state, as private Ivy League institutions with similar academic characteristics, a record of collaboration, a record of innovation, budget challenges, and the will and interest to work together in new ways. We are initially focusing our work on technical services (i.e., acquisitions, cataloging, e-resource management), collection development and global resources, and technology infrastructure and digital preservation. A Mellon Foundation grant supports consultation (Ithaka) to provide project management, meeting facilitation, work plan development, research, independent perspective, data mining and analysis, governance, business planning and legal support, and meeting travel and teleconferencing equipment.

Another important new collaboration to consider is a program being developed among the libraries at NYPL, New York University (NYU), and Columbia University. The recently developed scope statement defines the purpose. The three comprehensive research libraries in New York City—NYPL, Columbia, and NYU—have a long history of cooperation and coordination. At the same time, that long history has also been, in some sense, stagnant and constrained. With major changes in the economy, in technology, in the patterns of library use, and in the expectations of library users, it is time to take an entirely fresh and more aggressive look at mutually beneficial programs of shared collecting and access. What greater access can each institution provide to the user populations of the other? If we can bring access to a new level, how can we then benefit from truly collaborative collecting? The goal of our meeting will be to identify how we can take advantage of our shared New York City location and our shared mission as comprehensive research libraries to move beyond our traditional programs of cooperation and coordination to a new level of deep collaboration that will actually change what we collect and how we do business with each other.

The initial planning meeting, involving management teams from the three libraries, considered as a first step the following questions:

1. What are the current areas of explicit and implicit collaboration among and between the three libraries?
2. What do we want to achieve through expanded and enhanced collaboration?
3. What do our users expect and require as they work across the three libraries?
4. What are the barriers to shared collections and access?
5. What are model efforts among other research libraries that we can explore and evaluate?
6. What are the three actions that we can take immediately to create expanded access?
7. What are the three actions that we want to pursue as priorities to test our ability to coordinate collection development?
8. How will we measure and evaluate progress?
9. How should we communicate with our user communities and administrations on our collective efforts?

The discussions on collaborative collection development echoed the "conspectus" model promoted by the Research Libraries Group 30 years ago. The goal will be to define both the historical depth of collections in designated areas and the current and continuing investment. The discussion on access encouraged barrier-free access across the three libraries for the research users of the three institutions, these communities requiring clear definition and refinement, as well as expedited physical and electronic document delivery. The key barriers are physical, operational, policy, and financial. The discussions on electronic resources highlighted the need to negotiate for a collective collection that provides more content and more favorable terms than the three institutions could achieve separately.

Rosabeth Moss Kantor, a researcher at Harvard Business School has identified the characteristics of successful partnerships (Kanter, 1994).

- *Individual excellence*, in that the partners are strong and have something to contribute to the relationship.
- *Importance*, in that the relationship fits the strategic objectives of the partners and they want to make it work.
- *Interdependence*, in that the partners need each other and have complimentary assets and skills.
- *Investment*, in that the partners are willing to show tangible signs for a long-term commitment.
- *Information sharing*, in that communication is open and critical data is shared freely.
- *Integration*, in that the partners develop linkages and share in joint activities.
- *Institutionalization*, in that the relationship may adopt a formal status with clear responsibilities and decision processes.
- *Integrity*, in that partners behave towards each other in honorable ways that justify and enhance mutual trust.

This is the substance of a successful library and faculty collaboration.

Kantor also posits the key mechanisms for successful partnerships.

- *Self analysis*. Know yourself and your business and be able to evaluate a potential partner.
- *Personal chemistry*. The need for rapport among the players, a sense of commitment and respect.
- *Compatibility*. Shared values and aspirations. A compatible assessment of benefits and opportunities. Integration, including strategic and sustained contact focusing on broad goals and trends, tactical plans for specific projects and joint activities, operational through day-to-day work together,

interpersonal through regular meetings and contacts, and cultural awareness and communication skills to bridge differences.

These characteristics and mechanisms will serve well the expanding collaborative venues being pursued by academic research libraries. The arenas and examples outlined in this article testify to the rich possibilities and the prospective benefits.

REFERENCE

Kanter, R. M. (1994, July/August). Collaborative advantage: The art of alliances. *Harvard Business Review*, pp. 96–109.

Repackaging the Library: What Do Faculty Think?

KEVIN GUTHRIE and ROSS HOUSEWRIGHT
Ithaka, New York, NY, USA

ABSTRACT. *Ithaka S+R's Faculty Survey 2009, the 4th iteration since 2000 of this survey of faculty members at colleges and universities across the United States, offers insights into how faculty attitudes about electronic media and technology have evolved over the last decade. In this article, the authors focus on the aspects of the survey that most directly relate to the work of research libraries, including commentary on information discovery and use, the evolving role of the library, and changing attitudes toward access and preservation of journal current issues and backfiles. The responses to this survey point to some of the more valuable services libraries offer (or could offer), as well as highlighting the many challenges facing libraries and putting an exclamation point on the widely shared view that the libraries cannot rely on what have been their traditional strengths.*

It is a pleasure and privilege to have been asked to participate in "Climbing Out of the Box: Repackaging Libraries for Survival" and to contribute to this collection of articles. We are in the very early stages of a dramatic transformation, where the primary mechanism for transmitting knowledge is shifting from print on paper to digits on the wire. The fundamental challenge facing all of us who operate in the scholarly communications environment is that the infrastructure that has served us so well for centuries is not optimized for storing, preserving and disseminating knowledge in digital form.

Research libraries are an absolutely critical component of the traditional knowledge dissemination infrastructure. But as one looks to the future and imagines the extreme case—a day when all knowledge is available in digital form—it becomes obvious that the buildings, shelves, and systems designed to efficiently and effectively store and make accessible books and other physical objects will no longer be valuable. Someday the "warehousing" role of libraries may not be necessary at all, or at the very least will be profoundly diminished. This is not to argue that we will see such a day soon, but large amounts of content, led by journal literature over the last decade, are now used primarily in electronic form. Consequently, in response to user preference and pressures to reduce costs, libraries are canceling print subscriptions in favor of electronic access and moving print off shelves. Moreover, publishers increasingly are naming the e-journal as the copy of record and are beginning to consider ceasing print publication. "Climbing out of the box" will require that libraries shift the emphasis of their activities away from the management of physical objects to the provision of services to support and care for electronic content.

Our contribution to this conversation is to share initial findings from a survey of faculty at institutions in the United States conducted during the fall of 2009. This survey, the fourth in a series that has been conducted every 3 years since 2000 (2000, 2003, 2006 and 2009), offers insights into how faculty attitudes about electronic media and technology have evolved over the last decade. In this article, we focus on aspects of the survey that most directly relate to the work of research libraries, including commentary on information discovery and use, the evolving role of the library, and changing attitudes toward access and preservation of journal current issues and backfiles.

Before presenting our findings, we would like to offer some general context about our research and highlight how we think the results should be used. We surveyed a large number of faculty at 4-year colleges and universities in the United States. Since no definitive census of this population exists, there is inevitably risk of sample and response bias in the results. The ways in which we have worked hard to manage this bias are discussed briefly in the *Methodology* section, and we have also developed increasing confidence over the years in the reliability of the results as we have developed tracking data from survey to survey. Nevertheless, these results should not be regarded as definitive statements about faculty attitudes as a population. This is business-oriented market research, not academic social science. When we refer to faculty in the ensuing discussion, we are discussing the views of the faculty who responded to this survey. Over the years, these responses have proven to predict future developments and trends, but we do not assert that they are representative of all U.S. faculty.

Our objective is to offer data that will provide valuable input to libraries (and societies and publishers and others working in scholarly communications) as they develop strategies to continue to serve the academy during this time of change. The availability of responses to the same questions over a period of time is extremely important to the interpretation of our findings. We present many of the findings in terms of the percentage of faculty that have responded to a question in a specific way (e.g., rating a view as "very important"), but we regard the absolute value of those responses as less important than the trend represented by a series of responses over time. These trends are the data that we believe most reliably point to the direction in which faculty views are headed, and that should be most useful in guiding the development of strategies. We encourage readers to compare the findings with your own experiences interacting with faculty and combine them with data you collect in your local institutions to develop your strategies for the future. We hope these results contribute to the collective understanding of the rapidly changing environment, and that they prove helpful in pointing the way to effective approaches.

METHODOLOGY

Since 2000, our faculty surveys have examined how new technologies are impacting faculty attitudes and behaviors. Every 3 years, we have conducted large-scale studies of faculty members to learn more about their attitudes toward the ongoing transition to an increasingly electronic environment. These surveys have been limited to faculty at colleges and universities in the United States that grant bachelor's degrees or higher. They have been designed to allow for stratifications in each of the major arts and sciences disciplines, as well as in a number of professional fields. We conducted these surveys in the fall of 2000, 2003, 2006, and most recently 2009, updating the questionnaire to match the rapidly changing environment but keeping many questions unchanged to allow for tracking and analysis of the evolution in faculty attitudes and practices (Guthrie & Housewright, 2008; Housewright & Schonfeld, 2008; Schonfeld & Guthrie, 2007). Unless specified otherwise, all findings presented in this report are based on the 2009 responses.

The faculty responses were collected from a survey that was mailed to 35,184 faculty members in September 2009. The names and addresses of these faculty were purchased from a commercial service's list of 661,000 faculty in 34 higher education disciplines. Certain fields were oversampled to ensure adequate responses for analysis, with an every nth randomization mechanism to select the target number of faculty members in each field.

A total of 3,025 complete responses were received and tabulated, for a response rate of approximately 8.6%. Demographic characteristics, including discipline, are self-reported, and disciplinary weightings are utilized to construct aggregate findings. Table 1 and Table 2 contain information on the breakdown of responses across demographic categories. In 2006, we deposited the data set with ICPSR for long-term digital preservation and access, and we intend to do so again with the 2009 data set.[1] code following the

TABLE 1 Respondents by Institution Size

Institution size	Respondents	Share (%)
Very large	893	29.5
Large	482	15.9
Medium	1038	34.3
Small	361	11.9
Very small	251	8.3

word "Share" in Table 1 without my version of Word crashing. Please note that the Table 1 Head ends there.

With thousands of survey responses and hundreds of data points for each returned survey, this summary report can only scratch the surface of the amount of information available to us. We have focused this analysis and the report on findings to the data that we think are most relevant for leaders of research libraries.

DISCOVERY AND THE EVOLVING ROLE OF THE LIBRARY

Scholarly use of information services has changed substantially in recent years. Research practices and teaching methods are shifting and evolving in ways that seem to vary by discipline. The availability of new network-level services, such as digital content resources, a variety of new kinds of discovery tools, new services for information organization and use, and scholarly and pedagogical interaction and collaboration tools, have been the most important factors in motivating these changes. This section examines some of the most important trends in information discovery and use, as well as the profound challenges posed for information service providers and intermediaries, caused by the fact that these services are increasingly provided online rather than locally.

Traditional research practices relied on access to physical materials held in a library and locally implemented library-provided tools for discovery of these materials (e.g., books, journal articles, manuscripts). Today, there are numerous alternative avenues for information discovery, and libraries

TABLE 2 Respondents by Disciplinary Grouping

Disciplinary grouping	Respondents	Share (%)
Area studies	191	6.3
Humanities	652	21.6
Social sciences	1154	38.1
Sciences	791	26.1
Other	237	7.8

are challenged to determine what role they should appropriately play in this new environment. Changing behaviors and practices increasingly put the academic library at risk of being disintermediated from the discovery process, a possibility that, if realized, could cause libraries to be irrelevant in one of their core functional areas. This section examines how patterns of information discovery and usage by faculty members are changing and the implications of these changes for their perceptions of traditional and emerging roles of the library.

Information Discovery and Use

Since our first faculty survey in 2000, responses have indicated that faculty members are steadily shifting towards reliance on network-level electronic resources, while relying less on locally provided tools for discovery. This section examines this trend through the lens of several questions posed to faculty about their information discovery and usage behaviors.

Versions of this study since 2003 have asked faculty to select their "starting point" for research from a list of four broad categories:

- the library building,
- your online library catalog,
- a general-purpose search engine on the Internet or World Wide Web such as Google or Yahoo, and
- a specific electronic research resource / computer database.

As Figure 1 illustrates, the library's physical edifice and catalog have declined steadily as starting points for research. The research process is no longer likely to begin with a face-to-face consultation with a librarian, a visit to the library's special collections service points, or a search of the online library catalog. Rather, our respondents most often turn to network-level services, including both general purpose search engines and services targeted specifically to academia. These services have steadily grown in importance to a growing share of faculty members, and there is every reason to expect this pattern to continue. Although they may rely on resources licensed by the library, their pathway for discovery of these materials no longer goes through the library, except in a very technical sense; their access is only facilitated by the library "behind the scenes."

Of all disciplines, respondents in the sciences remain the least likely to use library-specific starting points; only about 10% of these scientists start their research at either of the library-specific starting points, whereas approximately 30% of the humanists do so (see Figure 2). Most of this difference is explained by their relatively different usage of the online library catalog. We expect this difference is because of the fact that humanists are

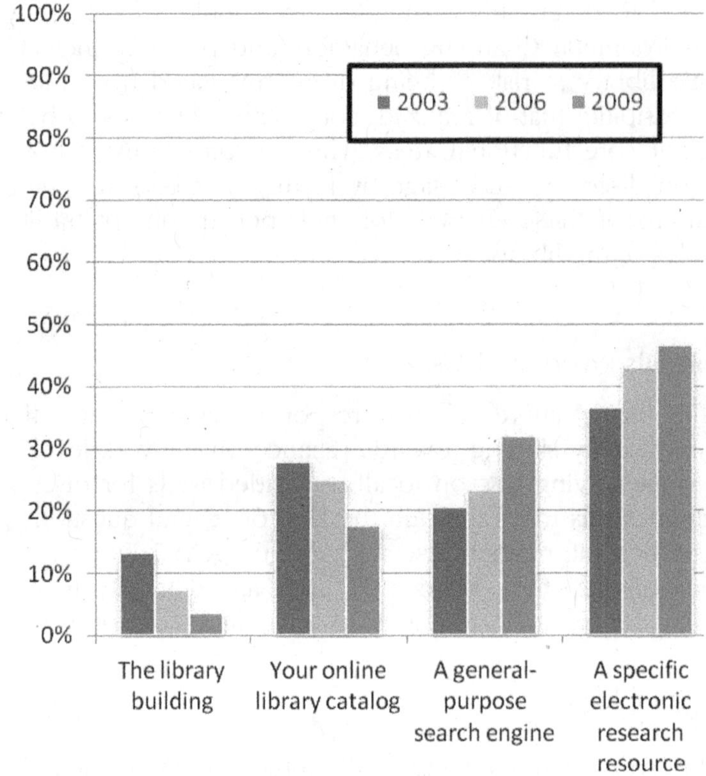

FIGURE 1 Starting Point for Research Identified by Faculty in 2003, 2006, and 2009.

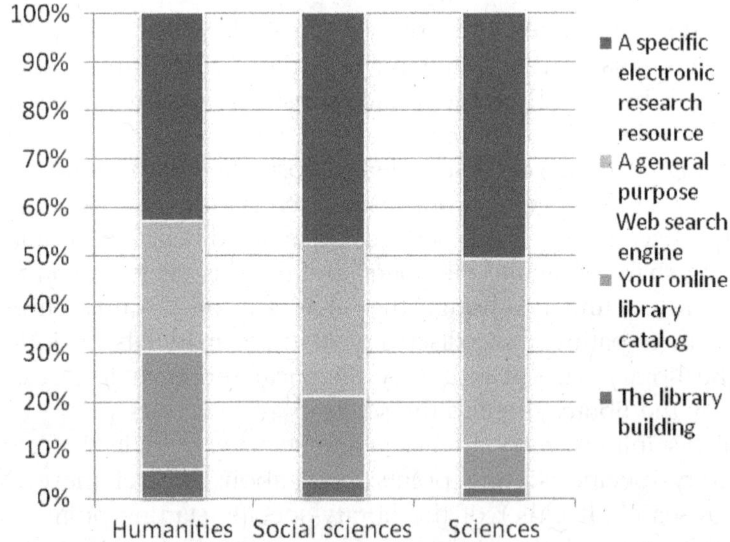

FIGURE 2 Starting Point for Research Identified by Faculty, by Disciplinary Grouping.

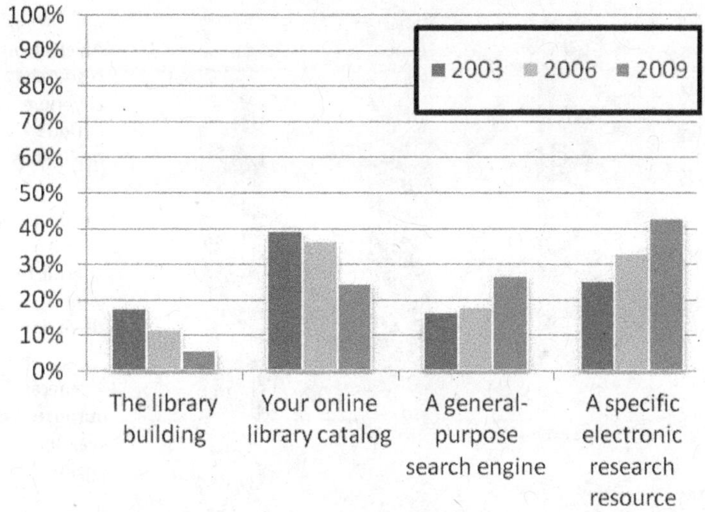

FIGURE 3 Starting Point for Research Identified by Humanities Faculty in 2003, 2006, and 2009.

generally more reliant than are social scientists and scientists on monographs for their research and teaching. Monographs have not made as complete a transition to digital formats as have journals.

Still, notwithstanding their reliance on books, respondents in the humanities have also trended steadily away from library-specific starting points and toward the network level (see Figure 3). These data indicate that network-level services are increasingly important for discovery, not only of monographs and journals but also of archival resources and other primary source collections. And, as book digitization projects advance and the opportunities to use full-text search more broadly in the discovery of monographs grow, this pattern seems likely to develop further.

In the 2009 faculty survey, we drilled deeper into this issue, asking faculty members who report starting their research with a specific electronic research resource a question about whether this resource is discipline-specific or covers multiple disciplines. Our respondents tend to prefer electronic resources specific to their own discipline over those that cover multiple disciplines (see Figure 4). This pattern holds across disciplines, although these social scientists are relatively more reliant on multidisciplinary resources than are the humanists or the scientists. We speculate that the use of resources focused on a specific discipline may simplify the research process for scholars, reducing their need to sift through unrelated materials in their search for items of interest. And targeted resources may be able to offer discovery mechanisms and other tools that speak directly to a discipline's unique research needs and practices, further facilitating an efficient and effective research process.

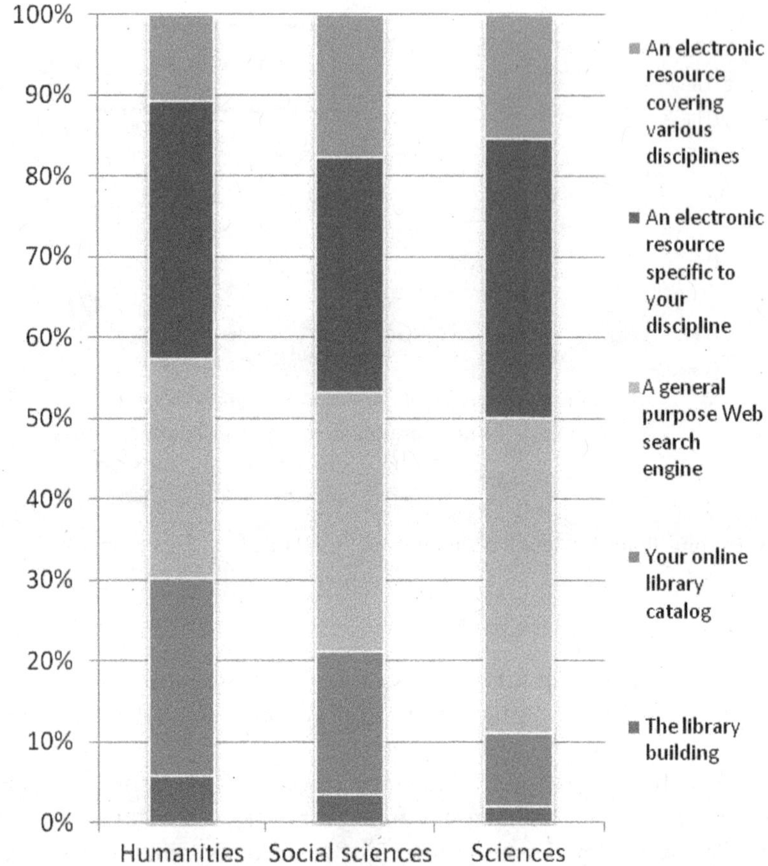

FIGURE 4 Starting Point for Research by Disciplinary Grouping, With Responses of "A Specific Electronic Research Resource" Broken Down Based on the Complementary Question "Which of the Following Types of Specific Electronic Research Resources Would You Be Most Likely to Start With?"

The Changing Roles of the Library

As faculty research and teaching practices continue to shift in response to their rapidly changing information environment, their uses of the library also change, as does their perception of the value the library offers. Faculty used to rely almost exclusively on the library for the scholarly materials they needed for research and teaching, and librarians guided faculty to and otherwise facilitated the discovery of these materials. As scholars have grown better able to reach needed materials directly online, going to or using the library is not essential to carrying out research and so faculty are turning to other options, as the previous section on shifting discovery practices illustrated. The library must evolve to meet these changing needs. To do so effectively requires awareness of how faculty members evaluate

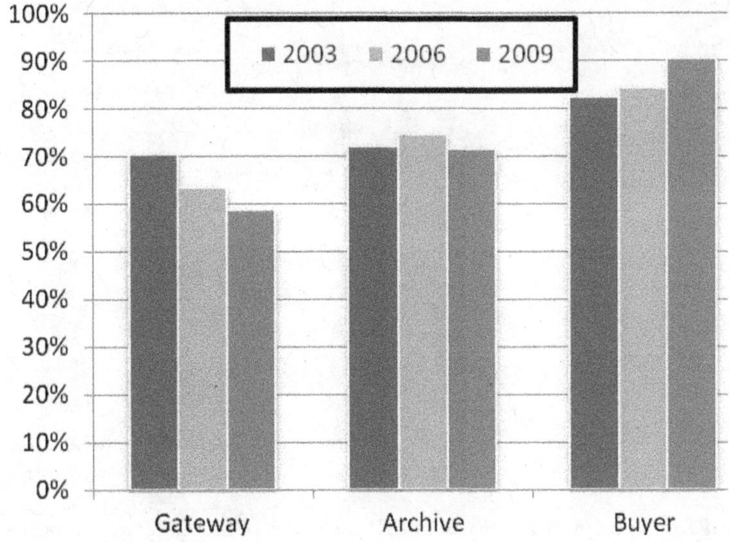

FIGURE 5 Percent of Faculty Rating These Roles of the Library as Important in 2003, 2006, and 2009.

different existing library roles and react to potential changes in library services. Since 2003, the Faculty Survey has asked about faculty perceptions of the importance of three traditional functions of the library:

- "The library is a starting point or 'gateway' for locating information for my research" (which we refer to as the "gateway" function)
- "The library pays for resources I need, from academic journals to books to electronic databases" (which we refer to as the "buyer" function)
- "The library is a repository of resources—in other words, it archives, preserves, and keeps track of resources" (which we refer to as the "archive" function)

Figure 5 illustrates the gradual decline in the perceived importance of the gateway function over time and the gradual increase in the perceived importance of the buyer function among our faculty respondents. Over time, the gap between roles has grown substantially. While the buyer role has always been important to the most faculty members, it is now *by far* the most important of the three: while 90% of faculty members view this buyer role as very important, 71% and 59% now view the archive and gateway roles as very important, respectively. As individual faculty subscriptions have declined in favor of an increasingly broad set of library-licensed resources, faculty perceptions of the importance of the library as their "purchasing agent" has steadily increased.

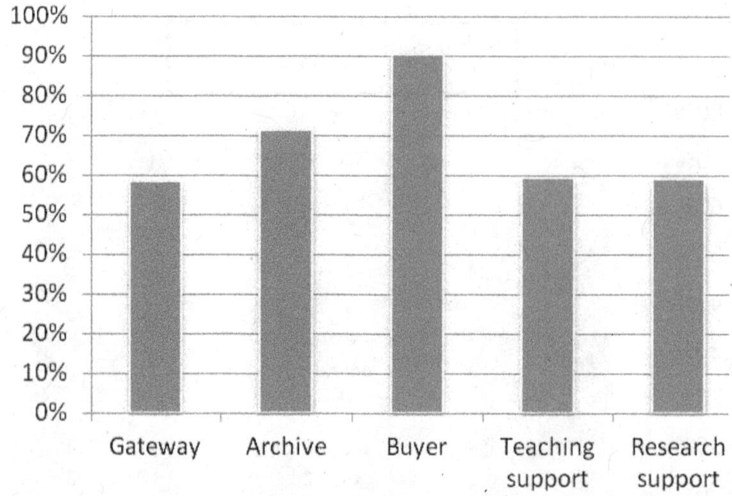

FIGURE 6 Percent of Faculty Rating These Roles of the Library as Important.

The gateway, archive, and buyer functions are among the core traditional roles of the library. But many believe that these historical roles will not be the main focus of libraries in the future, and envision the transformation of the library from an institution focused on acquiring, maintaining, and providing services centered on a local print collection into a more electronic hub offering a variety of services to support campus needs for research, teaching, and learning (Esposito, 2006; Lewis, 2007; Ross & Sennyey, 2008). Many libraries have made significant investments in such a transformation, reducing print collections or moving them to less central locations to enable the use of prime real estate for new learning and collaboration services such as information commons (Lippincott, 2010). In addition, libraries are taking on new research-support roles, providing digital information curation and management services and even establishing a new professional identity for themselves as "informationists" (Brandt, 2007; Oliver, 2005).

To evaluate the impact of these transformative services, our 2009 faculty survey asked faculty about their perceptions of two additional roles for the library beyond the three already reviewed:

- "The library supports and facilitates my teaching activities" (which we refer to as "teaching support")
- "The library provides active support that helps to increase the productivity of my research and scholarship" (which we refer to as "research support")

As Figure 6 illustrates, a roughly equal share of faculty members rate these roles as very important, and the importance of both of these roles is rated at almost exactly the same level as the library's gateway function. Both fall short of the high importance expressed for the library's buyer role. In the absence of tracking data, we are not prepared to speculate on whether recent library investment in these roles has positively affected their value to faculty members or if they will over time come to be among the most widely valued roles of the library. There are strong indications, however, that many libraries will increasingly focus on these roles going forward, both developing new services and seeking to direct faculty attention to existing activities. It is our intention to track the change in perceptions about these services with future surveys. As libraries continue to invest in developing new emphases on these sorts of services, active evaluation of their impact will be crucial to help libraries direct limited resources to the most valuable activities.

There are several deeper patterns in response to this question that may have important strategic implications for libraries. Significantly more of our faculty respondents who consider themselves as "more of a teacher" rather than "more of a researcher" rate both the library's teaching (67% vs. 45%) *and* research (62% vs. 51%) support roles as valuable. And faculty members at the very largest research universities are less likely to appreciate the library's research and teaching support roles. Taken together, these patterns suggest that the relationships built through engaging faculty in supporting their own teaching activities (which have historically proven harder to scale at the largest institutions) may be an especially beneficial way to build relationships with faculty members more broadly.[2]

As is the case with most discussions in academia, disciplines matter (see Figure 7). Virtually all faculty respondents in all disciplines uniformly rate the buyer role as very important. A large majority of the humanists also value several other library roles highly, but for social scientists and scientists the buyer role is by far the most important role of the library. It is striking how faculty members have come to universally perceive the library role as purchasing agent for institutional information resources as essential.

But for other library roles, there are noteworthy disciplinary differences in faculty perceptions. Almost three-quarters of the humanities faculty who responded indicated teaching support is a very important role of the library, while a notably lower share of social scientists and scientists saw teaching support as very important. This finding raises some questions for validation locally and for further study. Is this role really most strongly valued by humanists, and if so, why? Alternatively, is there some reason that perceptions vary so significantly? As numerous libraries have invested in building information commons over the past decade, are there alternative or additional teaching roles that would be valued by social scientists and scientists?

The library's role as archive is very important to a very high share of the humanists (82%), a relatively close second to the buyer function. For social scientists and scientists, however, the archiving role is a distant second, with 66% and 65%, respectively, ranking the archival role as very important.

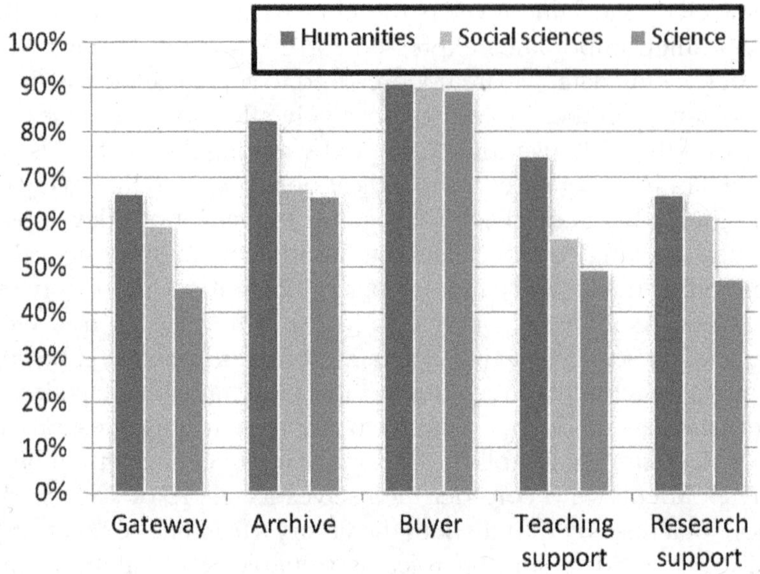

FIGURE 7 Percent of Faculty Rating These Roles of the Library as Important, by Disciplinary Grouping.

Perhaps this pattern is unsurprising, given the humanities' continuing reliance on print monographs, paper archives, and special collections, which have not yet seen the same dramatic format and preservation shift to the digital and the network level as have journals. Over the next few years, it will be interesting to track this question as more and more monographs are readily available to faculty members as e-books.

Finally, the library's role as a gateway demands attention. Helping users "locate information for their research" has become a far more competitive endeavor than it was in the days of print, and the library now competes with Google, publishers, aggregators, and other network-level services to serve its constituents. The fact that the perceived value of the gateway role has declined is a point that must be factored into libraries' resource allocation decisions; the trend over the last decade makes an even more powerful argument that libraries need to consider very carefully the investments they make in search and discovery services. The decline in the library's perceived role as a gateway among our respondents matches the shift to network-level discovery and has been steady and consistent over the last 10 years, holding across disciplinary groupings (see Figure 8).

A particularly small share of scientists (less than half) see this gateway role as very important, and notwithstanding efforts to provide advanced alerting and discovery services to faculty members at some institutions (Schecker, 2008), the scientists in our surveys have expressed dramatically declining reliance on the library since 2003. Libraries need to regularly assess whether their constituents continue to use and value the gateway services that they

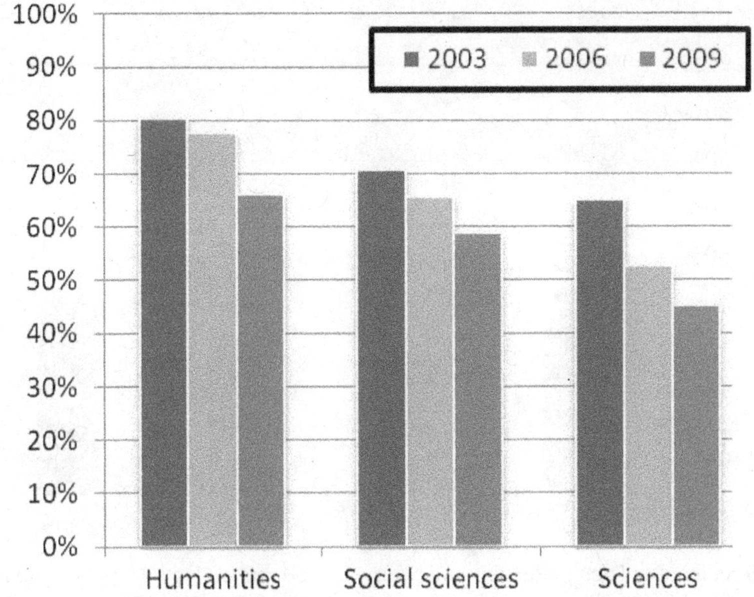

FIGURE 8 Percent of Faculty Rating the Library's "Gateway" Role as Very Important, by Disciplinary Grouping in 2003, 2006, and 2009.

provide to ensure that the level of investments being made are justified by the benefits being delivered and valued by their constituents. Libraries should also give careful consideration to ways to deliver these services more efficiently through collaboration and participation in services delivered "in the cloud" or at the network level.

Despite the reported declines in importance of all the library's roles other than as a buyer, the 2009 study saw a slight rise among respondents in their perceived general dependence on the library (see Figure 9). Given the trend established in previous surveys, these data surprised us. In fact, in each disciplinary category, faculty rated their dependence on the library higher in 2009 than they had in 2006, and in some cases at their highest level since 2000. We do not have definitive evidence to explain whether this is an aberration or represents a reversal of the trend, but one possible explanation for the increase is the substantial growth in the value placed on the buyer function by the respondents. As mentioned previously, 90% of our respondents rate the value of the buying function as "very important," a result that is universal across disciplines. If this is in fact the reason for the general increased perception of dependence on the library, this would represent a kind of victory for libraries. When we presented findings from these surveys early in the decade, librarians generally expressed frustration that faculty were not more aware that many of the resources they were accessing via the Web were paid for by libraries. Libraries have taken a variety of steps to raise awareness of that role. In addition, increased attention to open access,

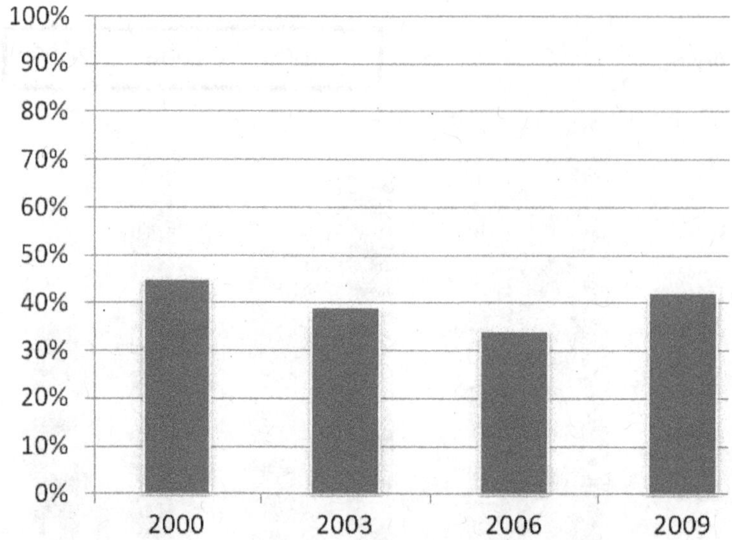

FIGURE 9 Percent of Faculty Responding "Very Dependent" to "How Dependent Would You Say You Are on Your College or University Library for Research You Conduct?"

which libraries have played an active role in raising, makes it clear that many resources are not free and require the payment of often substantial subscription fees. Finally, the challenging economic climate of the last two years and the resulting cuts and cancellations to subscriptions surely must also have brought into higher relief the important role libraries play in making resources available to the campus community.

Summary

Network-level discovery tools include disciplinary resources and powerful search tools that dramatically improve research efficiency while also increasing effectiveness. Faculty members responding to our survey indicate that discovery practices across all disciplines have continued their marked shift to the network level. These faculty members are reducing their use of local library services for discovery purposes and therefore seem to put less value on the library's traditional intellectual role as a gateway to information. However, these faculty members continue to strongly support the library's collection and preservation roles.

The positive response to two new roles introduced in our most recent survey, teaching support and research support, suggest an opportunity for libraries to further develop campus relationships. But notwithstanding noteworthy library investments in everything from the information commons to data curation services, faculty members across disciplines do not yet value the library's teaching and research support activities nearly as highly as they do acquisition and preservation. Based on our respondents, developing research and teaching services that are valuable to scholars in the science and social science fields seems to have been a particular challenge for libraries.

All this suggests a key dilemma for the libraries (and their parent institutions) as they make strategic decisions about where to invest resources and direct staff. On the one hand, the fields whose practices are most traditional also appear to contain the library's greatest supporters; therefore, if the library shapes its roles and activities based on what is currently most highly appreciated by faculty, it may lose a valuable opportunity to innovate and position itself as relevant in the future. On the other hand, if the library develops new and innovative roles and services that address unmet needs, becoming newly relevant and even essential to those scholars who have moved farthest away from it, in the near term it may lose the support of its most ardent supporters. Can the academic library reengage with scientists? If not, is it realistic to expect humanists to remain loyal given that the trend indicated by faculty responses in the humanities over the years demonstrates declining support for the library's gateway role? While there is more support for the library's gateway role in the humanities than in the sciences, the trend is totally consistent. This would indicate that humanists may be following in the footsteps of their peers in other disciplines, a pattern which may only accelerate as a broader range of humanistic scholarly materials is made available in digital form. Addressing this dilemma is perhaps the most urgent strategic challenge facing academic library leaders.

No libraries possess the resources to pursue every strategic opportunity they confront. For this reason, many may face a strategic choice between investing to reengage with scientists and certain social science fields or building on their existing strength with humanists to develop durable services for an increasingly online future. In contemplating such decisions, it is necessary to examine the range of feasible services needed or wanted at a disciplinary level. Moreover, many libraries will find it useful to consider unique assets and opportunities on their own campuses in the context of this broad strategic backdrop, perhaps investing in individualized strategy analyses for their own institutions (University of Minnesota, n.d.; NYU, n.d.; Studying, n.d.). Certainly, in this environment, academic libraries can benefit from a culture of regular experimentation, assessment, redirection and reinvestment to keep pace with this dynamic environment.

THE FORMAT TRANSITION FOR SCHOLARLY WORKS

As more and more new scholarly works are produced in digital form, and as increasing waves of digitization have brought a wide range of primary and secondary scholarly materials online, faculty attitudes and behaviors regarding digital scholarly materials have evolved rapidly, altering needs and expectations for scholarly materials in physical form. Scholarly journals have been at the forefront of this transition. Responses to our surveys suggest that a tipping point has been passed for current issues of journals, and that, with certain narrow exceptions, print editions of current issues of scholarly journals will rapidly become a thing of the past. And although faculty attitudes on journal backfiles do not yet appear to have experienced the same nearly-complete shift, they are changing in parallel with library resource constraints such that backfile print collections will increasingly be replaced exclusively by digitized versions. Our findings raise key strategic questions for publishers and libraries alike on when and how to wind down print publishing and collecting programs and on how digitization will reshape collections management for print collections of journal backfiles.

Current Issues of Scholarly Journals

Faculty responses to our survey confirm what we all have observed: that journals have continued their transition to digital format, with growing acceptance and in some cases enthusiasm for the substitution of electronic for print journal materials. Long-standing disciplinary patterns continue to hold: humanists remain more attached to print than their colleagues in the social sciences and, especially, the sciences. Our survey indicates that faculty are widely prepared for a complete transition away from print to digital-only for current issues of scholarly journals.

For current issues acquisitions, there is widespread agreement that the ongoing transition meets the needs of faculty. Nearly three-quarters of faculty agreed strongly that it would be "fine" with them for their library to cancel current issues of a print version of a journal while continuing to make them available electronically, a figure that has steadily and substantially risen over the years (see Figure 10). This trend is surely going to continue through a complete transition, as publishers increasingly identify the electronic format is the "version of record" and in many cases have added content, features, and functionality to their electronic versions that are not available in print.

This attitude is almost universally shared by our respondents in the social sciences and sciences (see Figure 11), with less than 10% of these faculty members holding a negative perception about print cancellations. Even among humanists, strong support for this point of view has continued to grow over time, and a solid majority of humanists have asserted their comfort with such substitution for current issues of journals.

There are, certainly, differences even between humanists. Art historians and Asian studies faculty are the only disciplines in which less than a majority support the transition of current issues to electronic media, while philosophers are relatively more accepting of this transition than are most

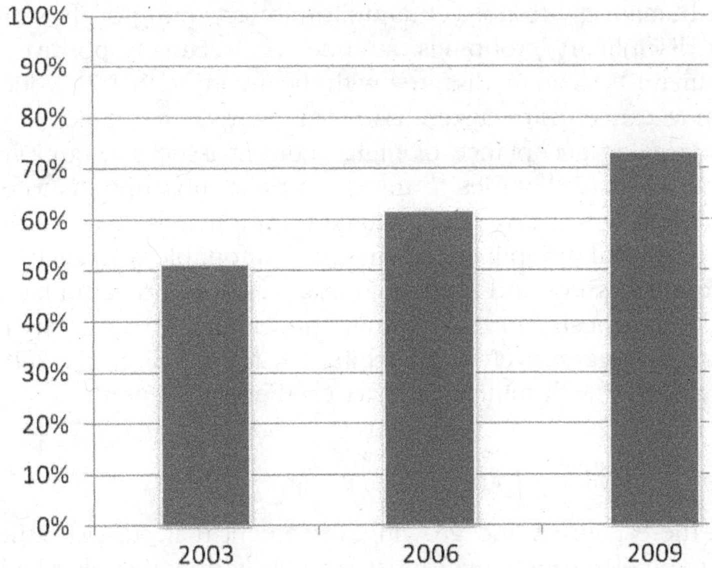

FIGURE 10 Percent of Faculty Strongly Agreeing With the Statement: "If My Library Cancelled the Current Issues of a Print Version of a Journal but Continued to Make Them Available Electronically, That Would be Fine With Me" in 2003, 2006, and 2009.

humanists. But even among more "conservative" faculty, attitudes have continued to shift and comfort with this transition has continued to grow. For example, although still less accepting than their peers, art historians' comfort with the transition has grown at about the same rate as their humanist peers.

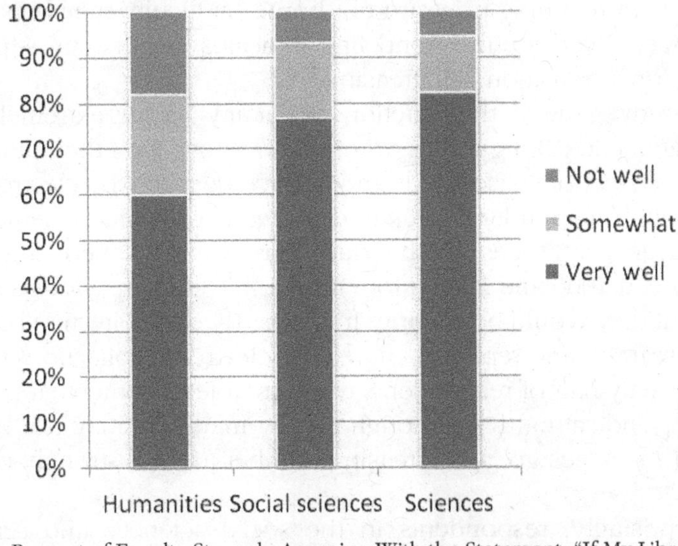

FIGURE 11 Percent of Faculty Strongly Agreeing With the Statement: "If My Library Cancelled the Current Issues of a Print Version of a Journal but Continued to Make Them Available Electronically, That Would Be Fine With Me," by Disciplinary Grouping.

Although humanists are not yet as uniformly accepting of this transition as the other disciplinary groupings, attitudes are relatively positive; less than 20% of humanists strongly disagree with the assertion that it "would be fine" with them to cancel print current issues in favor of electronic.

This growing acceptance of digital current issue substitution validates the choices of many libraries to transition their subscriptions to electronic-only. Although a sensitive and nuanced approach is needed—as already mentioned, several disciplines remain less comfortable with such a transition even for current issues and local circumstances (and powerful faculty!) must be considered—these national findings suggest that libraries may be able to move relatively aggressively in switching most remaining print subscriptions to electronic-only with minimal impact on their constituents.

Backfiles of Scholarly Journals

Although there is great and growing agreement that current issues can be migrated to an electronic-only format, especially now that electronic is often the "format of record," faculty responses to questions about the retention of journal backfiles are somewhat more mixed. For backfiles, a variety of providers, including but not limited to publishers, have digitized thousands of journal titles, at various levels of quality that may at times diverge to at least some degree from the original published print version, with a variety of provisions for digital preservation and postcancellation access. It is therefore understandably more difficult for faculty members to contemplate removing a resource currently available to them than to consider foregoing purchase of the new digital "format of record," especially if the opportunity costs associated with retaining print are not borne by faculty members but rather by the library. Even so, the trend line indicates that faculty support for a backfiles format transition is increasing.

Our study gauged the reaction of faculty to an extremely strongly worded statement, asking if they would be "happy" with their library having "hard-copy collections discarded" and replaced entirely by electronic collections. Although respondents prepared to agree with that statement were a distinct minority, attitudes on this question seem to have changed significantly between 2006 and 2009. More than a third of respondents now agree strongly that they would be "happy" to see hard-copy collections of scholarly journals discarded and replaced entirely by electronic collections (see Figure 12). And exactly half of respondents respond at least somewhat positively to this notion,[3] indicating that although faculty members may not be "happy" to see print backfiles go, an increasing number are not strongly opposed to the idea.

Unsurprisingly, respondents in the social sciences and sciences are more comfortable with such a substitution than are their colleagues in the humanities, but attitudes have shifted substantially among all disciplinary

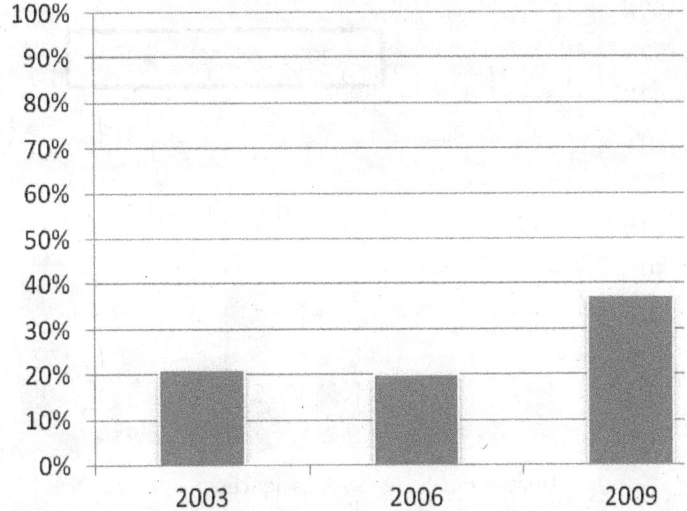

FIGURE 12 Percent of Faculty Agreeing Strongly With the Statement: "Assuming That Electronic Collections of Journals Are Proven to Work Well and Are Readily Accessible, I Would Be Happy to See Hard-Copy Collections Discarded and Replaced Entirely by Electronic Collections" in 2003, 2006, and 2009.

groups since 2006. Even among scientists, the majority of respondents are still not "happy" about the prospect of wholesale electronic-for-print substitution, but the jump in comfort level in the 2009 responses may signal the beginning of a broader shift that should be assessed in a future survey (see Figure 13).

When asked about their continuing need for access to backfiles in print form, a complementary picture emerges: only slightly more than a third of faculty respondents indicated their sense that it would *always* be *crucial* for *their own* college or university library to maintain print journal collections (see Figure 14). These overall figures mask dramatic differences among individual disciplines' reactions to print backfiles deaccessioning. Faculty in business, economics, and several of the sciences are among the most enthusiastic about the transitioning of print backfiles to electronic only, offering an opportunity for immediate impact, whereas humanities disciplines like art history and classics are not ready for local print holdings to be replaced with electronic resources.

Declining faculty reliance on local print collections may pose a challenge for libraries, as local investment in print preservation efforts may go unrecognized and unrewarded just as efforts to withdraw local print holdings may elicit controversy. Notably, looking at responses to these questions by faculty at large research institutions compared with those at smaller ones shows that there is no more interest in local print preservation efforts among faculty at the largest institutions, which are assumed by many to bear the lion's share of responsibility for preservation, than at other institutions. New

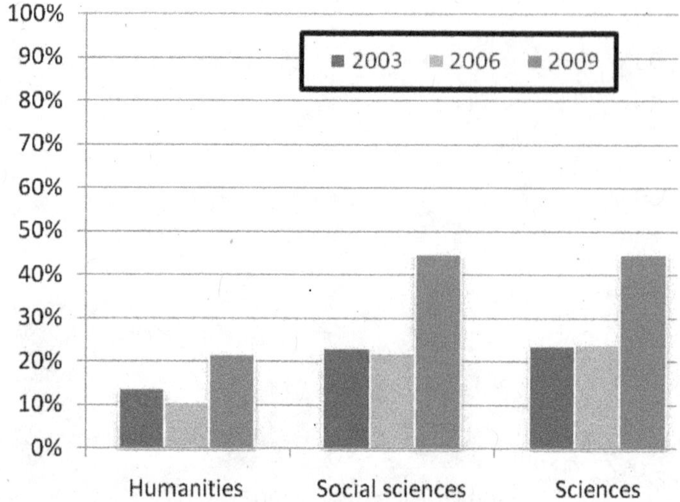

FIGURE 13 Percent of Faculty Agreeing Strongly With the Statement: "Assuming That Electronic Collections of Journals Are Proven to Work Well and Are Readily Accessible, I Would Be Happy to See Hard-Copy Collections Discarded and Replaced Entirely by Electronic Collections," by Disciplinary Grouping, in 2003, 2006, and 2009.

methods to more efficiently distribute these responsibilities and costs across the library community and balance the economics, system-wide needs, and perceptions of faculty are needed and are the principal motivation behind the library movement to develop print repositories (Reilly, 2003).

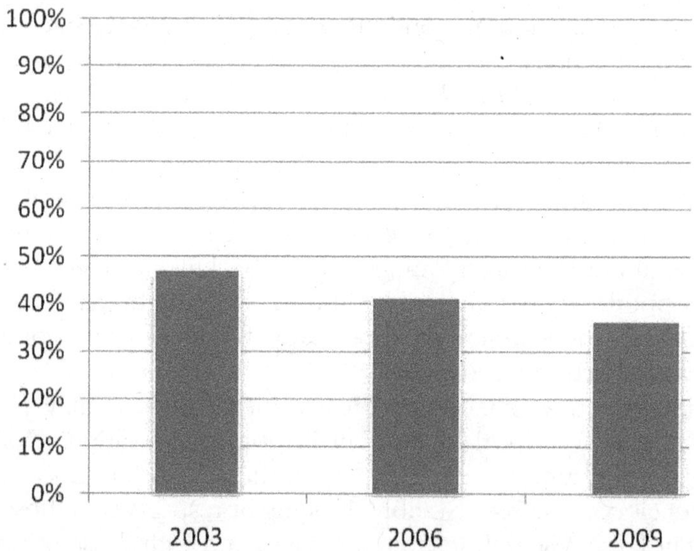

FIGURE 14 Percent of Faculty Agreeing Strongly With the Statement: "Regardless of How Reliable and Safe Electronic Collections of Journals Are, It Will Always Be Crucial for My College or University Library to Maintain Hard-Copy Collections of Journals" in 2003, 2006, and 2009.

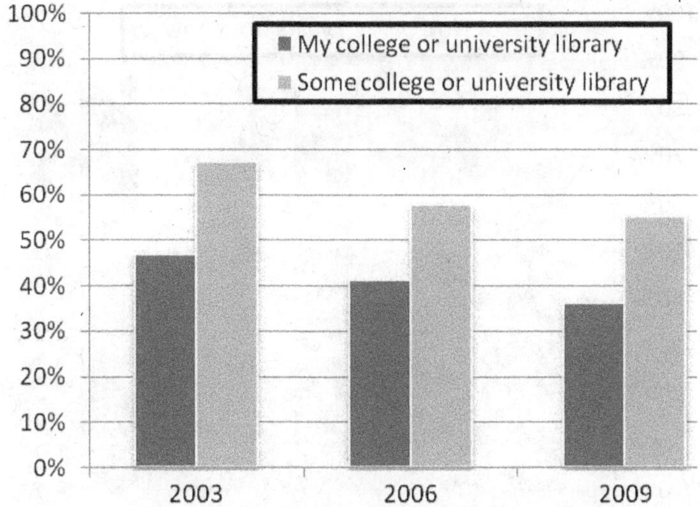

FIGURE 15 Percent of Faculty Agreeing Strongly With the Statement: "Regardless of How Reliable and Safe Electronic Collections of Journals Are, It Will Always Be Crucial for _____ to Maintain Hard-Copy Collections of Journals" in 2003, 2006, and 2009.

In comparing the previous statement about local retention with a similar question about retention *somewhere* in the library community, it is clear that, although these faculty continue to value print preservation, they seem to be feeling less of a need to have immediate access to print journals locally. Both figures have drifted downward over the last decade (see Figure 15). They have varied predictably by discipline—both numbers are substantially higher for humanists than for scientists. Overall, over time and by discipline, concern that print be maintained *somewhere* has consistently trumped interest in local print preservation. These attitudes do not give libraries a clear mandate with respect to print preservation: they neither indicate that local print collections remain functionally relevant to faculty work processes nor suggest that faculty are increasingly willing to see local print collections discarded and rely on remote access; rather, they seem to demonstrate a slowly declining valuation of print preservation in general.

These faculty attitudes may in the long term prove challenging to the print repository strategy that many libraries and consortia are today pursuing. Today, a slim majority of our faculty respondents agree strongly that print collections should be retained remotely following their digitization, but long-term trends indicate a continuing decline in prioritization of these activities. Just as decreasing faculty support for local print preservation activities shapes the environment for library investment in these areas, so the declining mandate from faculty members to support remote preservation activities may have an impact over time. A print repository strategy therefore must also incorporate system-wide efficiencies in print collection management

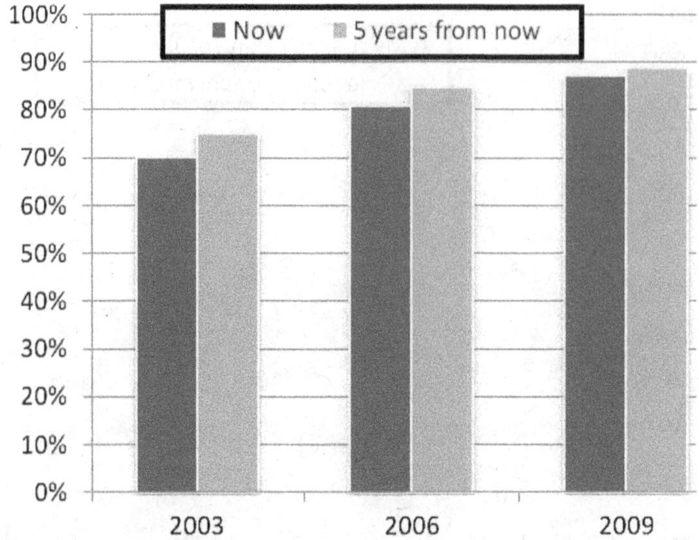

FIGURE 16 Percent of Faculty Responding "Very Important" to the Question: "How Important Is the Long-Term Preservation of Electronic Journals to You Today?" and to the Question "Thinking About 5 Years From Now, How Important Do You Think the Long-Term Preservation of Electronic Journals Will Be to You?" in 2003, 2006, and 2009.

that reduce the burdens of preservation while still prioritizing the responsible maintenance of print.[4]

Preservation of Electronic Journals and Other Scholarly Materials

Our survey respondents' attitudes with respect to electronic preservation of journal materials appear much less complex; these faculty members' sense of the significance of long-term preservation of electronic journals has steadily increased since 2003 (see Figure 16). Interestingly, faculty assessments of the importance of these preservation activities have grown even faster than faculty themselves expected. There is now virtually unanimous agreement on the importance of long-term e-journal preservation, suggesting that faculty care most about the preservation of those materials that they make greatest use of today and expect to be important to them in the future.

Libraries may be able to harness this near-unanimous agreement to garner support for a more holistic view of the preservation of the intellectual contents of journals across formats, linking up their diverse preservation activities into a coherent vision. Publishers may also find guidance in these findings, which suggest that a transparent program for long-term electronic preservation of their publications may be viewed positively by, and afford value to, many of their faculty constituents. In any case, effective and

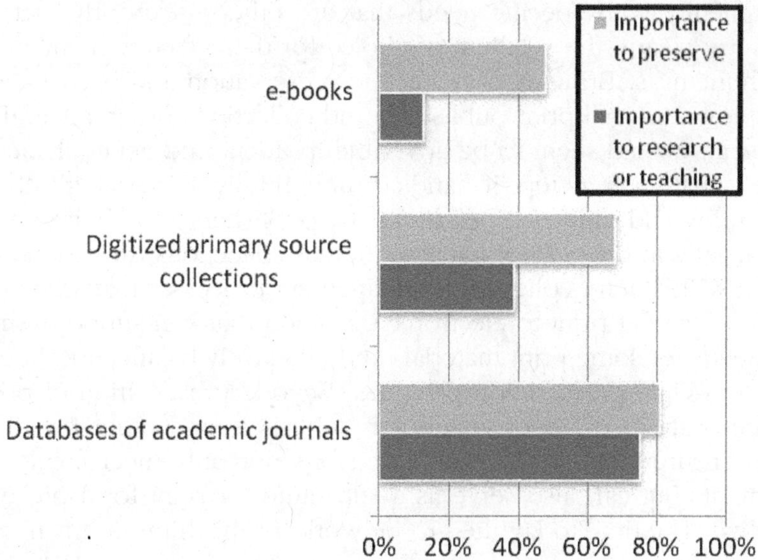

FIGURE 17 Percent of Faculty Responding "Very Important" to the Questions: "How Important Is This Item to Your Research or Teaching?" and "How Important Is the Long-Term Preservation of This Type of Digital Materials?"

sustainable models for the preservation of electronic journals are likely to be widely supported by faculty (Sustainable, 2010).

Although scholars across disciplines highly value the electronic format for journals, opinions on the importance of other types of digital materials vary more widely. Broadly speaking, our respondents, regardless of field, indicate a general preference that digital materials be preserved. We also asked faculty to rate the importance of various forms of electronic content to their research and teaching. While there is parity in faculty views about the importance of preservation and access in the case of journal databases, in the cases of both e-books and digitized primary source collections, far more faculty feel that it is important that these materials be preserved than feel that these types of materials are important to their research and teaching at this point in time (see Figure 17).

We do not have evidence as to why this may be the case, although we speculate that it reflects a general sense of the importance of preserving electronic materials, as well as possibly an indication that they expect these other electronic materials to be more important in the future.

Summary

In the eyes of the faculty we surveyed, electronic versions of journals are now utterly mainstream. Although print journals may continue to play a limited role for faculty with specific needs that are otherwise poorly met, digital versions are clearly the medium of choice for these faculty members, even among humanists. Bringing together the preservation and business models to wind down journal print publishing and collections programs in the next several years would seem to be advisable, prudent and generally accepted. It is likely that such a step, if handled thoughtfully and strategically across the system, would reduce expenditures by publishers and libraries alike.[5]

Especially in the case of backfile journal collections, structural changes in system-wide library collections management processes may be needed in order to facilitate a print-to-electronic transition that will support remaining faculty needs for some print materials and effectively balance local flexibility with system-wide preservation priorities. Beyond preservation of print versions, there are also opportunities for publishers and other backfile suppliers to ensure that their digitized versions not only meet faculty access requirements but can also serve as a substitute for print for a preservation perspective. The time to lay the groundwork for this transition is now.

THE GENERAL SENSE OF LIBRARY IMPORTANCE

Many aspects of the faculty responses to our specific questions about library roles convey a challenging picture for libraries. There is considerable evidence that the importance of some of the library's roles could be decreasing, and libraries may understandably feel threatened by these changes. Consequently, in addition to these questions about the specific roles of the library, we asked faculty about their more general impressions of the changing importance of the library in the digital age. Their answers suggest that although usage patterns and evaluations of specific library roles have shifted, overall support for the library as a campus entity remains strong; libraries are still generally operating from a position of strength.

For example, we asked faculty whether money should be redirected from the library to other needs. Whatever practical changes have occurred in their behavior, extremely few of our faculty respondents feel that the print-to-electronic transition has made the library and librarians obsolete. When presented with a strongly-worded statement suggesting that "colleges and universities should redirect the money spent on library buildings and staff to other needs," only about 10% of faculty indicated strong agreement (see Figure 18). Support for such a radical reconsideration of the library does vary slightly by discipline—virtually no humanists agreed with this statement, and a handful of disciplines may reach closer to 20% agreement—but remains low across the board. Moreover, these responses did not increase markedly between 2006 and 2009.

We also asked faculty members about their level of agreement with the strongly worded statement, "Because faculty have easy access to academic

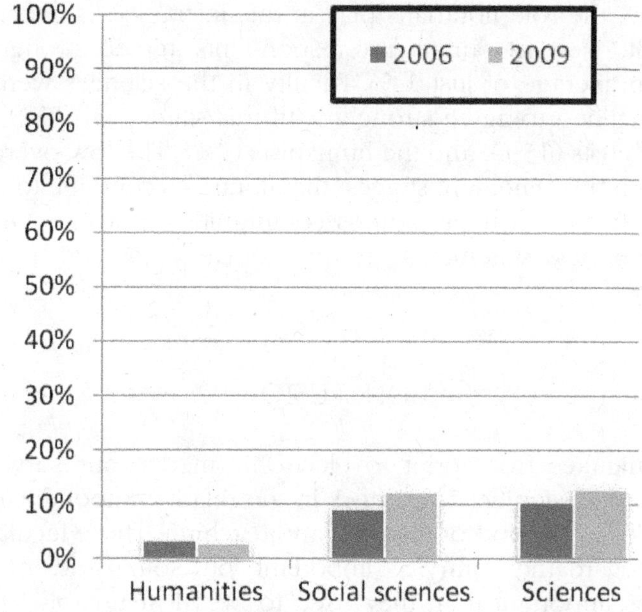

FIGURE 18 Percent of Faculty Agreeing Strongly With the Statement: "Because Scholarly Material Is Available Electronically, Colleges and Universities Should Redirect the Money Spent on Library Buildings and Staff to Other Needs."

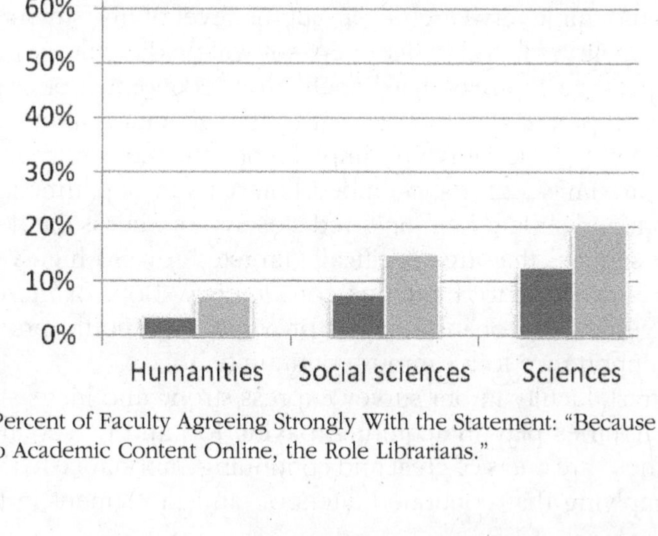

FIGURE 19 Percent of Faculty Agreeing Strongly With the Statement: "Because Faculty Have Easy Access to Academic Content Online, the Role Librarians."

content online, the role librarians play at this institution is becoming much less important." Few of our faculty respondents agreed strongly with this statement—an average of just 14%. Faculty in the sciences were comparatively more inclined to agree strongly with this statement (20%), than were the social scientists (15%), and the humanists (7%). The low overall levels of agreement with this statement suggest that librarians continue to have strong support from faculty in their campus communities. But in each discipline, agreement with these statements has approximately doubled since 2006 (see Figure 19).

CONCLUSION

As content migrates from print to electronic media, our survey suggests that faculty expect significant changes in the relative importance of various library activities in support of research and teaching. These faculty members continue to regard the library as important, but some roles of library are becoming less important than they used to be. Most notably, the ubiquity of the network and the rapidly increasing availability of electronic resources on that network is diminishing the centrality of the library in helping faculty discover and use content. This trend is not only evident in the attitudes expressed in this survey, but is observable in the behaviors of faculty and students evident everywhere we look. Although these attitudes and behaviors are most advanced in the sciences and social sciences, the trend in the humanities is consistent. As scholarly resources become available in digital form, users want to use them in that form, and they will use whatever tools are most convenient to get to them.

There is every reason to believe that this trend will continue, and that libraries' role in providing access to widely available resources will diminish. Libraries should think very carefully about the level of investment they make in tools and resources to aid in discovery—it will be difficult to compete with the likes of Google in areas that benefit from economies of scale in technological development. The one caveat to this general statement would be if libraries are able to identify and implement valuable services that rely on geographic proximity. Efforts to embed librarians in departments represent such an effort, and should be monitored closely. Another is the development of discovery services that are specifically targeted toward high value collections that are available to a campus constituency. Both of these strategies depend on geographic or institutional proximity and could prove to be of sustainable importance to a campus community.

By contrast, faculty in our survey express strong and increasing support for the role libraries play in acquiring, paying for, and preserving scholarly resources. These are areas of great and continuing importance to these faculty members, implying that continued attention and investment in these areas will be welcomed. With the nature of those activities also changing due to the transition in medium—preservation of e-resources is very different from preservation of print—libraries will need to work collaboratively and strategically to manage this transition in ways that take system-wide needs and available resources into account.

While the changes we have seen in attitudes and behaviors related to journals have been profound and rapid, these materials represent a relatively small amount of the collective footprint of library activity. With Google digitizing millions of out-of-print books and the Kindle, the iPad, and the Nook offering easy access to hundreds of thousands of e-books, the transformation of libraries that looms ahead is massive and unprecedented. If books experience a print-to-electronic transition similar to what we have seen for journals, a significantly larger share of libraries' core activities may be impacted profoundly. The responses to this survey point to some of the more valuable services libraries offer (or could offer), as well as highlighting the many challenges facing libraries and putting an exclamation point on the widely shared view that the libraries cannot rely on what have been their traditional strengths.

NOTES

1. The data set for the Faculty Survey 2006 is available at http://dx.doi.org/10.3886/ICPSR22700.
2. Karen Williams's forthcoming "Transforming Liaison Roles" report (part of the Association of Research Libraries' *New Roles for New Times* series) may offer valuable insight on these questions, especially in the context of large institutions. See http://www.arl.org/rtl/plan/nrnt/nrntliaison.shtml
3. While we measure "strong agreement" as responses of 8-10 on a 1-10 scale, positive responses include the wider range of responses from 6–10.
4. Ithaka S+R's "What to Withdraw Initiative provides a framework for balancing these considerations from a system-wide perspective to enable library action (Schonfeld & Housewright, 2009).
5. It certainly would do so for nonsubscription costs for libraries (Schonfeld, King, Okerson, & Fenton, 2004).

REFERENCES

Brandt, D. S. (2007, June). Librarians as partners in e-research: Purdue University Libraries promote collaboration. *C&RL News*, *68*(6), 365–396.

Esposito, J. (2006). What if Wal-Mart ran a library? *Journal of Electronic Publishing*, *9*(1). Retrieved from hdl.handle.net/2027/spo.3336451.0009.104

Guthrie, K., & Housewright, R. (2008). Attitudes and behaviors in the field of economics: Anomaly or leading indicator? *Journal of Library Administration*, *48*(2), 173–193. Retrieved from http://dx.doi.org/10.1080/01930820802231369

Housewright, R., & Schonfeld, R. (2008, August 18). *Ithaka's 2006 studies of key stakeholders in the digital transformation in higher education.* Retrieved from http://www.ithaka.org/ithaka-s-r/research/faculty-and-librarian-surveys

Lewis, D. W. (2007). A strategy for academic libraries in the first quarter of the 21st century. *College and Research Libraries*, *68*(5), 418–434.

Lippincott, J. K. (2010). Information commons: Meeting millenials' needs. *Journal of Library Administration, 50*(1), 27–37.

NYU. (n.d.). *NYU 21st Century Library Project: Designing a research library of the future for New York University*. Retrieved from http://library.nyu.edu/about/KPLReport.pdf

Oliver, K. B. (2005). The Johns Hopkins Welch Medical Library as base: Information professionals working in library user environments. In *Library as place: Rethinking roles, rethinking space*. Washington, DC: Council on Library and Information Resources.

Reilly, B. F., Jr. (2003). *Developing print repositories: Models for shared preservation and access*. Washington, DC: Council on Library and Information Resources.

Ross, L., & Sennyey, P. (2008). The library is dead, long live the library! The practice of academic librarianship and the digital revolution. *The Journal of Academic Librarianship, 34*(2), 145–152.

Schecker, J. (2008, December). The unseen scholars: Researching information in the digital age. *1663: Los Alamos Science and Technology Magazine*. Retrieved from http://www.lanl.gov/1663/files/documents/Item/627/1663_dec08_dialogue.pdf

Schonfeld, R. C., & Guthrie, K. M. (2007). The changing information services needs of faculty. *EDUCAUSE Review, 42*(4), 8–9. Retrieved from http://www.educause.edu/EDUCAUSE±Review/EDUCAUSEReviewMagazineVolume42/TheChangingInformationServices/161752.

Schonfeld, R. C., & Housewright, R. (2009, September 29). What to withdraw? Print collections management in the wake of digitization. *Ithaka S+R*. Retrieved from http://www.ithaka.org/ithaka-s-r/research/what-to-withdraw.

Schonfeld, R. C., King, D. W., Okerson, A., & Fenton, E. G. (2004). *The nonsubscription side of periodicals: Changes in library operations and costs between print and electronic formats*. Washington, DC: Council on Library and Information Resources.

Studying students: The Undergraduate Research Project at the University of Rochester. (n.d.). Retrieved from http://hdl.handle.net/1802/7520

Sustainable economics for a digital planet: Ensuring long-term access to digital information. (2010, February). Retrieved from Blue Ribbon Task Force on Sustainable Digital Preservation and Access website: http://brtf.sdsc.edu/biblio/BRTF_Final_Report.pdf

University of Minnesota. (n.d.). *A multi-dimensional framework for academic support*. Retrieved from at http://www1.lib.umn.edu/about/mellon/UMN_Multi-dimensional_Framework_Final_Report.pdf

Times of Crisis Accelerate Inevitable Change

ALLEN POWELL
EBSCO Information Services, Birmingham, AL, USA

ABSTRACT. *Librarians, publishers, and vendors have all experienced a period of assessment, strategic review, and reaction as a result of not only the recent economic downturn but also the continued evolution from an industry that was primarily print-based to one dominated by electronic dissemination of scholarly information. This article addresses some of the important actions taken by vendors, publishers, and librarians as a result of the recent economic situation and the continued migration of scholarly resources to electronic formats. It explores patterns in publisher prices and pricing models, library content selection, and spending trends, as well as vendor strategies and tactics during a time of fiscal challenge and industry change.*

The economic crisis of 2009 and resulting recession has had a major impact on institutes of higher learning. The effects of the recession are well documented and there are a number of surveys and studies on the topic. The impact of this crisis on colleges and universities has had a direct and significant negative effect on these institutions' libraries. This negative impact has in turn trickled down to others in the information industry, namely publishers and vendors. Each of these organizations (libraries, publishers, and vendors) has had to react swiftly to the economic downturn to meet budgets and achieve their missions. This article will explore how the economic crisis has impacted academic libraries, publishers and information agents and what measures each have undertaken and are planning to employ to adapt and survive.

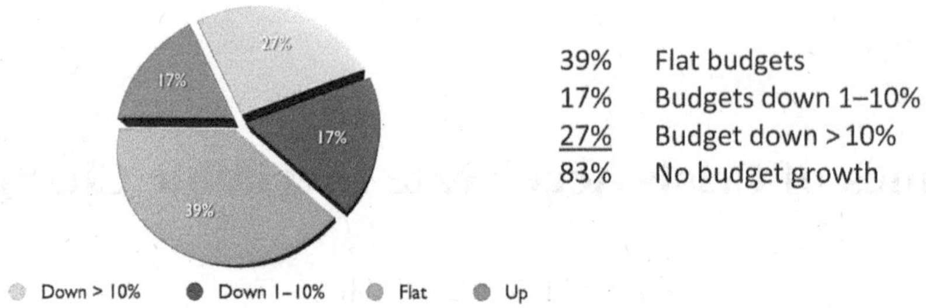

FIGURE 1 Budgets for 2009–2010 Versus Prior Year.

LIBRARIES

Several recent surveys seek to frame the significant impact of the financial crisis on libraries. One of these studies, presented at the Charleston Conference in 2009, clearly illustrated the dramatic impact of the economic crisis on library budgets. This survey, which summarized responses from 641 academic libraries from around the world, indicated 83% of academic libraries reported no budget growth for the 2009–2010 fiscal year including 44% reporting actual budget decreases (see Figure 1).

The same libraries' expectations for fiscal year 2010–2011 were similar to their experiences of 2009–2010 with 87% expecting no budget growth including 40% anticipating budget decreases (see Figure 2).

Finally, the longer term outlook was not much better with 71% of libraries reporting their 2-year outlook expected no budget growth (CIBER, 2009) (see Figure 3).

ARL libraries reported similar statistics in another survey earlier in 2009, with 70% of respondents indicating budget cuts for their 2009–2010 fiscal year and 60% expecting budget cuts of 5% or more (Anderson, 2009).

In February 2010 EBSCO conducted a survey of our larger customers in the United States and Canada in an effort to not only validate other studies but also to look ahead as we as a company prepare strategic and tactical plans

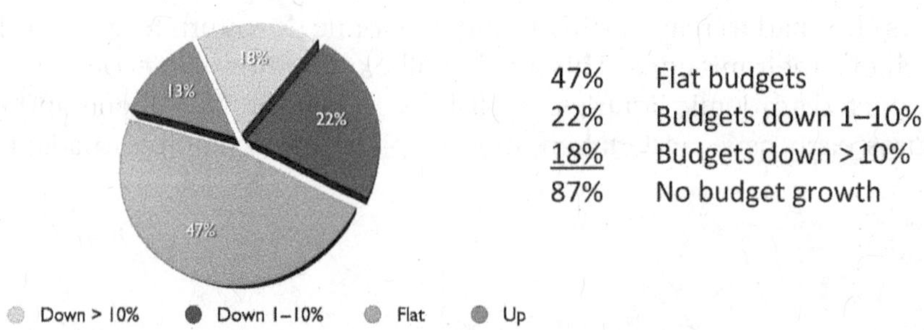

FIGURE 2 Expected Budgets for 2010–2011.

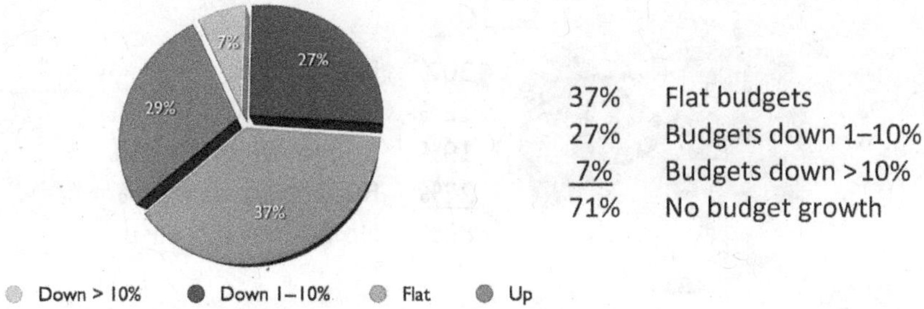

FIGURE 3 Outlook for Budgets in 2 Years.

that reflect the reality of what our customers are planning and expecting (see Figure 4).

The EBSCO survey, sent to 900 of our largest customers in the United States and Canada, had a response rate of 50%. The results of our study were in line with results from other surveys but with perhaps more pessimism toward the immediate future.

Fifty-three percent of respondents reported decreased budgets for their 2009–2010 fiscal year with another 30% reporting flat budgets for a total of 83% of libraries reporting no budget growth (see Figure 5). ARL libraries were especially hard hit with 64% reporting budget decreases.

Expectations for fiscal year 2010–2011 were similar with 49% expecting decreased budgets and 36% expecting flat budgets for a total of 85% expecting no budget growth (see Figure 6).

The Association of Research Libraries's (ARL) library expectations for fiscal year 2010–2011 were slightly more pessimistic than the average of all library types with 64% expecting decreased budgets and 24% expecting flat budgets for a total of 88% expecting no budget growth (EBSCO, 2010a) (see Figure 7).

It is notable that despite the continued rising cost of scholarly information, budgets of the libraries that purchase this information are not rising. The result is the continuation of a significant gap between the cost of scholarly

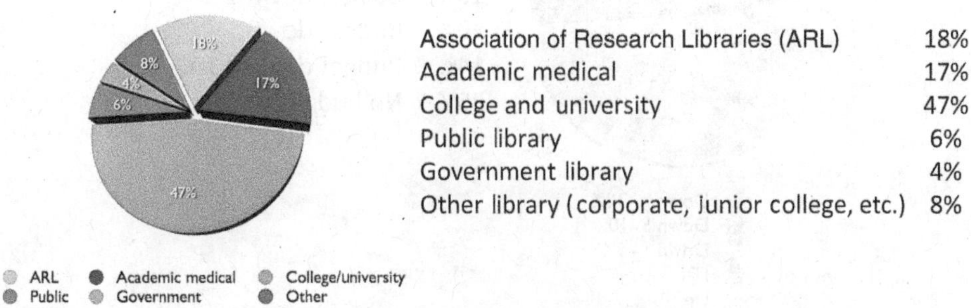

FIGURE 4 EBSCO February 2010 Survey of 449 Large Customers in the United States and Canada: Type of Library Responding to EBSCO Survey.

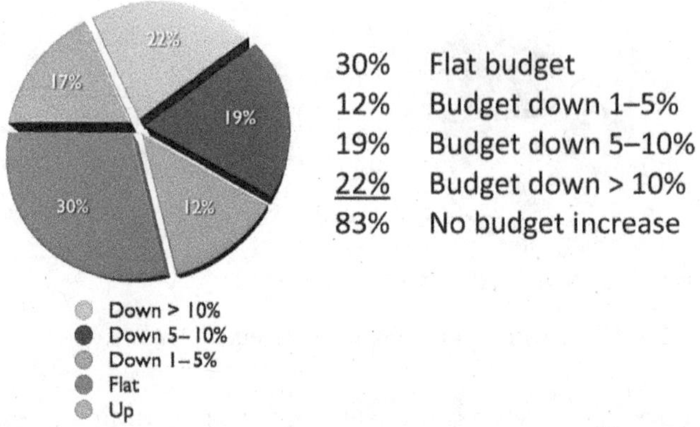

FIGURE 5 Budgets for 2009–2010 Fiscal Year (% of Libraries Reporting in a Category).

information and the funds to acquire it. This is not new news. The so-called "serials crisis" has existed for a very long time as evidenced by the ARL graph in Figure 8 (Association of Research Libraries, 2009). The only difference today is the magnitude of the crisis or gap between funding and costs.

When I first started in the information business 20 years ago, one of my first jobs at EBSCO was to assist with the annual production of a forecast of publisher pricing increases. Each year we would contact the top scientific, technical, and medical (STM) publishers asking for their estimated average price increases for the upcoming year. We would accumulate this data and then apply their estimated price increases across a significant sample of actual customer purchases to come up with an estimated effective price increase for the "average" customer in one of several categories (ARL libraries, academic medical libraries, college and universities, junior colleges, etc.). I

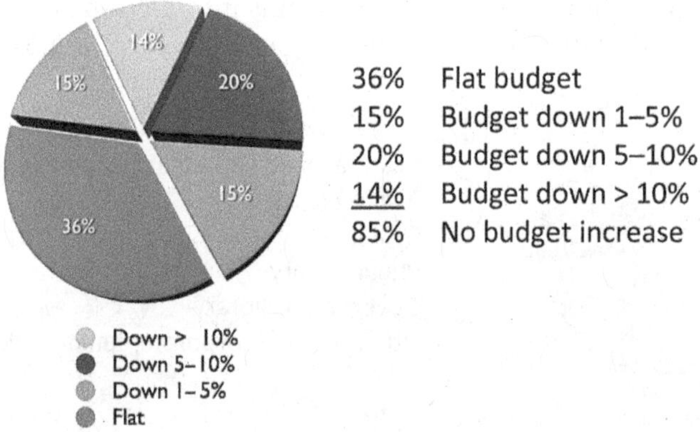

FIGURE 6 Expectations for Budget Year 2010–2011 (% of Libraries Reporting in a Category).

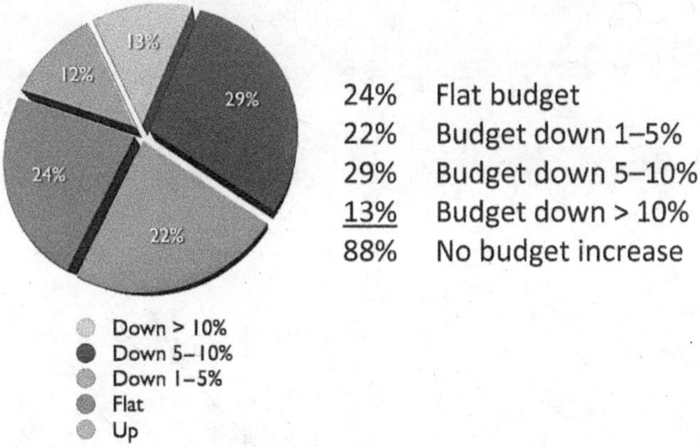

FIGURE 7 Association of Research Libraries's Library Expectations for Budget Year 2010–2011 (% of Libraries Reporting in a Category).

can remember years in which the average annual publisher price increases would be in excess of 10%. We even experienced years where prices for non-U.S. material could rise up to 15 to 20% depending on what happened with foreign currency markets and the relative strength of the U.S. dollar. During this time I recall many articles focused on the serials crisis, as it was well documented that price increases for scholarly information were generally well ahead of basic inflation. When EBSCO would ask publishers why prices would increase at such a significant rate their responses would generally be to provide a breakdown of several factors that were driving price increases and the relative percentage increase attributable to each. For example, a typical response might be as shown in Table 1.

Several observations could be made rather quickly from the publishers' annual responses, with perhaps the most important two being: (a) the assumption that there was a desire on the part of librarians to receive and pay for more scholarly information as publishers continued to publish more articles, more issues, and more volumes in various fields of study; (b) the demand for scholarly information is price inelastic. In other words, an increase in the price of a journal would not be met with the same percentage of decrease in the number of subscriptions purchased. The end result would therefore be more total revenue for the publisher as a result of the price increase. A simple way to think about this is to consider what would happen

TABLE 1 Example Breakdown of Typical Factors Causing Publisher Price Increases

General inflation	Additional pages/volumes	Cancellations	Postage increase		Final total increase
3–4%	2–3%	3–4%	1%	=	9–12%

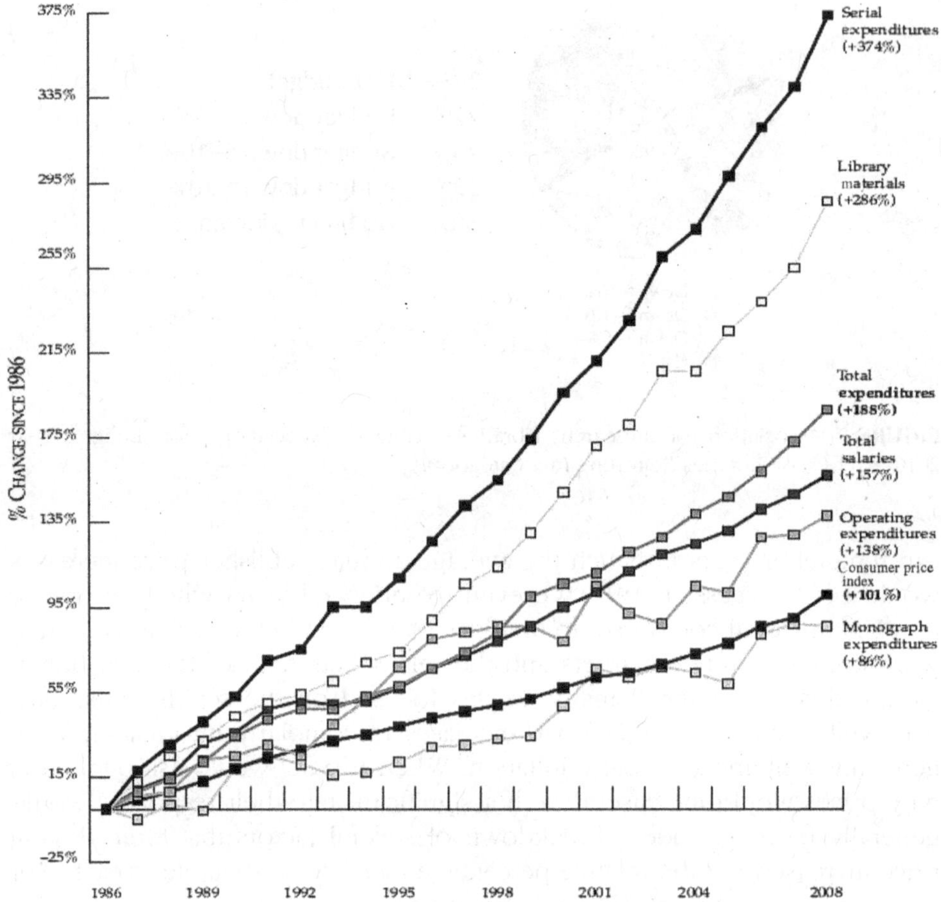

FIGURE 8 Expenditure Trends in Association of Research Libraries (ARL) Members, 1986–2008.

if the price were to go down as a result of cancellations instead of going up. If the demand for a journal were price elastic, then a reduction in price of that journal should result in at least a proportional increase in the number of units sold of that journal. Obviously this is not the expectation of those who price scholarly content.

EBSCO annually conducts a study of publisher prices. To do this we take the actual annual price increases of publishers and cross reference these increases across the actual purchasing patterns of customers to arrive at an "average annual price increase" for various subsets of customers. As you can see from the chart in Table 2, serials price increases have, over the past 10 years, risen at rates averaging at least 7–9%, outpacing inflation.

TABLE 2 EBSCO Annual Historical Price Analysis by Library Type (U.S. Libraries)

	2000	2001	2002	2003	2004	2005	2006	2007	2008	2009	2010
ARL	7.0%	7.3%	7.8%	8.7%	9.8%	8.4%	7.6%	8.5%	8.8%	8.8%	5.5%
College and university	9.5%	7.9%	7.9%	8.6%	9.3%	7.9%	7.8%	8.6%	8.8%	9.3%	5.5%
Academic medical	7.3%	8.2%	7.3%	9.0%	9.4%	8.6%	8.3%	8.8%	9.3%	9.9%	4.9%
Consumer price index	2.2%	3.4%	2.9%	1.6%	2.3%	2.7%	3.4%	3.2%	2.9%	3.8%	–0.4%

Note. ARL = Association of Research Libraries.

One notable observation is the significant drop in price increases for 2010. What has caused this drop in price increase percentage? Is this in response to the economic crisis? Is it a 1-year anomaly or the beginning of a trend? Whatever the longer term outlook, the data shows the drivers of the effective lower increases fall into two categories: (a) lower price increase percentages on individual electronic and print journals. Ostensibly in response to industry requests, many publishers have held prices flat for 2010 or committed to "lower than usual price increases" and this has had an impact on the overall effective price increase percentage; (b) lower price increase caps on large electronic journal package multiyear deals. With such a large percentage of library serial budgets now tied up with large packages, lower price inflation caps are having an impact on the overall effective average price increase percentage.

Although lower percentage price increases are certainly welcome news for librarians this is still little consolation as most libraries experienced decreased budgets for 2009 as compared to the prior year. As a result, the gap between the cost of information and the funding to buy the information has not only continued but widened. The chart in Table 3 which compares average increase percentages for serials prices and library budgets for 2008 and 2010 illustrates this reality.

Indeed, there remains the question of whether a lower price increase on a journal in a particular field of study from one publisher versus a higher price increase on a journal from another publisher in the same field will actually result in a shifting of purchasing dollars to the publisher with the

TABLE 3 Comparison of Average Serials Price Percentage Increases for 2008 and 2010

2008	**2010**
Avg. Price Increase 8.8%	Avg. Price Increase 5.5%
Avg. Budget Increase 2.5%	Avg. Budget Decrease (3.0%)
Gap 6.3%	**Gap 8.5%**

lower price or price increase. T. Scott Plutchak, director of Lister Hill Library of Health Sciences, University of Alabama at Birmingham, addressed this in a recent blog post, as he pointed to the list of publishers who had agreed to hold prices at 2009 levels for 2010. Plutchak speculated whether this pledge would actually result in a change of buying behavior: "*Will those publishers be rewarded with a disproportionally smaller number of cancellations from libraries struggling to deal with reduced acquisition budgets? Or as librarians scramble to find the funds to maintain the big packages from publishers they love to hate, will it be the 'good guys' who end up getting screwed?*" (Plutchak, 2010). Plutchak highlighted the struggle of wanting to move to titles of publishers who price material more affordably versus the compulsion to continue to order important content from publishers whose prices are less affordable. He particularly focused on titles which are included in publisher packages and collections.

At EBSCO, we are still analyzing our 2010 ordering data as many e-journal package purchase decisions were made very late by many customers. However, the data reviewed thus far indicates that the "good guys," those publishers listed on the Medical Library Association Web site (http://www.mlanet.org/resources/publish/sc_2010-prices.html) that kept price increases flat or to a minimum, actually saw proportionately more cancellations than other publishers.

One trend we have observed in the 2010 data is an increase in the number of e-packages being "broken up" or not renewed with publishers as compared to prior years. In an EBSCO analysis of orders of 205 libraries whose package orders were complete for 2010 we observed the following:

- *Number of e-packages ordered in 2009: 841*
- *Number of e-packages ordered in 2009 that were cancelled for 2010: 42 = 5% cancellation rate*

This data appears to corroborate anecdotal evidence that the growth of e-package purchases is slowing or even declining.

We believe a key reason for this emerging trend toward breaking up e-packages is the significant impact the purchase of a few packages can have on the overall library's buying power. It is not uncommon to see a few large packages consume much if not most of the library's serials information budget. A 2009 survey published by Jill Taylor-Roe, of Newcastle University in the United Kingdom, documented the impact of e-journal packages on libraries' serials budgets.

As you can see from the summary in Table 4, 41.9% of library respondents indicated so called "big deals" consumed 26 to 50% of their library serials budget and 38.7% of libraries said "big deals" consumed more than half of their serials budget. This same study also indicated 50% of respondents were now less happy with these deals and 37% had either cancelled

TABLE 4 Percentage of Serials Budget Consumed by Big Deals (% of Libraries Reporting in a Category).

41.9%	26–50% of serials budget
38.7%	>50% of serials budget

deals altogether or downgraded to smaller subsets of content. It also looks as if this trend will continue with the percentage of those planning on cancelling "big deals" for future years rising 250% (Taylor-Roe, 2009).

The dominance of library budgets by a few publishers who sell their content in packaged bundles can be further seen by the dispersion of worldwide sales for EBSCO for our fiscal year 2009 as compared to 1994. Assuming that EBSCO's sales roughly represent the buying habits of a large number of libraries, it is clear significant publisher consolidation has occurred within the last 20 years and with this consolidation, a concentration of serials expenditures with a relatively few publishers.

From the charts in Figure 9 you can see that in 1994, the 10 largest publishers in terms of overall sales revenue with EBSCO represented 19% of EBSCO's total sales revenue dollars as the ordering of serial content was widely dispersed across many publishers. In 2009, the 10 largest publishers accounted for 50% of EBSCO's total sales. This significant shift over the last fifteen years clearly shows the consolidation of the information industry and the concentration of library purchases among a few publishers. This consolidation has occurred over time primarily via publisher acquisition of other publishers' titles or entire publishing operations. As publishers have grown their title portfolios, they have sought various methods to increase the exposure, distribution and sales of their expanded content. A key method has been the bundling of this content into packages and collections.

Initially the purchase of packages and collections was met with enthusiasm within the library community as there was an opportunity to provide more content to users for "pro-rata less." However, as time has passed

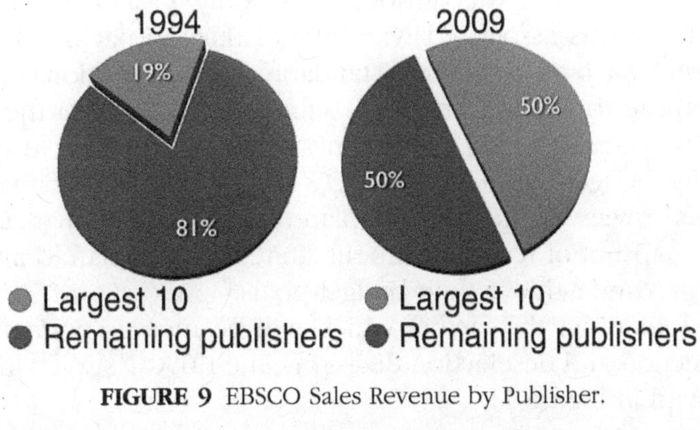

FIGURE 9 EBSCO Sales Revenue by Publisher.

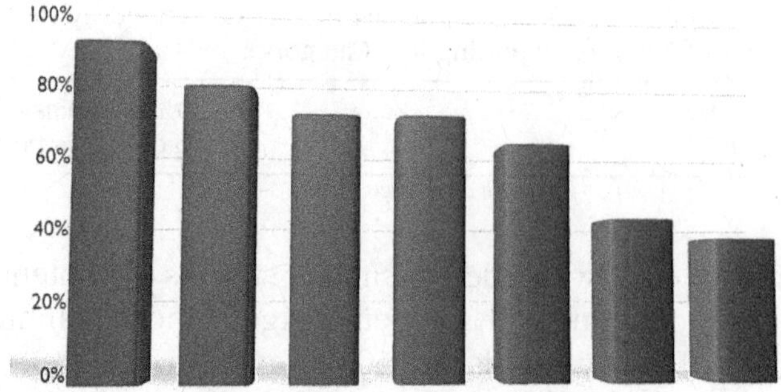

Move from print and electronic subscriptions to electronic only	86%
Cancel databases to eliminate duplicate content and retain databases with the most unique full text	75%
Break up e-packages and renew only the most used e-journals in a package	68%
Try to renegotiate multiyear e-package agreements (lower prices, lower annual price increase caps)	68%
Seek alternative open access content	61%
Consolidate subscription vendors for better pricing	42%
Consolidate software/access and management services (link resolver, A-to-Z lists, discovery, federated search, Electronic Resource Management System) to achieve better pricing	37%

FIGURE 10 Percentage of Librarians Indicating They Are Very or Somewhat Likely to Employ the Above Strategies.

packages have been met with a more critical view as they consume a larger proportion of library material budgets and their annual price increases become unsustainable, especially in this era of unprecedented budget cuts.

Another reason for the intense review of large packages is the increasing availability of usage statistics for titles within a package or collection. As online usage statistics become available, librarians are better able to analyze the use of their collections and determine if all of the content within a package is worth the money they are spending. In fact several recent studies have revealed significant gaps between what is purchased and what is used. One such study was presented in February 2010 at the Electronic Resources & Libraries (ER&L) Conference in Austin, Texas. Nisa Bakkabasi, head of electronic collections at Yale University Library, presented a case study which showed that 80% of use was attributable to only 24% of titles in packages and 90% of use was associated with 40% of titles in packages (Bakkabasi, 2010). Statistics such as these understandably lead to questions regarding the viability of these "big deals" and large subject collections for the future.

Evaluating e-packages is not the only strategy that will be used by librarians to bridge budget deficits; in EBSCO's survey, many librarians referenced other content review strategies they plan to pursue. The chart in Figure 10 provides a snapshot of responses about strategies they plan to implement to bridge the gap and achieve their budget goals.

When looking at the factors which will be most important in making content selection and deselection decisions, the EBSCO survey indicated the data portrayed in Figure 11.

Usage statistics/cost per use	85%
Faculty recommendation	57%
Historical price increases	37%
Value metrics (impact factor/eigenfactor)	33%
Local rating	24%

FIGURE 11 Percent of Librarians Indicating a Metric as "Very Important" When Making Content Acquisition/Deselection Decisions.

The overwhelming selection of usage as very important to most survey respondents could well mean that publishers who are not COUTER compliant and do not provide regular usage statistics could be at great risk of being marginalized.

Librarians are not only rapidly adapting to new methods of content evaluation to address their funding issues, they are also thinking more holistically about the overall costs of achieving their missions. In addition to adjusting materials buying, they are also addressing other costs within their organizations. For 2007–2008, ARL indicated 41% of library budgets were spent on library materials while 45% of budgets were spent on salaries (see Figure 12) (Association of Research Libraries, 2009).

With the amount of funds spent on personnel being roughly equal to the funds spent on materials, the economic situation has required that librarians also focus on the personnel piece of the budget pie to bridge the economic divide. A trend that seems to be emerging is institutions no longer looking at costs in "silos" or in separate categories but rather managing library expenditures in a more holistic method whereby the costs of staff, materials, infrastructure, and so on are all seen equally as "fair game." Librarians are seeking to find the most effective use of funds, or the expenditures most acceptable to cut, to meet the mission of the library. This has been seen as some libraries have begun to reduce or even eliminate positions once thought indispensable. EBSCO's survey shows this focus on the personnel part of the equation as indicated in Figure 13. Of those reducing staff,

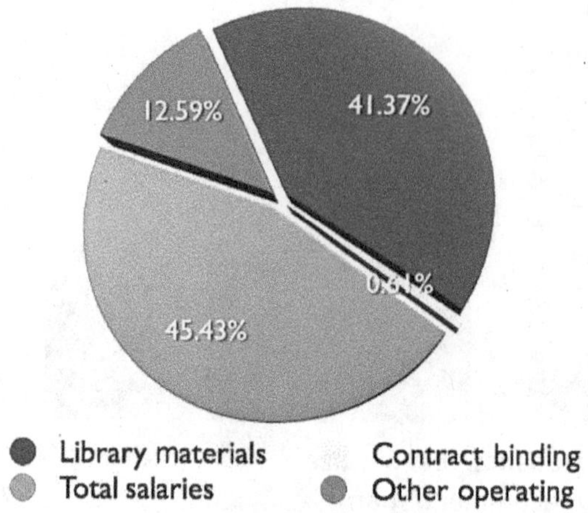

FIGURE 12 Budget Allocation in Association of Research Libraries.

librarians reported reductions in several categories of positions as indicated in Figure 14.

It is clear the cost of serial information for libraries has risen at a pace that has outstripped library budgets for decades. Cost containment approaches will be keys to survival. However, one wonders, even after we emerge from the current economic crisis, if this long-term problem will have been addressed at all. Will the gap between cost of material and funding continue? Or will the emergence of improved tools to measure key metrics such as cost per use finally break the grip of this long-standing problem?

Like any business or organization, libraries also continue to have issues on the revenue side of the equation. While very modest annual budget

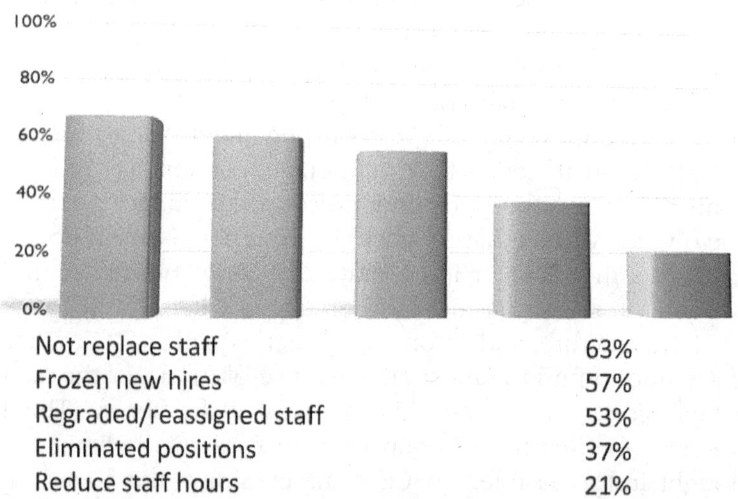

FIGURE 13 Percent of Librarians Indicating the Following Staff Actions.

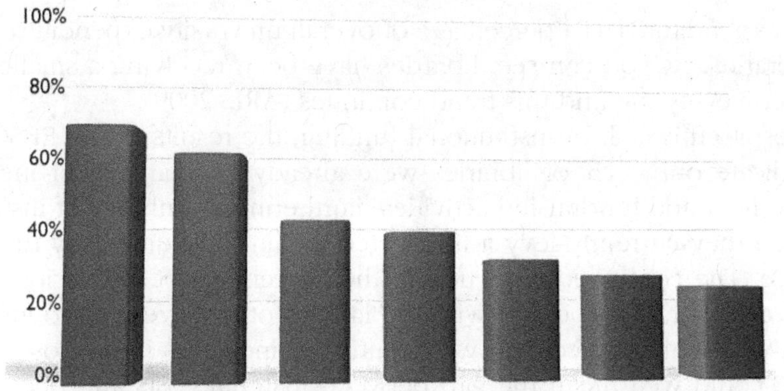

Technical services	65%
Public services	58%
Temporary staff	41%
Student workers	38%
Branch library staff	31%
Administration	27%
Information technology staff	24%

FIGURE 14 Of Those Reducing Staff, Percent of Librarians Reporting Reductions in the Above Categories.

increases were not uncommon before the recent economic crisis, such increases are now virtually nonexistent. This lack of funding or rather decrease in funding is disheartening but is further troublesome when studies indicate libraries have been receiving a reduced portion of overall university revenue despite the explosion in scholarly information. Figure 15 shows a trend of

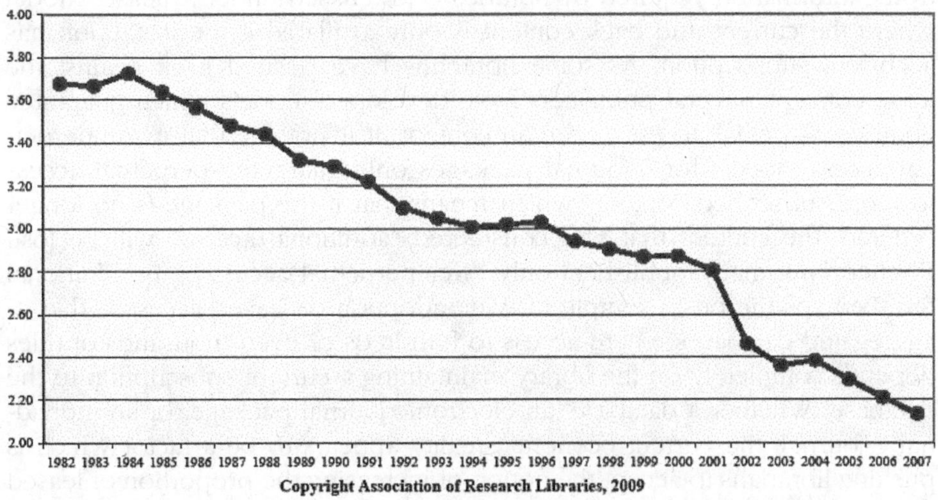

FIGURE 15 Library Expenditures as a Percent of University Expenditures for 40 Association of Research Libraries Member Libraries, 1982–2007.

library expenditures as a percentage of overall university expenditures for 40 ARL libraries. As you can see, libraries have been receiving a smaller piece of the university pie and this trend continues (ARL, 2009).

Despite this lack of institutional funding, the results of the EBSCO survey indicate only 41% of libraries were already engaging in or increasing development and fundraising activities. Furthermore, only 6% of institutions indicated they currently levy a library fee within their university tuition fee structure. The continued reduction in the percentage of university revenue allocated to libraries coupled with the lack of other revenue-producing activities, when taken in concert with continued increases in the cost of information, could well mean the gap between material costs and budgets will continue even after the current economic crisis abates.

Not only have librarians been faced with a continuation of the "serials crisis" but tough economic times coupled with the onset of electronic information have contributed to a migration away from individual libraries as "owners" of serial information they purchase for their patrons. Early in the migration to electronic content, there was an overt concern over the archiving of the information. This was taken into consideration by publisher pricing models that included "electronic free with print." This migrated to a "flipping" of the concept whereby the electronic version of a journal was the primary item purchased and the print version could be purchased at a deeply discounted price (DDP). Now, with severe funding constraints, the notion of retaining print is quickly disappearing as evidenced by 86% of respondents to EBSCO's survey indicating they were likely to utilize the strategy of moving from print and online to the online-only version of a title to save money and meet budget goals.

In addition to the loss of print ownership, much of the remaining electronic information acquired by libraries is purchased under a "lease" model where the current and back content is only available if the institution has a current subscription. As some librarians have pushed back against the lease concept, several publishers have developed models which guarantee libraries perpetual access to certain content. It is notable that many perpetual access models for e-journal packages only guarantee perpetual access to "core subscribed content" which means that if the package is no longer ordered, the content that was considered "additional access" will be lost. Furthermore, many publishers only offer perpetual access at an additional fee. Perhaps the best example of wide adoption of leased access is that of aggregated databases where access to hundreds or even thousands of titles depends completely on the library maintaining a current subscription to the database. Whether a database, an electronic journal package, or an individual e-journal, the current economic reality appears to be a factor which is pushing librarians to accept the notion of increasing the proportion of leased information in their collections.

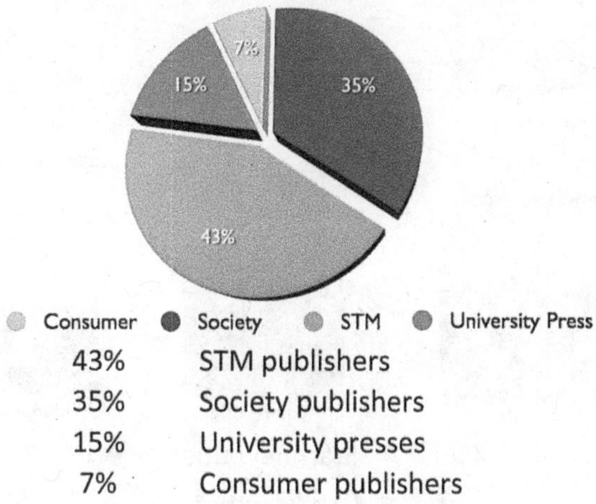

FIGURE 16 Type of Publishers Responding to EBSCO Survey.

PUBLISHERS

Understanding publishers also provides some insight into how the economic crisis may impact libraries. To assess the effect the current economic situation is having on publishers, EBSCO surveyed the largest 100 publishers with whom we do business based on dollar volume. We received responses from 82 of these top 100 publishers. The breakdown of the type of publishers responding to our survey is shown in Figure 16.

Sixty percent of the publishers responding to our survey indicated the economic downturn had a negative impact on their business for 2009. Of those publishers reporting declines, the percentage of declines is shown in Figure 17.

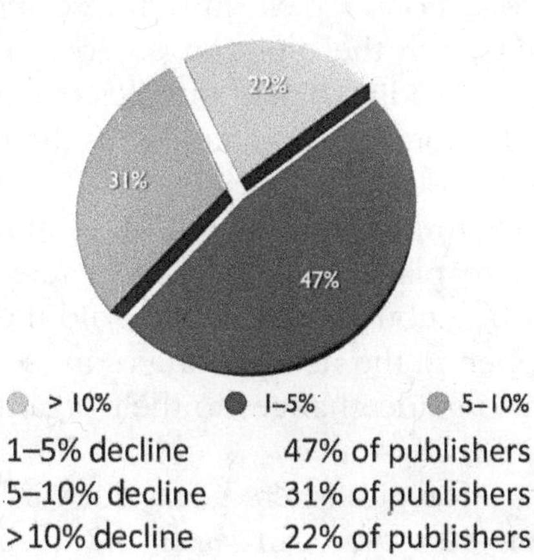

FIGURE 17 Percent of Publishers Reporting Declines in Revenue.

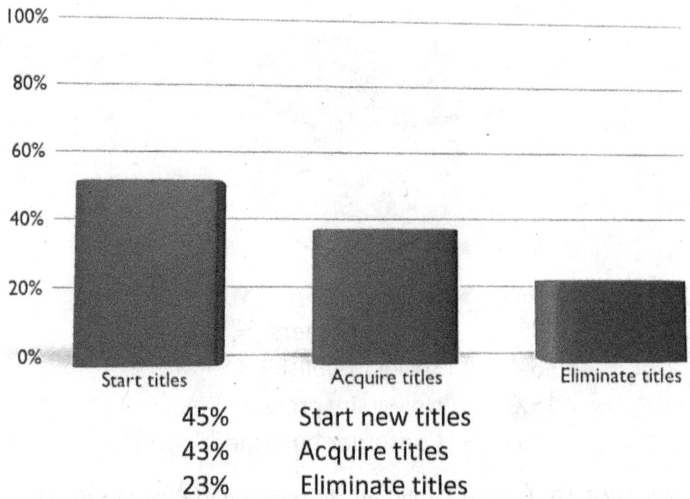

FIGURE 18 Percent of Publishers Very or Somewhat Likely to Do the Above.

It is clear publishers believe the economic downturn has fundamentally changed the way they will do business in the future with 56% of publishers indicating *the downturn had changed the way they do business.*

Title portfolio management continues to be an area of focus for publishers as they look at titles that are not profitable or are marginally profitable with an eye to eliminating these and acquiring new titles that show more promise. Despite the economic downturn many publishers indicated finding new titles to publish was still a key part of their strategy (see Figure 18).

Some publishers appear to recognize the early market trend of customers potentially breaking up packages and have responded by offering smaller sets of e-journals or becoming more flexible in allowing libraries to purchase custom collections ("pick and choose models"), with 49% of publishers likely to engage in these offerings. However, 51% of publishers continue to believe that providing bigger bundles of content at higher prices but with the promise of "more for pro-rata less" is the right strategy, even in the midst of the economic downturn (see Figure 19).

The EBSCO survey further indicates 47% of publishers believe "big deals" will have a secure place going forward while 25% indicated a belief that packages will be unbundled and 28% said they did not yet have a view on what will happen in the near-to-long term (see Figure 20).

Publishers have also made changes to their organizations as a result of the downturn as Figure 21 illustrates.

The staffing picture for publishers going forward for the next twelve months is somewhat mixed as you can see from the chart in Figure 22.

The economic downturn has caused publishers to consider other cost-cutting moves (see Figure 23).

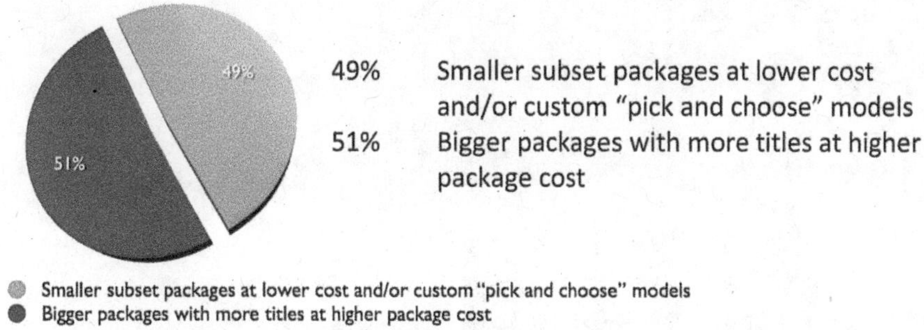

FIGURE 19 Percent of Publishers Likely to Offer the Above.

Although publishers are definitely looking at cost control, the majority of publishers appear to be focusing more on the revenue side of the equation in the coming twelve months as evidenced by their responses to the EBSCO survey as illustrated in Figure 24.

Clearly these actions indicate a primary focus of publishers this coming year will be on finding ways to increase revenues despite significant negative economic headwinds.

VENDOR (EBSCO)

The economic crisis has also had a negative impact on vendors like EBSCO. Stated simply, as libraries have less money to spend, they spend less with vendors. A decrease in the budgets of EBSCO customers translates into less revenue for EBSCO. Just as our customers have had to make adjustments, EBSCO is also making changes. Through February 2010, EBSCO sales

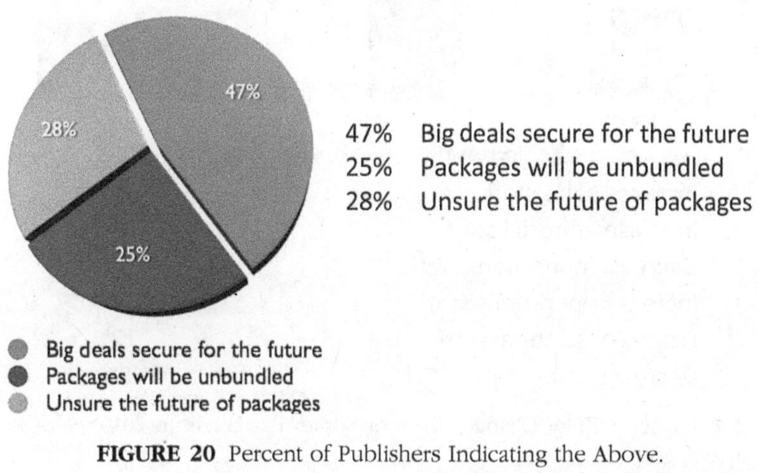

FIGURE 20 Percent of Publishers Indicating the Above.

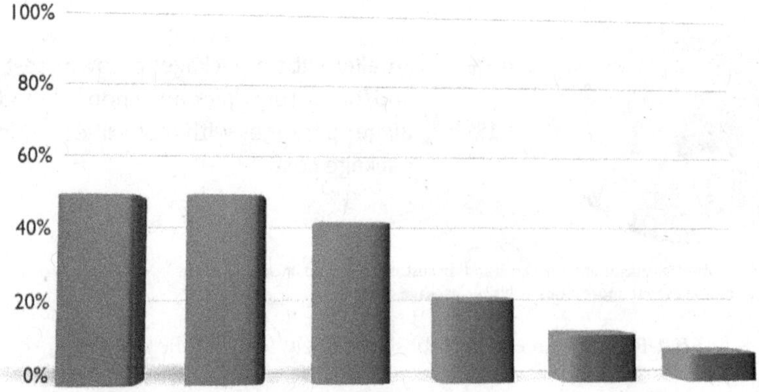

Not replaced staff who left	47%
Regraded/realigned staff	47%
Instituted freeze on new hires	40%
Cut staff	21%
Reduced hours	12%
Put staff on unpaid leave	7%

FIGURE 21 Publisher Staffing Changes in 2009 (% of Publishers Reporting by Category).

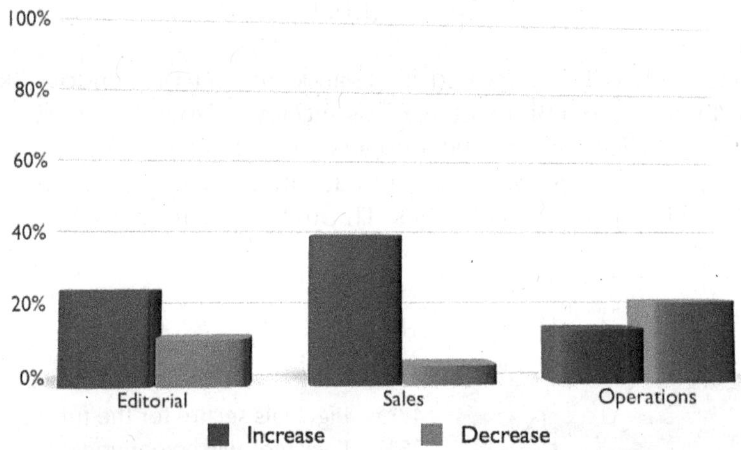

Increase sales staff	38%
Increase editorial staff	24%
Decrease operations staff	21%
Increase operations staff	14%
Decrease editorial staff	12%
Decrease sales staff	5%

FIGURE 22 Publisher Staffing Changes Very or Somewhat Likely in 2010 (% of Publishers Reporting by Category).

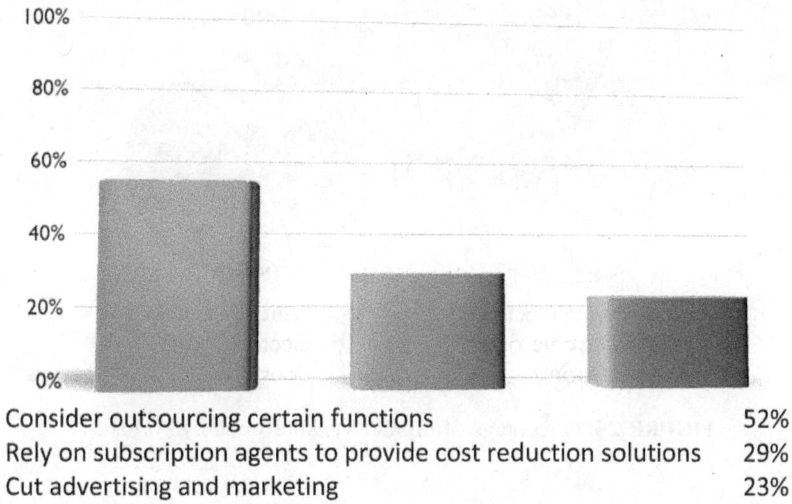

FIGURE 23 Publisher Actions Very or Somewhat Likely in 2010 (% of Publishers Reporting by Category).

revenues in North America are down 7%. A look behind the numbers indicates that the decrease is not due to lost customers but rather due to customers spending less because of reduced budgets. So many of our customers are spending less that new revenue we are adding as we gain new customers is being consumed by the drop in spending from existing customers. In contrast with the decrease in North America, EBSCO's sales outside North America are rising, especially in Europe, and this has resulted

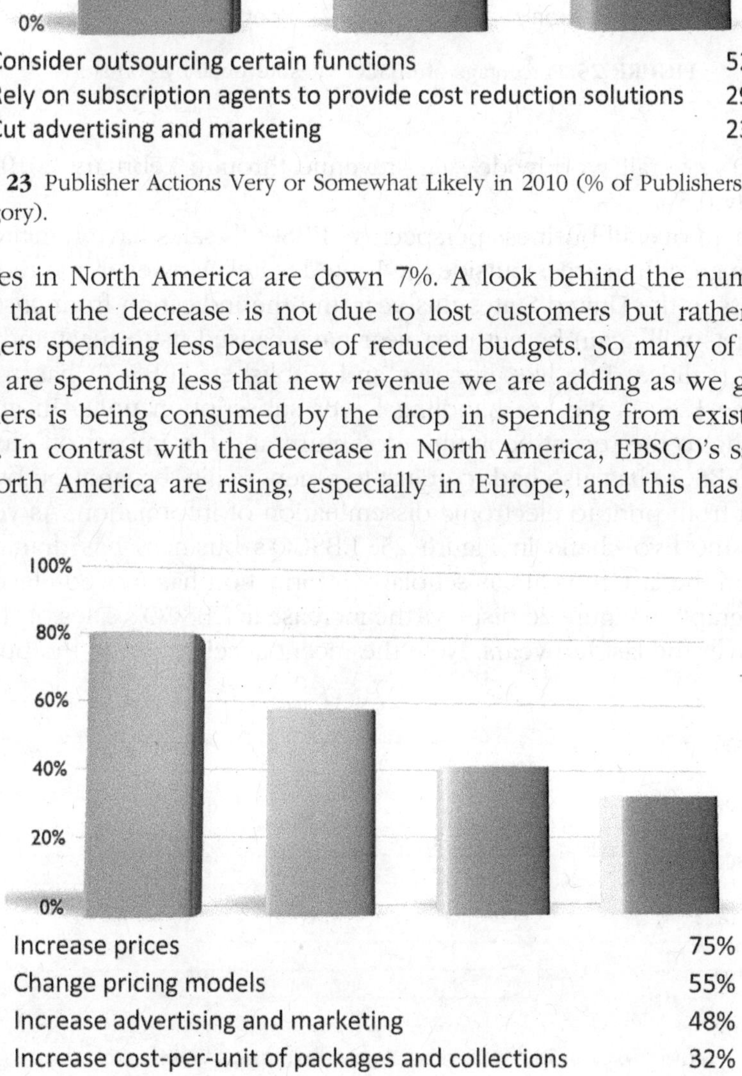

FIGURE 24 Publisher Actions Very or Somewhat Likely in 2010 (% of Publishers Reporting by Category).

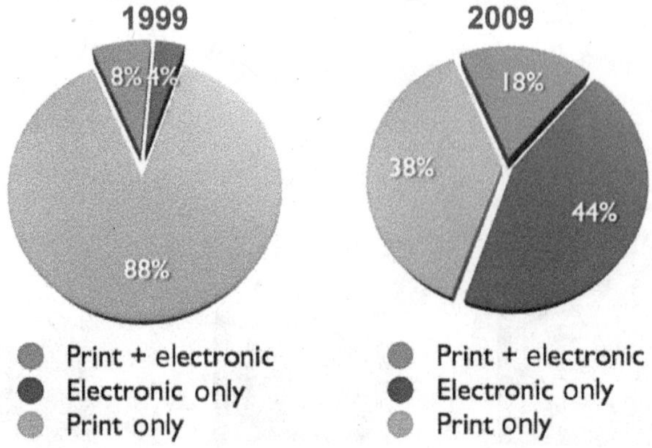

FIGURE 25 Percentage of EBSCO Sales Revenue by Format.

in EBSCO's overall worldwide sales revenue through February 2010 being down only 0.5%.

From an overall business perspective, EBSCO's sales have remained flat due to the growth in areas outside the United States. However, the reduction in business in the United States this year and the indication from customers that budgets will again be cut next year have caused us to react and adjust for these realities. Just like libraries and publishers, EBSCO has reduced staff in the U.S. as we are handling fewer subscription units. In addition to adjusting to the recent economic downturn and the impact on customer budgets, EBSCO has also had to adjust to a new reality brought on by rapid migration from print to electronic dissemination of information. As you can see from the two charts in Figure 25, EBSCO's business has dramatically changed in the last 10 years as scholarly information has moved electronic.

The graph in Figure 26 displays the increase in EBSCO's sales of "E-only" content over the last ten years. Note the recent acceleration in the purchase

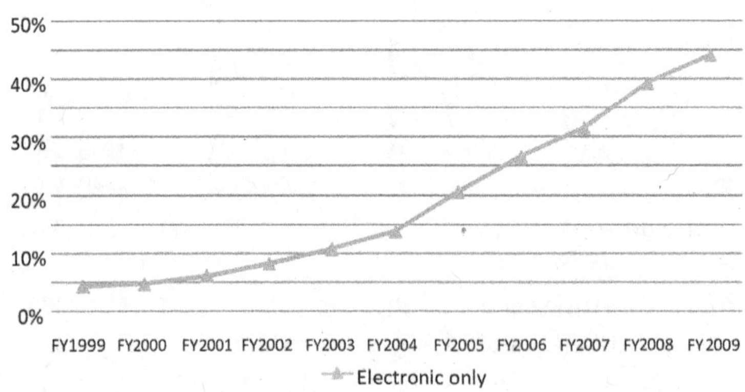

FIGURE 26 E-only Content as a Percent of Total EBSCO Sales.

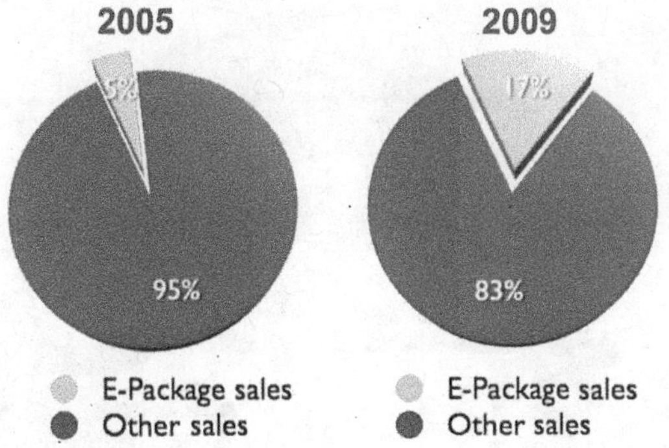

FIGURE 27 Percentage of EBSCO Sales Revenue From E-packages.

of "E-only" as indicated by the relative steepness of the curve over the last five years.

Not only has the type of information ordered via EBSCO changed, but the packaging of this information has also changed. From the two charts in Figure 27, you can see how the proportion of EBSCO's sales attributable to electronic journal packages has changed dramatically in the past few years.

How has EBSCO responded in the wake of the economic downturn, continued rapid migration to electronic formats of information and packaging of content? First, as indicated previously, we have reduced our cost footprint in the United States. We have eliminated positions to mirror the lower volume orders and continue to retool and reorient the organizational structure of the company to ensure we provide top-level service for our customers' electronic content purchases. Also, now that more business is transacted via the Internet, we have reduced costly duplication by continuing to consolidate our regional office structure. Additionally, we are consolidating certain "back office" functions not visible to customers into a centralized "center of excellence" at our Headquarters in Birmingham, Alabama, in order to increase economies of scale, improve efficiencies, reduce costs, and improve quality consistency. In Europe, where our business is rapidly expanding, we are adding staff and upgrading our support infrastructure.

Second, EBSCO continues to seek revenue from new sources. An example of this is our MetaPress division which hosts online content for primary publishers. MetaPress has been steadily growing and now manages content for 155 publisher imprints and hosts more than 3,200 e-journals, 36,000 e-books, 1,000 e-series and over 4.9 million content contributions. Another revenue source for EBSCO is our database division, EBSCO Publishing, which offers via its EBSCO*host*® interface more than 300 online hosted databases, most of these being full-text databases.

Third, we have observed the need to provide more integrated solutions for our library customers to help save them time and improve the overall experience of both librarians and their patrons and we have invested in

FIGURE 28 EBSCO Integrated Discovery and Management Solutions.

research and development to enter a "new space" with products that facilitate the discovery of more content, improve access, and provide integration with our existing products and services. In January 2010 we launched two new products, a discovery service and an electronic resource management system (ERMS), rationalized our product offering into the two categories of *Discovery* and *Management* solutions and connected all products with an integrated knowledge base. In 2011 we also plan on releasing a usage consolidation product which will allow customers to more easily retrieve and manage usage statistics. A diagram which illustrates these integrated solutions is presented in Figure 28.

Fourth, we are carefully watching market trends with an eye toward quickly reacting to help librarians and publishers as necessary. For instance, noting the breaking apart of e-packages as a likely emerging trend, we have further enhanced our e-package renewal system for 2011 orders to be prepared to help library customers handle a potential increase in the number of customized packages from a wider array of publishers.

Finally, we have recognized the need to take a more holistic approach to helping librarians both save money and better serve their institution and patrons. In this regard, EBSCO's role as a vendor is being morphed into that of an organization that is also in some senses a consultant whose job it is to understand a broad array of issues and to recommend solutions to help our customers achieve their goals. Two recent examples illustrate this:

A. We were approached by a group of libraries seeking to achieve several goals: (a) reduce overall costs; (b) preserve the content of the larger institutions in the group; and (c) expand content of the smaller institutions in the group. We evaluated the subscription lists, databases, and e-access and management products of the members of the group and came back with a proposed solution with several components. First, we offered a reduced subscription service fee for consolidation of all accounts, which allowed us to reduce service fees for the entire group. Second, we identified database content overlap and recommended the elimination of certain databases and the addition of others. Third, we proposed group pricing for an A-to-Z listing service, link resolver, federated search and ERMS. This is an example of the "win–win" concept where EBSCO was able to make price concessions in exchange for additional business in several areas. We see such consultation and collaboration as keys to the future.
B. A second example involved a large customer who desired to rationalize their database collection to reduce costs and free up money for the purchase of a discovery service. We evaluated the customer's database collections and e-access and management products. Our recommended solution included the elimination of certain overlapping databases, the addition of other databases, the purchase of a several e-journals to fill gaps created by the elimination of databases, and the replacement of the A-to-Z product. The result of these actions was a cost reduction of over $40,000, an increase in access to unique peer-reviewed content (an addition of over 3,300 unique journals), a reduction in patron interfaces and improved integration.

STRATEGY OR TACTICAL REACTIONS?

The recent economic crisis, as well as the change in the way scholarly information is disseminated, has had a profound impact on libraries, publishers and vendors. In response, these three parties have all responded in ways they judge best for their organizations and customers. Some responses have been straightforward and some more creative than others. What seems clear is that organizations in all three categories are having to assess and make adjustments more rapidly than they might otherwise. Some actions may even be seen as more reactive or tactical than strategic. In a January 25, 2010, *Wall Street Journal* article entitled "Strategic Plans Lose Favor" authors Joann S. Lublin and Dana Mattioli reported that more business leaders now value flexibility and quick decision making over strategic planning and further indicate strategic planning does not always work. In the article, Walt Shill, head of the consulting firm Accenture Limited, is quoted as saying "strategy, as we knew it, is dead" and "corporate clients decided that increased flexibility and accelerated decision making are much more important than simply predicting the future." Lowell Bryan, senior partner for consultants McKinsey and Company, contends "just-in-time" decision making is a tactic that will spread during the economic recovery (Lublin and Mattioli, 2010).

Whether the response to the economic crisis is called tactical reaction, accelerated strategic development, or just-in-time decision making, it is clear that librarians, publishers, and vendors all find themselves in this same situation where nimble and decisive action in the face of severe economic pressure and changing business climate is a required approach. All of us are responding in different ways based on immediate perceptions of the situation at hand and what we believe is best for our organizations and our customers. We are all faced with the prospect of adjusting our cost profiles and personnel; however, libraries and vendors like EBSCO appear to be taking a more aggressive approach in this area. Publishers continue to focus on new ways to generate revenue via title portfolio management, bundling of content, annual price increases and hopefully discovering new markets for their content. And if EBSCO is any indication, vendors are looking for revenue via new products and services which are more integrated as they seek to bring better value to help librarians and publishers do more with less and coming up with more creative offerings where improved pricing can be offered in exchange for more business. This might be subscriptions or electronic access and management tools or content offerings based on overlap analysis projects that pinpoint duplicate content that can be eliminated in favor of additional and valuable new content at the same or a lower price. Librarians appear to be ready to adopt new philosophies and approaches such as increased use of "leased" content models; using metrics such as cost-per-use to make tough buying decisions; breaking apart packages to save money on low-use content in the package; and aggressively managing their organization's cost holistically instead of via distinct allocated silos. All of these actions and others no doubt were at some point on the decision continuum and would ultimately have been considered. However, dire economic times and immediate pressures have resulted in these plans being accelerated as organizations seek to survive and fulfill their institutional missions.

REFERENCES

Anderson, I. (2009). *Our common future: Libraries and sustainability in the 21st century*. Presentation at the Charleston Conference, South Carolina.

Association of Research Libraries. (2009). *ARL statistics 2007–2008*. Washington, DC: Association of Research Libraries.

Bakkabasi, N. (2010). *Selecting and assessing e-resources in libraries*. Presentation at E-Resources in Libraries Conference, Austin, Texas.

CIBER Research Group. (2009). *The economic downturn and libraries: Survey findings*. London: University College London. Retrieved from http://www.ebrary.com/corp/inforequest/survey2009.jsp

EBSCO. (2010a). *Survey of 449 libraries in the U.S. and Canada*. Birmingham, AL: Author.

EBSCO. (2010b). *Survey of top 82 publishers*. Birmingham, AL: Author.

Lublin, J. S., & Mattioli, D. (2010, January 25). Strategic plans lose favor. *Wall Street Journal*. Retrieved from http://online.wsj.com/article/SB10001424052748703822404575019283591121478.html

Plutchak, T. S. (2010, February). *Incentives*. [Web log post]. Retrieved from http://tscot.typepad.com/tsp/2010/02/incentives.html

Taylor-Roe, J. (2009). "To everything there is a season": Reflections on the sustainability of the "big deal" in the current economic climate. *Serials*, *22*(2), 113–121.

From Surviving to Thriving

CARLA J. STOFFLE and CHERYL CUILLIER
University of Arizona, Tucson, AZ, USA

ABSTRACT. *This article focuses on the need for continual organizational change and new thinking about the work that libraries, librarians, and staff must do to remain key players in the academic world of the future.*

Academic libraries are facing a new reality. Even after the current economic crisis abates, no public university will ever be able to entirely recoup the funds that were once available, nor will our libraries. At private universities as well, steep endowment losses have taken their toll on many institutions' financial health (Blumenstyk, 2010). To thrive, libraries will need to use sound business-management practices, align themselves with campus learning and research goals, nimbly apply new technologies to improve service and reduce costs, utilize benchmarks in implementing best-services practices, and provide value-added library services—all while staying true to the guiding principles of librarianship. Although the way we work may change, our values remain the same. It is our responsibility, as the librarians and staff of today, to work together to build the successful libraries of the future.

Over the last 15 years, much has been written about how economics will drive libraries—especially large research libraries—to make organizational, structural, and cultural changes to maintain their roles as vital contributors to teaching and learning in their institutions (Stoffle, 1995; Stoffle, Leeder, & Sykes-Casavant, 2008). In 1996, Stoffle and her coauthors wrote that "the economic and political climate for higher education, especially public education, is more negative than it has ever been" (Stoffle, Renaud, & Veldof, 1996, p. 215). Unfortunately, that climate is even worse today. One only needs to read *The Chronicle of Higher Education* daily to see the financial and political hurdles that colleges and universities face (Blumenstyk, 2010; Hebel, 2010).

Stoffle's earlier articles focused on how library costs—skyrocketing information costs and the expense of introducing new technologies—would make it impossible to maintain the collections of the past, manage the libraries of today, and build the libraries of the future (Stoffle, Allen, Fore, & Mobley, 2000; Stoffle, Renaud, & Veldof, 1996; Stoffle & Weibel, 1995). After Stoffle served on the Project on the Future of Higher Education (2004) from 2001 to 2004, it became clear that libraries and research universities, especially public ones, would soon face an economic crisis that would not only threaten how libraries did business but the traditional way of doing business in the entire academy (Stoffle, Allen, Morden, & Maloney, 2003).

Stoffle's view of the changes needed to overcome these challenges has evolved over time and been shaped by experiences at the University of Arizona Libraries. Though we have had budget cuts 14 out of the last 18 years, our libraries are on the verge of greater integration into the campus's learning and research programs than ever before. That is not to say that we do not need more money (we lost nearly 20% of our wages/operations budget from fiscal year [FY] 2007–2008 to FY2009–2010) and are not stretched mightily (we are down more than 30 positions in that same period). But we are seen by the campus and our students as a strong, vital, contributing force to the university's excellence (University of Arizona, 2000, pp. 51, 77). Thanks to the sweeping changes we have made at the Libraries, and the hard work of our personnel, we are positioned to move forward with new programs.

We are not alone. Many library leaders—not wanting a serious crisis to go to waste[1]—are using the current economic downturn to make fundamental changes that have long been necessary. These changes will ultimately result in our ability to maintain the vitality of the library and allow our rhetoric to change from how we can *survive* to how we can *thrive* in service to our campuses.

As a preface to the rest of this article, it is important to stress that although the University of Arizona is used to illustrate what *can* be done, it is but one experience. It is not presented as *the* pathway to success, merely one of many possible paths. Each library must assess its own environment and the needs of its campus community to identify how it should adapt to the challenges. Many of the things done at the University of Arizona are not unique. Many libraries are using similar concepts to achieve similar goals. The University of Arizona has been very good at borrowing ideas from other library leaders (e.g., our colleagues at this conference, and people like Rick Luce and David Lewis; see Luce, 2008; Lewis, 1995, 2007). These University of Oklahoma Libraries conferences and our "Living the Future" (University of Arizona, 2008) conferences also are sources of inspiration. Another influential conference was the Association of Research Libraries/OCLC Strategic Issues Forum for Academic Library Directors in 1999, which resulted in the Keystone Principles (Association of Research Libraries, 1999) that have helped to guide our activities.

It is the totality—the breadth and depth—of our efforts at the University of Arizona that may provide some insights into the magnitude of the work necessary to build the successful library of the future. Our basic approach has been to:

- Stay focused on our customers and their changing needs; and
- Enable the creation of library as service rather than library as collection.

Our efforts can be broken down into five general categories: organizational/cultural changes, planning and budgeting, new business practices, communication, and collection approaches.

ORGANIZATIONAL STRUCTURE AND CULTURE

Let us begin with organizational structure and culture. At the University of Arizona, our objectives are to:

- Empower librarians and staff by flattening our organization and pushing decisions down to the appropriate level.
- Let go of traditional divisions of work. Rather than maintaining rigid organizational hierarchies and bureaucratic rules, we have a team-based structure and have everyone working at the top of their job classifications, knowledge, skills, and abilities.
- Have staff—not librarians—managing in-building services and facilities. Librarians are involved in some training and assessment of these services, but they are primarily focused on integrating the library into instructional and research programs. Meanwhile, we have created four new job classifications for staff and hire at a higher level (Huff-Eibl, Ray, & Voyles, 2008).
- Optimize staffing resources by placing individuals on the projects and activities that are most important to the future, even at the expense of functional daily work.
- Ensure that people have the technology and resources they need do their work, even if it means there are fewer people.
- Encourage diversity and create a climate that welcomes different viewpoints.
- Reward continual learning and improvement.

In 1993, when we began the task of reinventing ourselves, we decided to begin with our organizational structure and culture. We started there because we felt we could not make fundamental changes in our focus and services using the same old priorities and assumptions, especially those about funding. We realized that we did not have the resources to continue traditional collecting and processing activities, nor could we sustain the resource-intensive bureaucracy that characterized our organization. We decided we had to maximize our human and fiscal resources and that we had to become more nimble and flexible. To get buy-in, we appointed library-wide project teams—ultimately utilizing more than 100 people in the organizational redesign (Bender, 1997)—and introduced the principles of Total Quality Management during the process (Owens, 1999; Phipps, 2001, p. 647; 2004, pp. 90–96). We also experimented with Six Sigma process-improvement techniques (Voyles, Dols, & Knight, 2009), including Balanced Scorecards (Holloway, 2004, pp. 11–16).

Our structural redesign in 1993 moved us from a traditional bureaucratic organizational structure that was focused on processing, managing, and storing *things* to a team-based organization focused on *customers* and providing value-added services (see Appendix A). We have changed our organizational structure four more times since 1993. The most recent structure was implemented in July 2008. It has been tweaked several times already, for example moving our education programs to the Undergraduate Services Team and changing its name to Instructional Services. Our new organization is composed of nine functional teams and six crossfunctional teams (see Appendexes B and C).

Ultimately, the numbers or names of units in our organizational structure are not important. The point is what our team-based structure has allowed us to accomplish. The 1993 reorganization reduced administrative overhead from four assistant university librarians and 16 department heads to 11 functional team leaders and one assistant university librarian. This streamlining enabled us to lower overhead and reallocate administrative positions to frontline services.

Crossfunctional teams, composed of librarians and staff members from various functional teams, were created with decision-making authority to do strategic long-range planning and annual budgeting (with governance representatives and administrators added for budgeting), and to solve overarching library service problems using process-improvement techniques and data-based decision making. Policy creation, day-to-day management of the strategic plan implementation, and library-wide budget monitoring were delegated to the Library Cabinet. All of these groups learned consensus-based decision making. Over time, most organizational decisions have been made by consensus.

Each time we reorganized, library-wide crossfunctional teams designed the new structure. Personnel were reassigned to new teams based on their knowledge, skills, and abilities. The daily work of all personnel changed (Diaz & Pintozzi, 1999). Our goal was to place people where they could be the most successful and where the Libraries could most benefit from their talents. In the first restructuring, every team leader but one was a librarian. Today, four out of nine team leaders are not librarians.

In our latest restructuring, services such as chat reference and information desk staffing were moved completely to classified-staff teams. As classified staff have been trained to take on greater responsibilities, librarians' work has shifted to make the best use of their library degrees and expertise—focusing on instruction, creating online credit-bearing courses, integrating the Libraries into the university's learning program through its course management system, providing in-depth research support to faculty and students, managing collections decisions, and creating and implementing new systems to allow access to information not previously available.

Today, librarians are primarily divided among the Instructional Services and Research Support Services teams. Instructional Services is currently charged with reconceiving our educational programs with the goal of integrating the library services and collections into every course on campus as well as creating online credit-bearing courses. Research Support Services is focused on supporting the research and teaching needs of faculty, students, and researchers, especially by providing increased access, assessing the effectiveness of our resources, creating new online resources, and helping the faculty manage content.

Our organizational redesigns were done in order to adapt to changing customer needs and in anticipation of shrinking resources. Our goal was to improve service, but hold costs steady or even reduce them. When planning each redesign, we relied on data and process-improvement techniques. Renaming teams and services to reinforce a focus on the customer has helped to shift thinking about the role of the library and library personnel, though not without some concern and resistance. This is to be expected. But as Gen. Eric Shinseki, former U.S. Army Chief of Staff, is quoted as saying in *The Rules of Business*: "If you don't like change, you're going to like irrelevance even less" (Fast Company, 2005, p. 7).

Over time, we have introduced a number of new positions with new duties within the Libraries. Early on, we created the position for organizational development, which has now morphed into the director of Project Management and Assessment position. Our Scholarly Communications position is now the director of Copyright and Scholarly Communications. Recently, arising from a need to provide greater direction for our systems and digital library efforts, we created the position of assistant dean for Technology Strategy and established the Technology Architecture Council (see Appendix C) to oversee the Libraries' technology policies, strategies, and directions. Other new positions created include our Director of Marketing & Public Relations, a metadata librarian, and a digital archivist. These represent organizational responses to changing needs and reflect the ability of the organization to respond to new service needs and specialties.

The most important resource that any library has is its personnel. When employees share the same vision, are empowered to make decisions, have the resources to do their work, and are able to continually learn and grow professionally, that is an environment in which they can thrive.

Despite our frequent budget cuts, the University Libraries have sustained a commitment to maintain funding for training, professional development, research, and the resources and equipment needed to perform the work expected (Amabile & Kramer, 2010). In addition, there has been a commitment to maintain salaries at peer average for librarians and academic professionals, and at midpoint for the classified staff. This has meant eliminating positions where necessary, using process improvement, eliminating work, outsourcing, reassigning work to appropriate levels, and other streamlining. We now have fewer people, but we are trying to provide more support for them and reward them appropriately.

All personnel are expected to work at the top of their classification or rank. They are rewarded for continually learning and applying that learning in service of our customers. People are cross-trained so that essential work is always covered. Core competencies (WebJunction et al., 2010; Holloway, 2003) have been developed for most positions so staff and librarians will constantly know what skills they are expected to possess. All new librarians and staff are hired with the understanding that they may not be in the same position forever. If there is a greater need for their skills and knowledge elsewhere in the Libraries, they could be moved. Staff who continue to learn and develop new skills will not be laid off if their present position is eliminated in a restructuring. This is to keep talent in the Libraries and to enable individuals to exercise creativity and do what is best for our customers rather than worrying about job security.

Each year, we set aside funds for professional development, training, and travel. For 2009–2010, close to $100,000 was available to faculty and staff. Up to 24 days of professional leave a year are granted to both classified staff and appointed personnel for professional development (e.g., conferences, workshops, institutes). We also make available several research grants of up to $2,000 for library faculty.

Diversity has been critical to the success of our Libraries. Competencies for working in a diverse environment have been developed and there are diversity criteria for recruiting all positions. Nearly 29% of our librarians and 37% of staff are from underrepresented groups.[2] In addition, there are individuals from countries all over the world, with different sexual orientations, and in different age groups. A diverse workforce helps to improve our overall decision making. Having different viewpoints based on life experience outside the dominant culture also helps in the creation of services and programs for our increasingly diverse customer base. More than 30% of students at the University of Arizona are ethnic minorities (primarily Hispanic; see Office of Institutional Research and Planning Support, 2009). Minority student enrollment has climbed steadily over the past 25 years (Office of Institutional Research and Planning Support, 2009) and the University expects it to keep increasing, reflecting the growth and diversity of our state (University of Arizona, 2010, p. 28). So diversity is also a customer-based business decision, not just a value we hold.

PLANNING AND BUDGETING

The second area to discuss is planning and budgeting. Our objectives here have been to:

- Align our strategic goals with the university's strategic plan.
- Anticipate and influence change, rather than being incapacitated or suffering wrenching change based on budget cuts or other sudden disruptions.
- Look 3–5 years down the road, rather than focusing all of our resources on today's services and collections.
- Make data-based decisions based on ongoing assessments, surveys, customer feedback, and other usage and cost statistics.
- Budget to our plan rather than adjusting our plan to match our budget.
- Reallocate resources based on our highest priorities.
- Have staff-driven planning and budgeting, involving personnel across library teams and job categories.
- Take advantage of new opportunities, such as collaborations and the use of technology, to minimize the impact of shrinking resources.
- Diversify and create new revenue resources to lessen our dependence on state funding.
- Stimulate innovation and creativity among library personnel by providing funding to try new things.

Strategic long-range planning is conducted by a crossfunctional team made up of faculty and staff members from across the University Libraries. This team starts with the university's strategic plan and, from those goals, assesses the environment: local library, campus, national trends, technology developments, and potential areas for collaborations. They identify service lapses, unmet needs, or emerging needs. The planning team then establishes library goals and identifies the critical few strategies that have to be accomplished in the next 3–5 years. Library-wide projects are identified, reviewed by our Project Management Group, and then project teams are appointed from personnel across the libraries. Functional teams then identify team goals and projects that align with the campus and the library goals. All the while, we are concentrating on improving library services and identifying activities, tasks, or services that need to be phased out (the concept of planned abandonment, which will be discussed later in this article).

Library-wide projects have priority over all other projects and functional work in the Libraries. If necessary to achieve our strategic work, team projects are put on hold and individual functional work or tasks are reassigned or dropped for the time being. Continually improving and developing needed new services is our highest priority, even at the expense of some functional daily work. Our approach and philosophy around planning and budgeting is to start with "What does it take to be successful three to five years from now?" then budgeting and working toward those goals. We are not focused on today because we will never have enough resources to do everything today, let alone do that and still build for success in the future.

One of our forward-looking strategies has been to make sure money is available for new opportunities. Regardless of our budget situation, we set aside $500,000 each year (less than 2% of our annual expenditures) to fund strategic projects. We have been doing this since 2006. In 2009–2010, funds enabled us to process and catalog new items donated to Special Collections, digitize materials for our institutional repository, provide training and buy software to develop new instructional materials, hire a graphic designer and extra graduate assistants for our new online class, buy new electronic resources, and support our Technical Report Archive & Image Library (TRAIL) Project (Greater Western Library Alliance, n.d.) with the Greater Western Library Alliance (GWLA, a consortium of 32 research libraries in the West and Midwest).

In addition to setting aside dollars for strategic projects, we actively seek ways to diversify revenue sources beyond our institutional allocations. The percentage of expenditures that the Libraries get from state dollars has shrunk dramatically, from 91% to 75%, over the past decade.[3]

We also are exploring other revenue sources. Like other libraries, we have invested in staffing for fundraising and grant writing. We have created a café (Arizona Student Unions, n.d.) within the Libraries, from which we receive 50% of the profits. We are building up our capacity for generating revenues from selling reproductions and licensing the rights to use some of our materials in Special Collections and the Center for Creative Photography. The center also is developing an active loan and traveling exhibition program, which will generate revenue and provide exposure to the collections. The main library also generates revenue from its Express Document Center (EDC), which offers a full range of printing, copying, and scanning services. It markets its digitization capabilities to other units on campus.

Our most successful revenue generator is the student library fee, which students have been paying since 2006. This fee provided about 3.5% of our total expenditures in FY2009–2010.[4] In April 2010, the Arizona Board of Regents approved an increase in the fee from $30/year to $120/year, so we should be receiving about $3.5 million in fee revenue in FY2010–2011. The process for getting student fees approved is political, very time consuming, and often frustrating, but worth it in the end when fees provide a steady and predictable revenue stream. We use student fee money to buy new electronic resources, upgrade equipment and software, do video streaming, increase network speed, provide loaner laptops, and fund digitization projects. The student fee also finances the extra staffing needed for the growing demand for services such as interlibrary loan (ILL), and to keep our facilities open longer. During the fall and spring semesters, our main library is open 24 hours a day, 5 days a week, with reduced hours on Friday and Saturday nights.

Essential to good budgeting is the ability to reallocate resources to higher-priority or new work. The planning and budgeting process is designed to use cost and usage data to identify work that can be eliminated, streamlined, or outsourced at a lower cost, or assigned to staff in lower pay ranges. To maximize collection resources, we have used leveraged buying (saving $1.6 million and avoiding $6.5 million in expenditures through consortial purchases in FY2008–2009), participated in Center for Research Libraries programs including cooperative buying with the Shared Purchase Program, and invested in the development of improved resource-sharing programs through GWLA, RapidILL, and the Research Libraries Group's SHARES Program. We agree with Dan Hazen (2010, p. 120) that "Cooperative activities will become increasingly central to library programs and strategies."

It's also important for libraries to calculate their return on investment (ROI). This can be challenging to do, especially for research. We participate in the University of Arizona's MINES (Measuring the Impact of Networked Electronic Services) study (Association of Research Libraries, n.d.), which examines the usage patterns of electronic information resources and the demographics of users. Results are used to identify the indirect costs of conducting grant-funded research and development. Our campus uses the percentage research use of electronic resources (as measured by MINES) to identify the Libraries' contribution to indirect cost recovery. We are investigating other ways to quantify the Libraries' ROI. Carol Tenopir and Paula Kaufman are conducting a three-phase study of academic libraries' ROI, "Value, Outcomes, and Return on Investment of Academic Libraries" (LibValue, n.d.), and we are looking at those findings (Kaufman, 2008; Tenopir et al., 2010).

USING GOOD BUSINESS PRACTICES AND BUSINESS TOOLS

Implementing new business practices is another key. Here, our objectives have been to:

- Focus on continual learning and constant improvement of services. This is done incrementally, rather than waiting for outside economic drivers to force immediate wrenching change or, worse yet, erode our ability to stay relevant.

- Apply new technologies at a faster rate to improve service and reduce costs rather than just increasing capacity.
- Evaluate current services and collections, planning the abandonment of those that will not be needed in 3–5 years.
- Improve our decision making by involving those with the knowledge, skills, and abilities (rather just administrators) in the decision-making processes. This also creates buy-in among employees.
- Increase our flexibility and responsiveness.
- Make customers more self-sufficient in their research and learning activities.
- Design services with scalability in mind. By scalability, we mean the ability to ramp up these services and serve more people without needing more staff.
- Eliminate silos and look for improvements in systems and processes rather than tasks and individual jobs. This often means looking for partners and solutions outside the walls of the library.
- Assess staff productivity, schedule staff to the work, and reallocate resources to higher-priority work.
- Only do locally that which MUST be done locally—such as collecting unique items and providing access to these collections. We outsource or give up doing what is already available elsewhere, including at other libraries, even if we have to give up some control.
- Do not let "perfect" get in the way of "good enough." When it comes to service, it is not a choice between "perfect" or "imperfect"—it is a choice between "some" versus "none." We have decided that something is better than nothing at all. Of course, once we get a good service into production, we work to improve it and make it great. But we are not striving for perfection before we implement.

When we embarked on our reengineering adventure, the decision was made to identify and use new management tools and sound business practices to make improvements. We began by adopting Total Quality Management concepts—team-based management, focus on the customer, assessing customer satisfaction, continual learning and improvement, process improvement, and data-based decision making.

Early on, we identified three essential services that were not satisfactory to our customers—reshelving time, ILL delivery, and reserves processing times. Using process improvement, we reduced reshelving time from weeks to hours, reduced ILL processing time to less than 24 hours, and reduced reserve processing at the beginning of the semester from three weeks to 48 hours. All of these processes were improved while saving tens of thousands of dollars.

Later, we studied the processes of our Technical Services Team—from acquisitions to cataloging to book processing—and reduced book order time from 40 hrs to 8 hrs. By using Blackwell's shelf-ready book services and streamlining our other cataloging processes, we were able to move 11 librarian positions to frontline services and eliminate many staff positions, reducing staffing in Technical Services and Archival Processing over the last 15 years from 46 full-time equivalents (FTE) to 14, which now includes acquisitions and 3 FTE for archival processing. At the same time, we have eliminated cataloging backlogs (except in Special Collections and the Center for Creative Photography) and are getting new books from the loading dock to the shelves in less than 24 hrs.

In 2004, we began analyzing the types of questions received at our service desks and the levels of skill required to answer those questions. After tracking every question over three 2-week periods, our analysis concluded that students and trained generalists could answer more than 95% of the questions asked at each service site. So we trained classified-staff members to take the place of librarians on service desks. When staff get questions that do require a librarian's expertise to answer, they refer customers to librarians for in-depth reference help. By redeploying librarians from service desks to other library work, we were able to reduce our costs while maintaining quality service and increasing our ability to add needed new services (Bracke et al., 2007).

Without a doubt, the use of technology has enabled service improvements and expansion in our libraries. We see technology as an enabler. It is not cheap, however, so we have had to find ways to introduce new technologies while reducing other costs. Customer self-sufficiency is one key to this. For example, we have more than 80% of our circulation going through self-checkout machines, virtually eliminating staff and student workers doing this function. (A side note on our express checkout service: When we called it "self-checkout," it was almost unused. When we renamed it "express checkout," it was suddenly an important service innovation.) Many ILL requests are now unmediated, reducing staff devoted to this function. The reserves function has been eliminated in favor of enabling faculty to link our electronic collections to the course syllabus in the course management system or to have resources scanned that they can then add to the course on their own. Movement to digital collections has reduced space devoted to print runs and time spent reshelving, while improving access. Ultimately, some jobs have been changed or replaced by technology.

To manage our technology and make sure we are using it effectively, we recently created a Technology Architecture Council. Led by our assistant dean for Technology Strategy, this group is responsible for formulating our technology policies and making sure that technology architecture is consistent throughout the Libraries. A recent example is our "buy, borrow, or build" policy, which says we will buy or license an off-the-shelf software solution whenever possible rather than customizing or building from scratch.

Generating customer feedback and assessing the effectiveness of our services are critical to our ability to manage our budget resources effectively (Stoffle & Phipps, 2003). To gather customer feedback, we use the Association of Research Libraries' LibQUAL survey, have an online feedback form called library report card, conduct usability studies and focus group sessions, log customer feedback at all of our desks using Desk Tracker software, and survey Information Commons users and do a gap analysis of their responses.

We also measure our performance against quality standards we have set. These standards include:

- The ratio of acquired electronic resources vs. print resources (80% electronic to 20% print by 2012);
- The percentage of holdings open to Web browsers (100% open to most Web browsers by 2012);
- Shelving times (95% of materials shelved within 48 hours);
- Paging requests (100% paged within 24 hours); and
- ILL processing (90% of all lending requests responded to and/or shipped within 24 hours)

To manage our resources most effectively, we track more than 210 data points and use them to evaluate our operations. This information has helped us make better decisions about services, resource uses, and reallocation possibilities. Usage data—including time of service—allows us to schedule staff to the work, increasing our effectiveness and productivity. For example, we are able to process interlibrary loans virtually 24 hours a day by using the overnight staff at our service desks (Voyles, Dols, & Knight, 2009). From 2:00 a.m. to 6:00 a.m., when there are fewer customers to assist, overnight staff process ILL requests in their spare time.

Recently, we have initiated the use of project management techniques based on training by Ernie Nielsen, managing director of Enterprise Services Portfolio Management at Brigham Young University (Pintozzi, 2008). Since we use so many project teams, we wanted to ensure that the time spent by staff members was optimized. Becoming more efficient and effective in creating new services not only helps us improve more quickly, but has helped us free up resources for other services and work. To date, we have trained more than 115 personnel in project management. Creating and using road maps is an important aspect of project planning for us. These road maps, which will be managed by librarians and high-level staff, provide a detailed 3–5-year plan for the development of all of our products and services.

A fairly controversial practice is the use of planned abandonment (Stoffle, Leeder, & Sykes-Casavant, 2008, pp.19–20)—identifying services and activities for elimination before their use and demand have completely abated. We make these decisions based on use and cost data, as well as customer feedback, rather than waiting until there is no demand or wasting critical resources that could be redirected to reach a broader audience. Recently, we used this technique to phase out print and electronic reserves. We still digitize journal articles, book chapters, audio selections, and video for online course access—but now we encourage faculty to add these to the course management system, Desire2Learn (D2L). Student groups had pushed for reserve materials to be consolidated in D2L. Now, face-to-face instruction—the 50-minute library instruction session—is in the process of being eliminated in favor of more scalable instruction activities.

COMMUNICATION

The fourth area to address is communication. Here, our objectives are to:

- Create many opportunities for two-way dialogue inside and outside the library, ensuring that personnel have the information they need to do their work and understand the context of decisions.
- Be actively involved on campus.
- Continually build a jointly shared vision of the libraries.

Good communication—both inside and outside the library—is another key to thriving (Diaz & Pintozzi, 1999). Dean Stoffle stays in frequent contact with the President and Provost, networks with other deans and key administrators, and meets regularly with students. She and other library personnel are involved in key task forces and committees on campus. All of this helps keep us in the information loop, makes the Libraries more visible, and fosters important allies on campus.

When we are considering major changes at the Libraries—such as our recent identification of $976,000 in materials to be cut during spending reductions—we seek faculty and student input. We have found that it is important to stress the *context* of decisions, not just the *outcomes*. For these recent spending reductions, we set up a Web site (University Libraries, 2009) to collect campuswide input and explained in detail why the cuts were needed. We also met with key faculty and administrators several times during the process.

We take advantage of multiple channels of communication to reach students, faculty, and staff. We use Facebook postings, e-newsletters to faculty, campuswide e-mails, advertisements on 14 security monitors scattered throughout the libraries, and librarians' interactions with faculty and students. Now we are working on adding mobile communications to the mix. Internally, we hold monthly all-staff meetings and several Conversations with the

Dean each month (informal sessions that allow library personnel to ask the dean questions or share what is on their minds). We also hold Team Report Open Houses. Teams produce three reports a year, detailing their progress on projects, listing accomplishments, describing obstacles they have encountered, and reporting whether they have met their quality standards.

Regular contact with student governance groups, student advisory groups, and the Faculty Senate has been critical to garnering support for our student fee increase. Students say they appreciate our receptiveness to their input (not only asking for their ideas, but acting on them) and our track record of transparency and accountability (such as providing quarterly student fee reports). We have worked very hard to communicate our financial needs to students and provide plenty of data.

COLLECTIONS, DISCOVERABILITY, ACCESS, AND DELIVERY

The last area to explore is collections. We are managing information, not collections. Our objectives are to:

- Move to primarily digital collections and remove duplicate print copies from our stacks;
- Rely more on patron-driven selection of materials;
- Constantly push the library to our customers so they can have anytime–anyplace access to needed information resources, regardless of who owns them or where they are located;
- Put discovery and desktop delivery of information at the top of our priorities;
- Rely on collaborations with other libraries to jointly buy and keep little-used materials rather than trying to maintain large "just-in-case" collections; and
- Support regional and national efforts to create shared print and digital repositories.

In the past, large portions of library budgets went to buying, processing, managing, and storing large print collections. Maintaining this focus is economically unsustainable. Libraries must shift their spending from collections to new services and infrastructures to ensure long-term success. We agree with Lisa Spiro and Geneva Henry that "What makes a library unique today is not the size of its holdings but the quality and innovative nature of its services" (Spiro & Henry, 2010, p. 9). As David W. Lewis predicted in 2007, "Academic libraries must find and articulate their roles in the current and future information ecology. If we cannot or will not do this, our campuses will invest in other priorities, and the library will slowly but surely atrophy and become a little used museum of the book" (Lewis, 2007, p. 419).

We already have described the reallocation of processing staff that resulted from process improvement and outsourcing. Additional reallocation has recently become possible due to declining purchases overall and a switch from print purchasing to purchasing materials in digital format (91% of our current serials and 34% of our new monographic purchases are digital). A conscious decision has been made to make the digital format the format of choice for purchases, except in Special Collections and the Center for Creative Photography. We decided in 1999 to no longer purchase both print and digital copies of materials. In 2005 we became the first official "Virtual Federal Depository library" in the United States. We began removing print versions from the collections that duplicated electronic holdings. This freed up space for users and also provided easier access to remaining collections since our shelves were less crammed. We are not maintaining offsite storage facilities for these materials, although some have been sent to the Center for Research Libraries.

We are working with the University of California Libraries and other regional partners to create the Western Regional Storage Trust (WEST; see California Digital Library, 2010), a shared print repository service. One of our librarians leads the TRAIL Project, mentioned earlier, which is a massive digitization project involving Google, the Center for Research Libraries, and a number of GWLA academic libraries. For preservation access to the electronic materials we have, we have joined Portico (ITHAKA's digital preservation service; see ITHAKA, n.d.) and Stanford's LOCKSS (Lots of Copies Keep Stuff Safe) Program (Stanford University Libraries, n.d.) rather than building local infrastructure for this purpose.

Having less print requires less storage and management, including binding, repairs, and shelving. While we must admit that electronic book collections are mostly not yet ready for prime time with their usage difficulties, search limitations, and restrictions on number of simultaneous users (and some of our customers are quite unhappy with this option), e-book publishing is improving and gaining a greater market share each year. During 2010, many e-book readers appeared in the marketplace and the release of Apple's iPad had an immediate impact. In July 2010, Amazon.com announced that e-book sales for its Kindle exceeded the sales of hardback books for the first time (Miller, 2010). Academic libraries cannot afford to buy everything so, like many others, we have shifted from a "just-in-case" to a "just-in-time" philosophy (Association of College & Research Libraries Research Planning Committee, 2010, p. 286) and are moving resources from diminishing areas (print) to growth areas such as e-books.

In addition to moving to digital content, we have decided to reduce the staffing going into the selection and purchasing of materials, especially monographs, relying instead on patron-driven acquisitions[5] to determine what will be added to the permanent collection. With the huge increases in the amount of available information, even the largest libraries are struggling to meet users' information needs solely with local collections (Jan, 2010). Digital content from suppliers such as Ebook Library (EBL) (Ebooks Coorporation, n.d.), ebrary (n.d.), MyiLibrary (Ingram, n.d.), and NetLibrary (EBSCO, n.d.) can provide our customers with access to thousands more titles than we could purchase. Only items that show multiple uses are added to our permanent collection.

With the improvements made in the supply chain for books, it is now possible to move to patron-driven acquisitions for print as well (Hendrix, 2010, pp. 9–10). Records for available materials are exposed to users through the local catalog and/or OCLC and then only materials selected by users are purchased. Materials can be delivered to the patron in a short period of time, similar to a users' retail book-buying experience. A local Espresso (On Demand, n.d.) print-on-demand system can provide users with nearly immediate access to print content available on that platform.

We also are engaged in ongoing efforts to make more materials discoverable and accessible to users. Ninety-three percent of our collections are now discoverable via Google and other Web browsers. In January 2009, we made WorldCat Local the default search tool on our Web site. Now, instead of searching our library catalog first, faculty, staff, and students can search the collections of 72,000 libraries around the world. If customers find an item we do not own, they can request it through ILL with the click of a button. From 2008 to 2009, we saw ILL requests rise more than 50%.[6]

In response to requests for best sellers and other popular materials, which we typically do not buy, we recently began a partnership with our county library system. The public library sends its full-service Bookmobile to campus once a month during the school year, allowing people on campus to check out books, magazines, DVDs, books-on-CD, and other items. The Libraries' only cost is $25/month for Bookmobile parking.

In Special Collections and the Center for Creative Photography, we are concentrating on adding *unique* images, archival, and rare manuscript materials. We are stressing processing of the collection backlogs and expanding the online availability of finding aids to increase discoverability and access. In addition, projects are under way to digitize these collections and make them available 24/7.

To make more materials discoverable and accessible, we have begun a process of adding other campus collections to the Libraries' catalog. By March 2010, our catalog contained more than 36,000 items from the University of Arizona Poetry Center collection, 15,700 items from the children's literature collection in the College of Education, and nearly 4,300 media titles held by the School of Media Arts (and now available for video streaming in courses).

Our repository efforts have been all over the map. We have an institutional repository, UAiR (University of Arizona, n.d.f), but have not really concentrated on building the traditional repository. Instead, we have experimented with the "library as publisher" model, creating two electronic journals with faculty (*Journal of Ancient Egyptian Interconnections* [University of Arizona, n.d.b] and *Journal of Insect Science*)[7], publishing an electronic book (*Latino Politics* [University of Arizona, n.d.d]), digitizing and hosting several campus-produced scholarly journals (such as *Rangelands* [University of Arizona, n.d.e]), building digital libraries (such as the Geotechnical, Rock & Water [GROW] Digital Library) (University of Arizona, n.d.a), creating access to campus-created instructional materials for use in K–12 instruction (LessonLink [University of Arizona Libraries, n.d.c]), and digitizing materials from the Center for Creative Photography and Special Collections. The money for these activities has come from our collection budget and our strategic opportunities funding. Our goal is to add value to campus research, learning, and outreach programs, and to expand national as well as local access to unique collections. We are currently exploring data curation options.

LIBRARY AS SERVICE

We frequently hear the phrase "library as place" in library discussions. But we want to focus instead on "library as service." Throughout all of the changes we have made at the University of Arizona, the concept of library as service has guided us. Library as service focuses on the customer. It results in everywhere-you-are access—pushing the library into the research and learning environment at the desktop, in the lab, and in the classroom. We are doing what Paula Kaufman predicted in 2007: "In the future, many libraries will choose to integrate information fluency instruction into course management systems, develop mass customized path-finding services pushed to students, and offer an array of classroom support services that integrate class readings, information instruction functions, and access to and delivery of content in all media and expertise into the systems the students and their teachers will be using characteristically" (Kaufman, 2007, p. 20).

Library as service penetrates deeply into the activities and programs of the campus, becoming an essential partner in achieving campus strategic goals in all arenas, including outreach. Library as service tries to anticipate needs *before* there are demands. It empowers and enables customers to be effective information users and creators.

Library as service not only owns resources, it provides discovery, access, and delivery. It also manages and curates campus information resources regardless of source or format.

Library as service collaborates to achieve national information objectives, and leverages and extends the resources of each individual library or other collaborator. It makes investments and engages in activities such as open access and system interoperability design that strengthen the national information structure. Library as service supports legislation and the creation and interpretation of information policies that make information available in ways fair to scholarship and education, as well as commercial entities involved in scholarly communication.

Library as service collaborates with other entities such as arXiv (Cornell's e-print repository for physics, math, and computer science; see Cornell University Library, n.d.), regardless of whether there are those who do not pay their share or whether the campus is unlikely to see immediate returns. Library as service shares the philosophy that information is a public good that libraries must protect. Library as service is ultimately an educational entity, teaching not only information discovery, evaluation, and use, but about privacy, intellectual property, information ethics, the cost of information, information politics, etc.

We could go on. Obviously, we do not view library as service as an end in and of itself. It is a special entity on campus closely aligned to the goals of the institution. It is a major player, not just a support service. It is constantly adapting and adjusting to further the goals of the institution. One characteristic of library as service is a commitment to ensuring that core services—those that impact the most people most often—are operating at the maximum quality level. That is why our libraries, after restructuring, focused on improving shelving, reserves, and ILL services. These improvements built confidence in the Libraries and gave us room to make other changes. Learning from this experience, we have made it a practice to improve some aspect of our performance when we move to change or abandon another service. Library as service also creates the physical library as learning and research space, focused on users and their needs rather than storage of large print collections.

As we said before, library as service focuses on the customer. Thinking about users' time has encouraged us to:

- Provide desktop delivery of ILL articles;
- Deliver articles and chapters from our print collections within 24 hrs (document delivery);
- Pull requested books from the collections for customer pick-up within 4 hrs (express retrieval);
- Stream videos through the course management system; and
- Integrate campus collections, such as the University of Arizona Poetry Center's, into our catalog.

Library as service has permeated our concept of space as well. Library space has moved from an emphasis on storage to an emphasis on creating learning environments. By removing print materials, we are putting space for users back into the library. Our 33,000-square-foot Information Commons, which opened in 2002, was designed to be a large, full-service center for students, not a computer lab (Stoffle & Cuillier, 2010). It features a centralized information desk, 254 networked computers loaded with software, 180 laptop computers available for checkout, 24 group study rooms, two presentation practice rooms, and an electronic classroom. To facilitate group activities, work areas have plenty of extra seating available. We have replaced some of our study carrels with hexagon-shaped tables to enable students to gather around a single computer and work on group projects.

Our instruction program is taking on new dimensions as well. Our organizational structure reflects this new emphasis with the creation of the Instructional Services Team. This team already has been involved in the development of several new products and services. A recently developed libraries "widget" enables students to access reference services through the university's D2L learning management system. The "widget" is embedded into course pages, giving students easy access to the libraries' Web site and catalog, online guides listing subject-specific library resources, the student's library account, and our ask-a-librarian service. Duke University has developed similar functions for the Blackboard learning management system (Daly, 2010). Use of our ask-a-librarian service has more than doubled since being added to D2L and being added to every single page of our Web site.

Our new Library Resource Organizer helps facilitate the creation of course-specific resource pages and automatically links them to D2L. The online tool guides faculty through a step-by-step process of creating these pages, customized with relevant library resources and services. Duke University uses the LibGuides application (Springshare, n.d.) to create course-specific guides and link them within Blackboard (Daly, 2010). In addition, we have taken our traditional support for the English Composition class and morphed the content into a one-credit online course that is under consideration for becoming a requirement in the University of Arizona's general education program.

CONCLUSION

So, how does this all relate to the theme of this conference—"Climbing Out of the Box: Repackaging Libraries for Survival?" What is the take-home message that you can actually apply to your day-to-day work?

We think it is that we must create the library as service, and that doing so is an ongoing, never-ending process. It is very hard work. There is no magic bullet, no shortcut, no easy way out.

We are in uncharted territory. Even though we have made many changes at the University of Arizona, our work is not over by a long shot. There is no way to say, "OK, we're done now." We have to keep refining and improving. We have to stay nimble, flexible, and always customer-focused. The new reality facing libraries is that change is rapid, constant, and unavoidable. As futurist Joe Flower wrote in "The Change Codes": "You can't 'go back to the way things were' any more than you can unscramble eggs" (Flower, n.d.).

Once again, "The choice is clear. Change now and choose our futures. Change later, or not at all, and have no future" (Stoffle, Renaud, & Veldof,

1996, p. 224). It is up to us to do whatever is necessary to thrive—and be prepared to do it over and over again.

NOTES

1. "You never want a serious crisis to go to waste. . . . it's an opportunity to do things that you think you could not do before," said Rahm Emanuel, White House chief of staff for President Barack Obama, at the *Wall Street Journal* CEO Council in Washington, DC, on November 19, 2008.

2. Figures are as of end of FY2008–2009.

3. Changes are from FY1998–99 to FY2008–2009.

4. $957,062 in FY2009–2010.

5. *Collection Management* published a special issue on patron-driven acquisitions in 2010, Vol. 35, No. 3/4.

6. ILL requests rose from 38,598 in January–November 2008 to 58,822 in January–November 2009.

7. This journal was originally hosted by the University of Arizona Libraries, but is now published online by the University of Wisconsin Digital Collections Center and the UW–Madison Libraries' Office of Scholarly Communication and Publishing, http://www.insectscience.org.

REFERENCES

Association of College & Research Libraries Research Planning and Review Committee. (2010). 2010 top ten trends in academic libraries: A review of the current literature. *College & Research Libraries News, 71*(6), 286–92.

Amabile, T. M., & Kramer, S. J. (2010). Breakthrough ideas for 2010. *Harvard Business Review, 88*(1), 41–45.

Arizona Student Unions. (n.d.). *Bookend Café*. Retrieved from http://www.union.arizona.edu/dining/ufs/bookend/index.php.

Association of Research Libraries. (n.d.). *MINES for libraries: Measuring the impact of networked electronic services*. Retrieved from http://www.arl.org/stats/initiatives/mines/index.shtml

Association of Research Libraries. (2010). *The keystone principles*. Retrieved from http://www.arl.org/bm~doc/keystone.pdf

Bender, L. J. (1997). Team organization–learning organization: The University of Arizona four years into it. *Information Outlook, 1*(9), 19–22.

Blumenstyk, G. (2010, June 10). Moody's sees continued financial challenges for private colleges. *Chronicle of Higher Education*. Retrieved from http://chronicle.com/article/Moodys-Sees-Continued/65847

Bracke, M. S., Brewer, M., Huff-Eibl, R., Lee, D. R., Mitchell, R., & Ray, M. (2007). Finding information in a new landscape: Developing new service and staffing models for mediated information services. *College & Research Libraries, 68*(3), 248–67.

California Digital Library. (n.d.). *WEST: Toward a Western Regional Storage Trust, Planning Meeting, January 7–8, 2010,* University of California. Retrieved from http://www.cdlib.org/services/collections/sharedprint/WESTMeeting1BackgroundDocumentFINAL.pdf

Cornell University Library. (n.d.). *arXiv.org e-Print archive*. Website: http://arxiv.org

Daly, E. (2010). Embedding library resources into learning management systems: A way to reach Duke undergrads at their points of need. *College & Research Libraries News, 71*(4), 208–12.

Diaz, J. R., & Pintozzi, C. (1999). Helping teams work: Lessons learned from the University of Arizona Library reorganization. *Library Administration & Management, 13*(1), 27–36.

Ebooks Corporation. (n.d.). *Ebook Library.* Retrieved from http://www.eblib.com

Ebrary. (n.d.). *ebrary.* Retreived from http://www.ebrary.com

EBSCO Publishing. (n.d.). *NetLibrary.* Retrieved from http://www.netlibrary.com

Fast Company. (2005). *The rules of business: 55 essential ideas to help smart people (and organizations) perform at their best.* New York, NY: Currency/Doubleday.

Flower, J. (n.d.). *The change codes.* Retrieved April 30, 2010, from http://www.well.com/~bbear/change_codes.html

Greater Western Library Alliance. (n.d.). *The Technical Report Archive & Image Library (TRAIL)—Project Site.* Retrieved from http://trail.gwla.org/

Hazen, D. (2010). Rethinking research library collections: A policy framework for straitened times, and beyond. *Library Resources & Technical Services, 54*(2), 115–121.

Hebel, S. (2010, March 14). State cuts are pushing public colleges into peril. *Chronicle of Higher Education.* Retrieved from http://chronicle.com/article/In-Many-States-Public-Higher/64620

Hendrix, J. C. (2010, February). *Checking out the future: Perspectives from the library community on information technology and 21st-century libraries.* Washington, DC: American Library Association Office for Information Technology Policy. Retrieved from http://www.ala.org/ala/aboutala/offices/oitp/publications/policybriefs/ala_checking_out_the.pdf

Holloway, K. (2003). Developing core and mastery level competencies for librarians. *Library Administration and Management, 17*(2), 94–98.

Holloway, K. (2004). The significance of organizational development in academic research libraries. *Library Trends, 53*(1), 5–16.

Huff-Eibl, R., Ray, M., & Voyles, J. (2008, December 8–10). *A new model at the University of Arizona: Are staff classification systems reflecting current and future library competencies?* Presented at the Arizona Library Association Annual Conference, Glendale, Arizona. Retrieved from http://intranet.library.arizona.edu/users/stofflec/Classified_staff_competencies_2008.ppt

Ingram Digital Ltd. (n.d.). *MyiLibrary.* Retrieved from http://www.myilibrary.com/

ITHAKA. (n.d.). *Portico: A digital preservation and electronic archiving service.* Retrieved from http://www.portico.org/

Jan, T. (2010, May 24). Harvard's paper cuts: School library works to maintain stature in the shift to digital. *Boston Globe.* Retrieved from http://www.boston.com/news/education/higher/articles/2010/05/24/for_harvards_library_an_arduous_digital_shift/?page=1

Kaufman, P. T. (2008). The library as strategic investment: Results of the Illinois return on investment study. *Liber Quarterly, 18*(3/4), 424–36.

Kaufman, P. (2007). It's not your parents' library anymore: Challenges and opportunities in the new webs of complexity. *Journal of Library Administration, 46*(1), 5–26.

Lewis, D. W. (2007), A strategy for academic libraries in the first quarter of the 21st century. *College & Research Libraries, 68*(5), 418–34.

Lewis, D. W. (1995). Traditional reference is dead, now let's move on to important questions. *Journal of Academic Librarianship, 21*(1), 10–12.

Lib-Value. (n.d.). Value, outcomes, and return on investment of academic libraries. Retrieved from http://libvalue.cci.utk.edu

Luce, R. E. (2008). A new value equation challenge: The emergence of eresearch and roles for research libraries. In *No brief candle: Reconceiving research libraries for the 21st century* (pp. 42–50). Washington, DC: Council on Library and Information Resources.

Miller, C. C. (2010, July 19). E-books top hardcovers at Amazon. *New York Times*. Retrieved from http://www.nytimes.com/2010/07/20/technology/20kindle.html?_r=1

Office of Institutional Research and Planning Support. (2009, September 20). *The University of Arizona: Total minority student enrollment trends, fall 1983 to fall 2009*. Retrieved from http://oirps.arizona.edu/files/Student_Demo/Enrollment_trends_for_minority_students_1983_2009.pdf

On Demand Books. (n.d.). *Espresso book machine*. Retrieved from http://www.ondemandbooks.com/the_ebm.htm

Owens, I. (1999). the impact of change from hierarchy to teams in two academic libraries: Intended results versus actual results using total quality management. *College & Research Libraries, 60*(6), 571–584.

Phipps, S. (2001). Beyond measuring service quality: Learning from the voices of the customers, the staff, the processes, and the organization. *Library Trends, 49*(4), 635–661.

Phipps, S. (2004). The system design approach to organizational development: The University of Arizona model. *Library Trends, 53*(1), 68–111.

Pintozzi, C. (2008, October). *Project, program, and portfolio management in the University of ArizonaL and CCP*. Retrieved from http://intranet.library.arizona.edu/xf/projmanage/documents/ProjectManagementOverviewPPT.pdf

Project on the Future of Higher Education. (2004). *Dealing with the future now: Principles for creating a vital campus in a climate of restricted resources*. Retrieved from http://www.wisconsin.edu/news/2004/02_Feb2004/UWPresentation-guskin_040205.pdf

Spiro, L., & Henry, G. (2010, June). Can a new research library be all-digital? In *The idea of order: Transforming research collections for 21st century scholarship* (pp. 5–80). Washington, DC: Council on Library and Information Resources.

Springshare. (n.d.). *LibGuides*. Retrieved from http://www.springshare.com/libguides/

Stanford University Libraries. (n.d.). *LOCKSS*. Retrieved from http://lockss.stanford.edu/lockss

Stoffle, C. (1995). The upside of downsizing: Using the economic crisis to restructure and revitalize academic libraries. In C. LaGuardia, S. Bentley & J. Martorana (Eds.), *The upside of downsizing: Using library instruction to cope* (pp. 1–13). New York, NY: Neal-Schuman.

Stoffle, C., Allen, B., Fore, J., & Mobley, E. R. (2000, November). Predicting the future: What does academic librarianship hold in store? *College & Research Libraries News, 61*(10), 894–897.

Stoffle, C. J., Allen, B., Morden, D. & Maloney, K. (2003). Continuing to build the future: Academic libraries and their challenges. *portal: Libraries and the Academy, 3*(3), 363–380.

Stoffle, C. J., & Cuillier, C. (2010). Student-centered service and support: A case study of the University of Arizona Libraries' Information Commons. *Journal of Library Administration, 50*(2), 117–134.

Stoffle, C. J., Leeder, K., & Sykes-Casavant, G. (2008). Bridging the gap: Wherever you are, the library. *Journal of Library Administration, 48*(1), 3–30.

Stoffle, C., & Phipps, S. (2003). Meaningful measures for libraries. *Library Issues, 23*(4), 1–4.

Stoffle, C. J., Renaud, R., & Veldof, J. R. (1996). Choosing our futures. *College & Research Libraries, 57*(3), 213–225.

Stoffle, C. J., & Weibel, K. (1995). Funding academic libraries. In G. McCabe & R. J. Person (Eds.), *Academic libraries: Their rationale and role in American higher education* (pp. 125–148). Westport, CT: Greenwood.

Tenopir, C., Love, R., Park, J., Wu, L., Baer, A., & Mays, R. (2010, June). *University investment in the library, phase ii: An international study of the library's value to the grants process.* Retrieved from http://libraryconnect.elsevier.com/whitepapers/roi2/2010–06-whitepaper-roi2.pdf

University Libraries. (2009). *Spending reductions for 2009/10 & 2010/11.* Retrieved from http://www.library.arizona.edu/spendingReduction

University of Arizona. (2000). *NCA 2000 self-study report North Central Association.* Retrieved from http://provost.arizona.edu/files/NCA2000_Self_Study_Report_Chp4_6.pdf

University of Arizona. (2008). *Living the future 7: Transformation libraries through collaboration.* Retrieved from http://www.library.arizona.edu/conferences/ltf/2008

University of Arizona. (2010). *Expanding our vision, deepening our roots: Five-year strategic plan 2011–2015.* Retrieved from http://plan.web.arizona.edu/strategic-plan.pdf

University of Arizona. (n.d.a). *Geotechnical, rock and water resources library.* Retrieved from http://www.grow.arizona.edu

University of Arizona. (n.d.b). *Journal of Ancient Egyptian Interconnections.* Retrieved from http://digitalcommons.library.arizona.edu/holdings/journal?r=uadc://azu_egypt/

University of Arizona Libraries. (n.d.f). *K–12 LessonLink.* Retrieved from http://lessonlink.library.arizona.edu/

University of Arizona. (n.d.c). *Latino politics (*eBook*).* Retrieved from http://uair.arizona.edu/item/292005

University of Arizona. (n.d.e). *Rangelands archives.* Retrieved from http://digitalcommons.library.arizona.edu/holdings/journal?r=http://rangelands.library.arizona.edu/

University of Arizona. (n.d.f). *UAiR: The University of Arizona Institutional Repository.* Retrieved from http://www.uair.arizona.edu

Voyles, J. F., Dols, L., & Knight, E. (2009). Interlibrary loan meets Six Sigma: The University of Arizona Library's success applying process improvement. *Journal of Interlibrary Loan, Document Delivery & Electronic Reserve, 19*(1), 75–94.

WebJunction, Carterette, P., Lenox, M., Houghton-Jan, S., Iaukea, E., & Gutsche, B. (2010). *Competencies for libraries.* Retrieved from http://www.webjunction.org/c/document_library/get_file?folderId=94651303&name=DLFE-25360002.pdf

APPENDIX A
THE UNIVERSITY OF ARIZONA LIBRARY ORGANIZATION

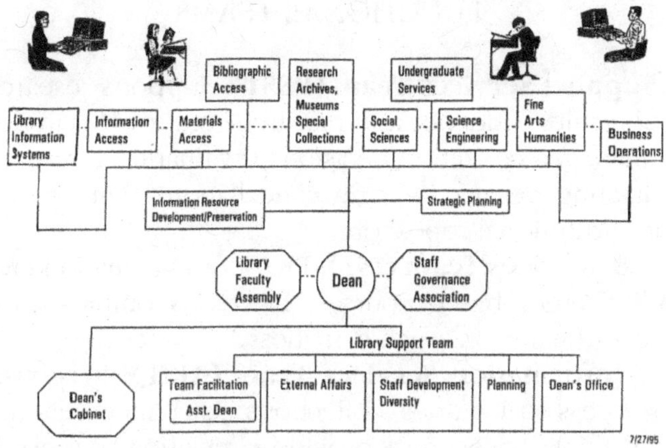

APPENDIX B
UNIVERSITY LIBRARIES AND CREATIVE PHOTOGRAPHY, UNIVERSITY OF ARIZONA: ORGANIZATIONAL CHART, FEBRUARY 2010

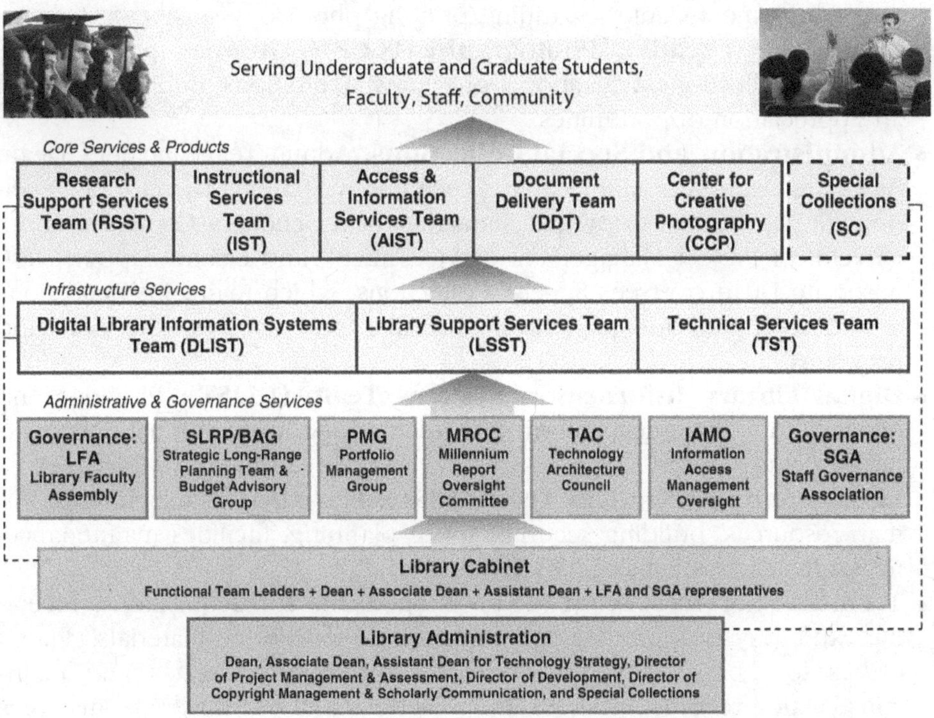

APPENDIX C

UNIVERSITY LIBRARIES, UNIVERSITY OF ARIZONA FUNCTIONAL TEAMS

- **Research Support Services Team (RSST):** Supports research and teaching needs of faculty, students, and researchers. Provides in-depth research assistance, manages collection decisions (evaluating resources and usage data, coordinating deselection and cancellations), and works on digital projects and institutional repository.
- **Instructional Services Team (IST):** Provides information literacy instruction, including credit-based courses. Develops online, learner-centered tools. Also coordinates outreach activities.
- **Access and Information Services Team (AIST):** Responsible for providing user access to Libraries' collections. AIST members house, shelve, and maintain these collections; provide circulation, basic reference, and billing/fees negotiation at the service sites; and answer queries concerning public service, collection maintenance, and billing/collections issues.
- **Document Delivery Team (DDT):** Provides on- and off-campus users with access to materials. Oversees borrowing and lending of materials (e.g., Interlibrary Loan), physical/electronic delivery of items, and Electronic Document Center (scanning/printing/photocopy services).
- **Center for Creative Photography (CCP):** Oversees photographic archives, collections, educational programs, exhibitions, publications, and art appreciation opportunities.
- **Administration and Special Collections:** Admin Team includes Dean, Associate Dean, Assistant Dean for Technology Strategy, Director of Development, Director of Copyright Management & Scholarly Communication, Director of Project Management & Assessment, and Dean's support staff. Associate Dean oversees Special Collections, which maintains collections of rare books and unique archival materials, and organizes exhibitions and programs.
- **Digital Library Information Systems Team (DLIST):** Provides and enhances the Libraries' information technology and information access infrastructure.
- **Library Support Services Team (LSST):** Encompasses accounting, human resources, building security, space planning, facilities maintenance, mail, grants coordination, and marketing.
- **Technical Services Team (TST):** Responsible for acquisitions, receiving, and physical processing of print and non-print materials. Places orders for library materials, renews subscriptions, creates and maintains catalog records, arranges and describes archival materials, manages commercial binding of journals and monographs, and repairs damaged materials.

CROSSFUNCTIONAL TEAMS

- **Strategic Long-Range Planning (SLRP):** Identifies key directions for next three to five years, enabling Libraries to focus resources and efforts on highest priorities. Creates strategic directions that clearly articulate Libraries' vision, mission, and values.
- **Budget Advisory Group (BAG):** Recommends budget allocations—including budget cuts, increases, onetime investments, or reallocations—to Cabinet yearly. BAG is made up of Strategic Long-Range Planning members, the Dean, Library Business Manager, Library Faculty Assembly chair, and Staff Governance Association member. Led by Library Support Services Team leader.
- **Portfolio Management Group (PMG):** Oversees day-to-day operations of project management. Prioritizes projects, monitors current status of projects, and makes team leaders aware of barriers facing projects. PMG is responsible for ensuring that programs and projects are strategic in nature, aligned with Libraries' goals, and that resources are allocated to highest-priority programs and projects. Director of Project Management leads group.
- **Millennium Report Oversight Committee (MROC):** Monitors and assesses progress on diversity goals developed by University. Assesses climate of Libraries, identifies problem areas, prioritizes these areas, and advises Dean and Cabinet on possible future actions. Provides educational sessions on diversity issues for Libraries' employees.
- **Technology Architecture Council (TAC):** Provides overall technical direction and strategy, addresses technology-related policies, decides whether Libraries have necessary resources/capacity to implement technology for particular projects, and approves technology decisions. Assistant Dean for Technology Strategy leads group.
- **Information Access Management Oversight (IAMO):** Assesses priorities for information resource spending, recommends allocations for Libraries' Information Access Budget (for books, serials, etc.), oversees expenditure of this budget, and makes recommendations concerning memberships and consortial/cooperative purchases. Materials Budget Procurement and Licensing Librarian leads group.

GOVERNANCE

- **Cabinet:** Provides leadership in establishing direction and vision for Libraries. Members include Dean, Associate Dean, Assistant Dean for Technology Strategy, team leaders, and designated members of Library Faculty Assembly and Staff Governance Association.
- **Library Faculty Assembly (LFA):** Advocacy group for all library faculty, including librarians, archivists, and curators.
- **Staff Governance Association (SGA):** Advocacy group for all classified staff in Libraries.

Index

Page numbers in *Italics* represent tables.
Page numbers in **Bold** represent figures.

Aardvark 4
Accenture Limited 127
access 140; anytime and anyplace 143; Arizona University Libraries 143–6; improved 50
accountability 70
acquisitions 67, 91; content evaluation factors **115**; cut in 44; patron-driven 144; reductions strategies *44*
adaptation 58
adaptive transformations 47
administration: reducing overheads 133
Alabama: Birmingham 125
Alabama University: Lister Hill Library of Health Sciences 112
Amazon 7, 8, 50, 61
American Libraries 58
American Library Association (ALA) 55
American Recovery and Reinvestment Act 40
antiquarian museums 56
Applications Programming Interface (APIs) 9
Archival Processing 140
archive: humanities 87; library as 85
archiving 67
Aristotle 33
Arizona Board of Regents 137
Arizona Poetry Center collection 145
Arizona University 2; Measuring the Impact of Networked Electronic Services (MINES) 138
Arizona University Libraries 131; access 143–6; approach 132; Center for Creative Photography 137, 140, 144–6; collections 143–6; communication 142–3; crossfunctional teams 155; delivery 143–6; discoverability 143–6; Express Document Center 137; functional teams 154; good business practices and tools 138–42; governance 155; Information Commons 147; library as service 146–8; organization 153; organizational structure and culture 132–6; planning and budgeting 136–8; Special Collections 137, 140, 144–6; thriving service 148–9; Virtual Federal Depository library 144
Art historians 92
arXiv 147
Asian studies 92
ask-a-librarian service 148
Assessing the Future Landscape of Scholarly Communication (Center for Studies in Higher Education) 26
Association of American University Presses 52
Association of Public and Land-grant Universities (APLU): *Coping Strategies of Public Universities During The Economic Recession (2009)* 39–40
Association of Research Libraries (ARL) 6, 27; budget allocation **116**; budget expectations (2010–2011) **109**; budgets 106; expenditure trends (1986–2008) **110**; fiscal survey 37–52; income 39; Institutions' Endowment Decline by Percentage **40**; LibQUAL survey 141; Lowry 1
audio files 63
Austin Conference: Electronic Resources & Libraries (ER&L) 114
authors 21
automation 51

backfiles: e-journals 94–8; suppliers 100
Bakkabasi, Nisa 114
Balanced Scorecards 133
Bell, Steven 58
Berry, Wendell 30
big deals: EBSCO survey 120
binding 144
Bing: Microsoft 4
biodiversity 62
Birmingham: Alabama 125
Blackboard learning management system 148
Blackwell's shelf-ready services 140
blended librarians 58
book barcodes 11
book digitization projects 83

Bookmobile 145
books: warehouses 56
bookstores 19
Boston Public Library 38
branch libraries: elimination and consolidation 48–9
Breeding, Marshall 5
Brigham Young University: Enterprise Services Portfolio Management 141
Bryan, Lowell 128
bubbles 23–5
Budd, John 58
budgets: 2009–2010 versus prior year **106**; Association of Research Libraries (ARL) 106; comparison of impact *42*; crisis 41; EBSCO (2009–2010) **108**; EBSCO expectations (2010–2011) **108**; expected (2010–2011) **106**; historic commitments 47; outlook in 2 years **107**; percentage of net change *42*; percentage net change for base *43*; reduction impact *44*; staff cuts 135
business faculty 95
buyer: library as 85; sciences 87; social sciences 87
buying decisions 128
buying power 112

campus-wide computer networking 23
Canada 10
capitalism 21
cataloging 67
catering 137
Center for Research Libraries 138
centres of excellence 67
change 48, 54, 58, 134, 148; economic crisis 105
chaos 19
chat reference 134
China 34
Christensen, Clayton: *The Innovator's Dilemma* 22, 26, 27, 32
The Chronicle of Higher Education 56, 131
civil liberties 70
Clark, Guy 29
Climbing Out of the Box: Oklahoma City (2010) 1
cloud computing 1, 19–20; benefits 9; definition 6
coffee shop 60
collaborations 31, 66; deep 68; digital libraries 69; for *just-in-case* collections 143; radical 67
collection development 69, 74, 90; obsessive 48
collections: Arizona University Libraries 143–6; storage facilities 68
Collins, Jim: criticism of 22; *How the Mighty Fall* 21, 24, 32
Columbia libraries (2CUL) 50–1, 73–4
Columbia University 14, 74
Committee on Institutional Cooperation (CIC) 50
Confucianism 34
conservation 70
conspectus model 75
consumers: library 71–2
content: bundling 128; investment 68; management 134
ContentDM 16; databases 64; software 63
Cooperative Collection Management Trust (CCMT) 51
Coping Strategies of Public Universities During The Economic Recession of 2009 (APLU) 39–40
copy cataloging 48
copying 137
copyright 69, 134
coral reefs 61–2
Cornell library (2CUL) 50–1, 73–4
cost: per use 116, 128
cost containment 116
Council on Library and Information Resources (CLIR) 58
creativity 136
credibility engine 5
Cuillier, Cheryl 2
customer focus 133, 135, 146, 148
customer self-sufficiency 140
cuts 44, 47; feedback 142; staff 115
cyberinfrastructure 71
Cynics 34

D2L learning management system 142, 148
Daoism 34
Darwin, Charles 3, 17
data capture 69
databases of academic journals: importance of **99**
datamining 74
decision making 133; quick 127
delivery: Arizona University Libraries 143–6
Deloitte Center for the Edge 22
demand: staff 48
Dempsey, Lorcan 6, 13, 59
Desire2Learn (D2L) 142, 148
Desk Tracker software 141
desktop delivery 143
Dewey, Melville 56, 57, 58
digital archivist 134
digital collections: movement towards 143
digital curation 86
digital graffiti 26, 27
digital ingestion 67

digital learning librarians 63
digital library: building 69
digital metaphors 61
digital preservation 74
digital record 94
digitization 50; legacy collections 49; repository 137; services 137
digitized primary source collections **99**
Dillon, Dennis 1
discoverability: Arizona University Libraries 143–6
Disney Corporation 57
diversity 135–6
document delivery 147
DSpace 51
duality 33–4
Dublin Core 64
Duke University 147
Duraspace 51

e-books 20, 21, 28, 49; importance of **99**; usage difficulties 144
e-journals 20, 78; acceptance of 94; backfiles of 94–8; custom collections 120; faculty need for keeping hard-copy **96**; long-term preservation of **98**; more for pro-rata less 120; packages 118; pick and choose 120; preservation 98–100; purchase decisions 112; support for back copies to electronic form only **95**; support for back copies to electronic form only by faculty **96**; support for by faculty **93**; support for **93**
e-newsletters 142
e-packages: breaking up of 112; evaluating 114; numbers ordered (2009) 112
e-printing 45
e-science infrastructure 71
eBay 7
Ebook Library (EBL) 145
ebrary 145
EBSCO: database division 125; dramatic change in business 124; Europe 125; *host* 125; impact of economic crisis 121–7; integrated discovery and management solutions **126**; MetaPress division 125; percentage of revenue from e-packages **125**; publishing orders analysis 112; purchasing decisions 112; sales 123; sales of e-only content **124**; sales in Europe 123; sales revenue by format **124**; sales revenue by publisher **113**; staff reductions 124; total sales 113
EBSCO Information Systems 2, 16
EBSCO Publishing 125
EBSCO survey: big deals 120; budgets 106–7, **107**; publisher prices 110; publisher prices analysis by library type *111*; publishers responding **119**
ecology 61–2
economic crisis: change 105; library budget 106; tactical reaction 127–8
The Economic Downturn and Libraries: Survey Findings (CIBER) 46
economics faculty 95
education programs 70
electronic collections 114
electronic research resources: starting point **84**
electronic reserves: phasing out 142
electronic resource management 67
Electronic Resources & Libraries (ER&L): Austin Conference 114
Eliot, Charles 59
embedded librarians 58, 102
endowments 40; decline **40**; percentage of change *43*
Enterprise Services Portfolio Management: Brigham Young University 141
Epstein, Jason: *New York Review of Books* 49
eSerials Holdings 7
Espresso: print on demand service 145
ethnic minorities 135
Europe: EBSCO 125
evolving role of library 80–91
expenditure trends (1986–2008): Association of Research Libraries (ARL) **110**
express retrieval 147

Facebook 4, 7, 11, 29, 60, 142
faculty: library classification 72; library taxonomy 72; opinions on libraries 77–103; relationships with 71–2
Federal Depository Library Program 48
Fedora 51
feedback: cuts 142
Fiels, Keith 55
FirstSearch service 15
flattening organizations 132
flexibility 127
Flower, Joe 148
Foglesong, Hortense 19, 33, 35
format of record: digital 94
format transition: scholarly works 91–100
France 10
free riders 49, 50
Friedman, Thomas: *The World is Flat* 22
Fritzler, Peter 61–2
fundraising 118

Gartner Inc. 6
gatekeeper 58
gateway: competition 88; library 85; role of libraries (importance) **89**; services 88

Germany 10
Gherman, Paul 51
Giesecke, Joan 2
Gilchrest, David 27
Glass-Seagal Act: repeal of 39
Google 4, 7, 61, 63, 88; competing with 102; digitization of books 31, 103; discovering materials via 145; efficiency 34; meets Amazon.com 64; search 26; TRAIL project 144; viewport 15
Google Book Search 15, 50; APIs 15; Library Project 16
Google Books 49
Greater Western Library Alliance: TRAIL project 137
Greece: libraries 56
Greenspan, Alan 38
Guthrie, Kevin 2

Haika Web site 4
hail: estimating size 55
Haithi Trust 14, 14–15, 16, 50, 68
hard-copy collections: replacements 94
Harvard 59
Harvard Business School 75
Hazen, Dan 138
Henry, Geneva 143
hermit publishing 25
higher education: income 39
Houston ARL Conference: Transformational Times 47
How the Mighty Fall (Collins) 21, 25
humanities: archive 87; print collections 95
hybrid librarians 58

image library 137
income: ARL 39; higher education 39
inefficiency: value of 34–5
information 30–1; as a commodity 2; value added 32
Information Commons 86; Arizona University Libraries 147
information desk staffing 134
information discovery and use 81–4
information policy agenda 70
informationists 86
infrastructure 67
innovation 66, 136
The Innovator's Dilemma (Christensen) 22, 26, 27
institutions: why they fail 21–3
Instructional Services 133
intellectual freedom 70
interlibrary loan (ILL) 138, 139, 141, 145, 147
International Standard Book Numbers (ISBN) 12
internet 22; access 73; development 70
iPad 103, 144
iPhone: RedLaser 11
Ithaka 2, 74
Ithaka S+R's Faculty Survey (2009): conclusion 102–3; evolving role of library 80–91; format transition for scholarly works 91–100; introduction 77–9; library importance 100–2; methodology 79–80; respondents by discipline *80*; respondents by size *80*

Jewitt, Charles Coffin 31
job classifications: librarians 132
job security 135
John Hopkins University 70
Jordan, Jay 1
journal bubble 24
journal market: consolidation 24
journals: cancelled 44; current issues of 92–4; format transition 91–100, *see also* e-journals
JSTOR archive 16
just-in-time 144; decision making 128

K-12 instruction 146
Kantor, Rosabeth 75
Kaufman, Paula 138, 146
Kilgour, Frederick G. 7, 9, 13
Kindle 103, 144
knowledge management system 57
Kuali Foundation 51

Lankes, R. David 59
laptop loans 138
lease models 118
leased content 128
legacy collections: digitization 49
Lewis, David W. 143
LibGuides 148
libQUAL priorities 31–3
LibQUAL survey: ARL 141
librarian and staff: pay increases *45*
librarian-educator 58
librarians 57–9; job classifications 132; staff actions **116**; strategies **114**
librarianship: mission 20
libraries: changing behaviours 81; changing views 56; funding crisis 131; funding for 39; genius of 34; images of 56; metaphors of 56–7; planning and design 71
library: as archive 85; as a body part 59; as buyer 85; consumers 71–2; as conversation 59–60; as gateway 85; as place 60–1, 146; as publisher model 145; as service 132, 146–9; strength of support 99–102, **101**;

values 33; vital position of 131, *see also* research library
Library Advisory Council 10
library automation 49
library budgets: addressing costs 115; economic crisis 106
library classification: faculty 72
Library of Congress 11, 33, 34, 35; 1897 book railroad 25–7
library costs 131
library expenditures: as a per cent of university expenditure **117**
library instruction session 142
Library Journal 61
library metaphors 58–62
library roles: importance **85**; importance by faculty **88**; rating by faculty **86**
library science: masters 58
library serial budgets 111
library space 71
library systems: evolution of 5–10; North America 5
licensing negotiations 67
licensing rights 137
Lincoln Public Schools: Nebraska 58
Lister Hill Library of Health Sciences: Alabama University 112
Living the Future conference 131
loans: collection 137
local catalog 145
local print preservation 97
LOCKSS (Lots of Copies Keep Stuff Safe) Program: Stanford 144
low-use collections: moving 49
Lowry, Charles 1
Lublin, Joann S. 127

MacArthur Foundation 4
McKinsey and Company 128
magazines 19
Malpas, Constance 14
MARC (machine-readable cataloging) 15, 64
mass production 67
Massachusetts Institute of Technology (MIT) 60
Mattioli, Dana 127
media services: microforms 63
Medical Library Association 112
Melbourne 12
Mellon Foundation 15, 51, 70, 74
Metadata Crosswalk 12
metadata librarian 134
metaphors 54–64
Michigan University 15
Microsoft: Bing 4
Missouri School of Library Science 58
Mizner, Wilson 27
monographs 49, 83
mp3 audio books 20
mutualism 61
MyiLibrary 145
MySpace 11

National Association of College and University Business Officers (NACUBO) 40
National Oceanic and Atmospheric Administration (NOAA) 55
national policy: lack of 69
Neal, James 2
Neal, Jim 58
Nebraska: Lincoln Public Schools 58
Nebraska Educational Television 63
Nebraska-Lincoln University 2, 60
Netherlands 10
NetLibrary 145
network level services 83
network speed 138
network-level discovery tools 90
New York Public Library 12, 38, 68, 74
New York research libraries collaboration: planning meeting 74–5
New York Review of Books (Epstein) 49
New York University 74
New York University Libraries 14
Newcastle University (UK) 112
newspapers 19
Newsweek 38
Nicholson, Scott 59
Nielsen, Ernie 141
Nitecki, Danuta 56, 57
Nitecki, J.Z. 59
Nook 103
North Atlantic Storage Trust 51
North Olmsted library 20

OAIster 16
OAIster database 15
Oklahoma University 1
Oklahoma University Library 131
online classes 137
Online Computer Library Center (OCLC) 50; increasing global relevance and position of trust 13–15; network 17; Question Point 4; text messaging 11; web services 6, 9–10, 12–13; WorldCat Registry 5
online databases 22
online library catalog 81
online reference 49
online resources: creating 134
open access 89
Open Archives Initiative Protocol for Metadata Harvesting (OAI-PMH) 15
Open Library Environment Project 51

open-access agenda 70
OpenURL Gateway 21
outsourcing 48, 135, 139
overnight processing: ILL 141
ox carts: supply chain 20–1

paging requests 141
partnerships: characteristics of successful 75; mechanisms of successful 75–6
patron-driven acquisitions 144
pay increases: librarian and staff *45*
Peer Behavioural Research (Loughborough University) 26
PhD professionals 58
philosophy 92–3
planning and design: libraries 71
Plutchak, T. Scott 112
popular materials 145
Portico: ITHAKA digital preservation 144
Powell, Allen 2
presentation practice rooms 148
preservation 49, 67, 69, 90, 98–100; lack of research 70
Princeton University 14, 68
print: retention 118; transition away from 92
print cancellations: support for 92
print collections: humanities 95; reduction of 86
print on demand service: Espresso 145
print preservation 97
print publications: end of 78
print repository strategy 97
print reserves: phasing out 142
printing 137
privacy 70
professional development 135
public good 50, 147
publishers 78, 98; considering new titles **120**; consolidation 113; cost saving measures 120; declines in revenue **119**; EBSCO survey **119**; factors causing price increases *109*; financial crisis solutions **123**; future of packages **121**; packages **121**; price analysis by library type (EBSCO survey) *111*; price increases 108; price increases for serials *111*; staffing changes **122**; staffing changes in future **122**; title portfolio management 120
publishing: new forms 25
purchase decisions: e-journals 112
purchasing agent 85

QuestionPoint: OCLC 4, 11; Qwidget 12

radicalization 66
RapidILL 138
Readex Digital Institute 59
recession: effects on libraries 37–52
RedLaser: iPhone 11
reductions: expectations **46**
redundancy 51
Reference Extract Project 5
remote collections 97
repackaging 54
repairs 144
repository fatigue 70
repository movement 70
research 27; dependence on library **90**; starting point 81, **82**
Research Collections and Preservation Consortium (ReCAP) 14, 68
research humanities: starting point **83**
Research Libraries Group 68, 75; SHARES Program 138
research library: core responsibilities 71; term 27, *see also* library
research support 86
Research Support Services 134
reserves processing 139
reshelving time 139, 140
return on investment (ROI) 138
revenue: diversification of 137
Rogers, Will 11
Rome: libraries 56
The Rules of Business (Shinseki) 134

salaries 115
scanning services 137
scholarly communication 25, 134
scholarly journals *see* e-journals
scholarly works: format transition 91–100
School Library Journal 60
Schrage, Michael 60
sciences: buyer 87
search engines 64; evolution of 4–5
searching tools 73
seating 60
Seattle 12
self-checkout 140
serials: price percentage increases (2008–2010) *111*
serials budget: percentage of big deals *113*
serials crisis 118
service: library as 146–8
service delivery: new models of 49
service desks 140
Shank, Jim 58
sharing information 29
shelving 144
shelving times 141
Shephard, Edward 59
Shill, Walt 127
Shinseki, Gen. Eric: *The Rules of Business* 134

Silverstein, Joanne 59
Six Sigma process-improvement techniques 133
Smithsonian Institute 31
snacking 63
social media 28
social networks 60
social sciences: buyer 87
Socrates 33
software negotiation 67
Special Collections 137
Spiro, Lisa 143
staff: budget cuts 135; demand 48
staff actions: librarians **116**
staff reductions: categories **117**
staffing changes: required *45*
staffing resources 132
Stanford: LOCKSS (Lots of Copies Keep Stuff Safe) Program 144
Starbucks 60
starting point: electronic research resources **84**; research 81, **82**; research humanities **83**
Sterling Memorial Library 59
Stoffle, Carla 2, 39, 130, 131
storage: shared 50
strategic planning 127
Strategic Plans Lose Favor (Lublin and Mattioli) 127
study zones 63
subprime mortgages 24
supply chain 145; ox carts 20–1
survival 54
Syracuse University 4
system-wide efficiencies: creating 15–16

tax funding 42
Taylor-Roe, Jill 112
teaching support 86
team-based work structures 132
Technology Architecture Council 140
TEI records 64
teleconferencing 74
Tenopir, Carol 138
Terlingua bookstore 18–19, 28–9
Texas cowgirl 29–30
Texas-Austin University Libraries 1
text messaging: Online Computer Library Center (OCLC) 11
Thoreau, Henry David 34
Titcomb, Mary 28, 33, 34
title portfolio management: publishers 120
Total Quality Management 139
training 135
Transformational Times: Houston ARL Conference 47
transitions 54
Twitter 60

United Kingdom (UK) 10
United States of America (USA) 10
University College London 46
UNL libraries: metaphors at 62–5
usage statistics 114
user environments: creating compelling 10–12
user satisfaction 70

value added information 32
value added services 133
video 63
video files 63
video streaming 138, 147
Virtual International Authority File (VIAF) 14
VuFind 15

Wall Street Journal 127
Walter, Scott 61
warehousing role 78
Washington 12
Washington University 4
Web 2.0: criticisms 28; trends 23
web sites: quality 73
web-scale 1; benefits 9; definition 6
Web-scale services: OCLC 6
Weisberg, Jacob 38
welcoming 60
Western Regional Storage Trust 144
Wolfram/Alpha 4
The World is Flat (Friedman) 22
WorldCat 16
WorldCat API 12
WorldCat Basic API 12
WorldCat Developers Network 12
WorldCat Hackathon 12
WorldCat Identities 11, 12
WorldCat Local 7, 10–13, 16, 51, 145
WorldCat Registry: API 11, 12, 13; functions 12–13
WorldCat Search API 11
WorldCat.org 9, 10, 12, 15

Yahoo 4
Yale University 59
Yale University Library 114